Educational Policy and the Just Society

Educational Policy and the Just Society

Kenneth A. Strike

UNIVERSITY OF ILLINOIS PRESS

Urbana   Chicago   London

This book is printed on acid-free paper.

LIBRARY OF CONGRESS CATALOGING IN PUBLICATION DATA

Strike, Kenneth A.
    Educational policy and the just society.

    Includes bibliographical references and index.
    1. Education—United States—Philosophy—History—
20th century.   I. Title.
LA209.S74   379.73   81-10479
ISBN 0-252-00908-8 (cloth)   AACR2
ISBN 0-252-00928-2 (paper)

To Janet and Daniel

Contents

Preface

Human beings have a tendency to solve problems at the lowest level of abstraction possible. That is no doubt a sensible procedure. One's central concepts are tools. They are meant to be worked with rather than worked on. When our intellectual tools are working well there is little reason to examine old ones or try out new ones.

Under stable conditions, philosophy will, therefore, not seem like a useful activity. Philosophers have a positive lust for examining fundamentals. They regard this activity as intellectually useful. After all everything else depends on our fundamental concepts. What could be more useful than examining them? But practical people know better. They intuitively understand that examining fundamental issues makes things more complicated. It is better to use our intellectual tools rather than examine them. Philosophy is like an automobile which never goes anywhere because its owner enjoys taking it apart too much. There is little intellectual mileage in a piece of cognitive machinery lying in disassembled glory in one's mental driveway. Philosophy is a bit of an intellectual disease which when contracted puts previously useful people in a state of articulate and sophisticated impotence. The disease and its carriers should be avoided.

Sometimes philosophy is a necessary evil. On these occasions our intellectual tools don't work very well. Then it is no longer practical to keep using them. We must stop and check them. Perhaps they will need to be modified or replaced.

I believe that in public education we need such a retooling. This study is based on the assumption that much of what we do in public schools is ultimately rooted in our concepts of rationality, liberty, and equality. Our understanding of these concepts has been inherited from the Enlightenment and forms an integrated ideology which I deem liberalism. These concepts are the intellectual tools that we have used to create public schools. And I believe that these tools have become problematic and need to be reexamined.

Perhaps this need to retool is best illustrated by the concept of equality. Two and a half decades ago the Supreme Court in *Brown v. Board of Education* ordered the desegregation of American public schools. Today in many northern cities fewer blacks attend schools with whites than was true when *Brown* was decided. We are not, however, even sure whether this is legally or morally objectionable. Segregation in urban schools is now largely a function of population migration. Is that as objectionable as the legislated segregation *Brown* outlawed? To answer such questions we need a clearer view of what equality of opportunity entails. We need to inspect our tools. We can no longer pursue equality without resolving our philosophical muddle.

Similarly our concepts of liberty and rationality no longer work well for us. We are unsure of the intellectual function of schools and of what role a rational person is to play. In many modern views of learning the learner is seen as a passive recipient of instruction rather than as a rational agent. Likewise we are unsure of how to partition the public and private aspects of schooling. Many feel that schools have encroached on the rights of parents. Demands that schools teach values are met by an equally energetic insistence that schools should be neutral about values. Here, too, we should examine our central concepts.

In this study I take the position that to a surprising extent the myriad problems of public schooling are rooted in the values and concepts of liberalism. It is liberalism that best captures the vision of justice which schools have been expected to promote. The contradictions of schooling are the contradictions of liberal ideology. The book thus involves a critique of a liberal theory of justice as an educational philosophy. It is also a defense, since I argue that an adequate philosophy of education can be stated in liberal terms. Liberalism has become problematic, but it also possesses the intellectual resource for renewal.

I proceed by examining a range of contemporary educational problems from a liberal point of view. The study employs a good deal of nonphilosophical material, but the point is to assess its philosophical relevance and to place it in a philosophical context. I have tried to select important current issues, to review both recent events and the best of current scholarship about these issues, and to inform the discussion by means of the best of contemporary philosophy. The "facts" I assume are often controversial, yet I do not normally argue them. Instead I see my task as setting the current empirical work in a coherent intellectual framework. Philosophy cannot be done without a view of the facts, but the philosopher's role is to interpret the facts, not to establish them.

I regard the study as a quasi text. I do not attempt to review the field. Nor am I neutral about the issues raised, but I do discuss a representative range of contemporary issues and integrate them into a discussion of the dominant public ideology. This study is therefore quite appropriate for classroom use. In my opinion the most effective use will be to base additional readings on the topics of the various chapters. A reasonable set of such readings can be inferred from the notes. The book can also stand alone as a text, or it can be used as one of several monographs.

The study's major virtue as a text is that it will allow the student to confront philosophically issues which even the least philosophically inclined among us will recognize as real. I hope that this will commend its use. It is not, however, easy reading. For the philosophically uninitiated student, it will need to be worked through and taught, not just read.

Before moving on to the argument of the book, I would like to make a few comments on the book's strategy. I hope that these remarks both will give the reader a sense of enterprise and will prevent misunderstanding.

This book is devoted to discussion of the educational significance of three liberal ideas. The ideas are that people should be rational and autonomous, that they should have equality of opportunity, and that there is a limit to state authority, a private sphere over which the individual, not the state, is sovereign. I have identified these as liberal ideas; I do not, however, identify liberalism with these ideas.

I do not propose the ideas I examine as a definition or a concept of liberalism. I doubt that political ideologies can be rigorously defined. Looked at long enough, ideologies will evolve in terms both of the concepts which are seen as central to them and of the formulation of particular concepts. Private property is less central to current liberal views of justice than was once the case. The concept of equality has changed substantially over several centuries. Political philosophies do not have essences. At any given time they will consist of a set of competing formulations of solutions to problems that are essentially agreed upon. Looked at historically they will exhibit an evolution of concepts and an evolution of problems. One identifies a given idea as liberal as much by its genealogy as by its actual content.

I do not claim therefore that the concepts here discussed define liberalism. I do claim, however, that they represent enduring and central themes in the liberal tradition. All three ideas had been formulated in a recognizable form by the nineteenth century. All three have roots in the liberal tradition which go back far earlier. And all three have endured into the twentieth century, but not without modification. They represent points of comparative stability in liberal thought.

I claim also for these ideas that they are useful tools for thinking about educational problems. How we understand these ideas is important for educational issues. Indeed many educational issues make little sense apart from these liberal ideas. But I assert few historical or empirical claims about the connections between liberal ideology and educational practice. I assume these liberal ideals are relevant to educational history, but ideas affect events in complex and circuitous ways. I do not deal with such causal issues and claim only that these liberal themes provide fruitful ways to analyze educational issues.

These ideas are formulated for systematic, not historical, reasons. Normally I state an idealized version of one of these themes and then use it to consider a set of educational issues. The criterion is that it illuminates the issue. The formulation may or may not have played a significant role in the history of the issue. What is important is its capacity to allow us to understand some problem in a philosophically fruitful way.

I have selected the topics because they are current, important, controversial, and because they can be illuminated by my philosophical tools. I have also tried to present a reasonable range of issues. Several factors are involved in the selection of nonphilosophical material. I have dealt with Skinner because he represents behaviorism. I have dealt with behaviorism because it is important and because it is rooted in the empiricist assumptions held by many liberals. I discuss numerous court cases. For the most part they are the leading precedents on their particular topics. I consider constitutional law at length because it is a major vehicle through which abstract philosophical commitments are turned into social reality. Often if one wants to identify a paradigm of how our society thinks about a certain issue, there is no better source than a court case or two.

I have focused on the Coleman report and the Westinghouse evaluation of Head Start because they are visible and have had substantial impact. Although not definitive they personify social and intellectual happenings which have been formative in our understanding of inequality. I use them to show that inequality of opportunity is not simply a product of overt discrimination; it is also a result of economic inequality and social class. This theme, which is crucial to the final section, is the phenomenon with which liberal views of equality must come to terms. Its truth does not depend on the accuracy of the details of the Coleman report or the Westinghouse study. They simply represent the larger claim that poverty and social class are inheritable when overt discrimination is absent.

My last point is that this book does not have an official foil. When I devote time to discussing or refuting views which differ from my own, I do so because I believe that the best argument which can be given for an idea is that it has the potential to solve the problems generated by its predecessors. For this reason I normally try to show that the educational problems I deal with are rooted in some traditional liberal, political, or epistemological conception. The major argument for my views is that they are a rational response to the particular problems generated.

While the book does not have a foil, it does contain a secondary theme. I regard the major competition to a liberal view of schooling to be to the left, particularly the work of recent neo-Marxists. I deal with various Marxist ideas lightly in the introduction and chapters 8 and 12. I have not wanted to lose the thread of my argument by looking at the competition too often. The reader who is knowledgeable concerning neo-Marxist writings will, however, find a fair amount of material in the volume which is relevant to an assessment of a Marxist view of education. Part of what I have wanted to suggest is that much of the leftist critique can be dealt with within the liberal tradition. One can accept many of the facts of the critique without buying the general Marxist intellectual package. I have argued this view only briefly in chapter 12. It deserves a far more extensive treatment. That treatment awaits another book.

The contribution of this book consists largely in its development of a set of intellectual tools, indeed a perspective, which can be used to think about real educational problems. I will not be crushed if the reader disagrees with much of what I say. There is little herein that is not speculative and uncertain. I will be disappointed if the reader does not find the book fruitful. Read it, please, with these perspectives in mind.

ACKNOWLEDGMENTS

Many people have helped with this manuscript. Sidney Siskin transcribed my scrawl on yellow paper into a first draft quickly, well, and without complaining about my writing. Marj Hulin has patiently retyped numerous revisions and inserted and deleted numerous paragraphs, tolerating my indecisiveness well. Don Habibi and Jeff Claus have helped with the proofreading and index.

Others have shared their ideas with me on the manuscript or its contents. They include Barry Bull, Lynn DeJonghe, Walter Feinberg, Peter Goldstone, Seymour Itzkoff, Donna Kerr, Hugh Petrie, and Jonas Soltis. My special thanks to Donna Kerr for helping to arrange the sabbatical leave at Washington during which the project was begun.

My thanks to all of these people. If I have neglected anyone, please attribute it to a memory like a steel sieve.

The truth of the matter is that the scientific attitude of mind is one of the highest values, and a primary value in democracy.

—F.S.C. NORTHROP

Introduction/
Liberalism and Education

American public institutions, including public schools, have roots in liberal views of social justice. One should therefore begin by explaining what liberalism is.

That is not a simple task. Liberalism has substantially evolved over the last several centuries. Moreover there exist significantly disparate strains in liberal thought. That there is some set of doctrines to which all liberals will subscribe is unclear.

For my purposes I shall treat three doctrines as central to liberal thought—rational autonomy, liberty, and equal rights. I do not claim that a commitment to some variant of these views is essential to liberalism. I do claim that these doctrines are central in the liberal tradition, and that they will prove a convenient vehicle for examining a variety of problems in public education.

An intuitive grasp of these doctrines may be achieved when they are contrasted with the views they replaced. Liberalism is the view which supplanted the social ideology which dominated Europe in the late Middle Ages. Perhaps the central doctrine of the period was the Aristotelian notion of natural place. The elements, earth, air, fire, and water were held to have a natural place in the world to which they return unless prevented by some external force. As a social doctrine this notion legitimated social hierarchies and inequalities of rights and status. Men have a natural place in the social world. Kings are kings and lords lords by virtue of natural superiority and divine appointment. It is their natural right to rule, and it is the natural duty of others to obey. A hierarchical ordering of society and an inherited status within that hierarchy is thus the natural state of affairs. Under this dispensation to resist the authority of those higher in the natural order was to war against God and the natural law.

This view is reflected in the conception of knowledge and in the conception of the individual's rights and duties of the period. Individuals were not regarded as able to think for themselves. Nor were they regarded as entitled to do so. The extant view of knowledge placed substantial emphasis on authority. Revelation as embodied in the Scriptures and the authority of Aristotle were the major intellectual forces. Knowledge was mediated to the common man by an ecclesiastical hierarchy.

Finally medieval society recognized few limits on the rights of the state or the church to regulate individual conduct. The church particularly felt itself entitled to oversee the spiritual health of the community. There was no sense that some areas of belief or conduct are the individual's private concern. The whole of conduct was a public matter.

Liberalism is the ideology which emerged from the collapse of these doctrines. Thus it can be formulated in opposition to them. It involves a commitment to a concept of rational autonomy which assumes that it is possible and obligatory to think for oneself. This doctrine has among its sources the Protestant Reformation and the emergence of the natural sciences. The Reformation introduced the notion of the priesthood of the individual believer. The individual was directly responsible to God for faith and conduct. The mediation of the church was not required. This meant that individuals must assume the responsibility to decide right and wrong for themselves. They must study and interpret the Scriptures.

The development of science also generated support for the idea of rational autonomy. Science provided a method whose results depended on experience and reason rather than on revelation and authority. More than this, it provided a method suitable to everyone. God may not speak to everyone, and not everyone can study Aristotle. But everyone has experience. If knowledge resides in experience and if the church and the philosopher are so many sources of bias, obstacles to learning from experience, wherein does the authority to judge for others lie? Are not people in a position to judge for themselves? How can one person presume to assume that duty for another?

The emphasis on experience and on moral autonomy is connected with the liberal rejection of inherited status and with the development of a concept of equality. The idea that everyone can learn from experience suggests the illegitimacy of inherited authority. People who can judge for themselves do not need the supervision of their betters. Moreover, those differences among individuals which seemed to justify one person's right to rule another are not a function of inheritance, but result from differences in experience. Perhaps rulers are made, not born. If this is the case, should not the higher places in society be earned? Is it not objectionable for social position or social authority to be inherited? Liberals, then, sought to replace aristocracy with meritocracy.

Is not the obligation of rational autonomy incompatible with authority at all? If I have a duty to do what I believe is right, I cannot simultaneously have a duty to obey another, regardless of what that person wishes me to do. If anyone is to have authority over me, must I not first agree to it and must it not be provisional? This seems the only kind of authority compatible with my duty to engage in independent judgment.

Such arguments lead to the liberal doctrines that social position must be earned rather than inherited and to the concept that government must rest on the consent of the governed. Ideas of equality and equal rights, thereby, replace older notions of inherited inequalities. Equality is man's natural condition, and inequalities stand in need of justification.

The final doctrine of liberalism is also suggested by rational autonomy. Liberals insist that governmental authority is limited. The obligation to decide for one's self requires the right to self-determination. Liberals have responded to this idea by attempting to limit governmental authority to public functions, leaving the rest of life to the individual's discretion. Thus liberalism does not claim the authority to regulate all areas of life. Instead it assumes that the exercise of authority has to be justified. An area to be controlled must be a legitimate *public* concern. Otherwise the area is a private matter. Liberal societies do not have a private morality.

Let me summarize these central ideals of liberalism. 1. Liberals assume that knowledge is a function of experience, not authority, and that individuals have the competence and duty to be rationally autonomous. 2. Liberals assume that there are limits on social authority and that there is a private sphere of beliefs and conduct over which the individual should exercise autonomy. 3. Liberals assume that social privilege and authority are neither natural nor inheritable. Social position must be earned and authority must be justified.

These ideas are characteristic of liberalism. It does not follow that they are always expressed in the way I have expressed them or that liberals always accept the arguments I have sketched. In the next several pages I will present a more detailed description of the view that knowledge rests on experience and will suggest a tentative liberal definition of the state. Here these same themes appear, but in different guises and argued for in different ways.

A. EMPIRICISM

The concept that knowledge comes from experience is usually labeled *empiricism*. Historically it is an attempt to make sense of the emerging natural sciences. Older epistemologies had taken geometry as their model of what knowledge entails. They understood knowing as a matter of deducing propositions (theorems) from self-evident truths (axioms). Knowledge began, then, in the intuition of innately known and/or self-evident ideas. We can know whatever is intuitively certain and whatever we can deduce from it. Experience was not a source of self-evident truths. It was regarded as capricious, and not a reliable source of knowledge.

But, empiricists claim, science does not fit this view. Scientific claims are neither self-evident, like the axioms of geometry, nor deducible from self-evident truths, like the theorems of geometry. Instead scientific claims are based on experience. While experience may appear capricious, underneath there is a basic regularity. Experiences follow one on the other in an orderly fashion. Experience is governed by laws. If we observe carefully, keep good records, conduct subtle experiments, and approach experience without preconceived ideas, we can discover these laws. Indeed all knowledge is like this. Knowledge does not originate in revelation, intuition, or innate ideas; it originates from the testimony of the senses. The empiricist motto assures us *There is nothing in the mind which was not first in the senses.*

This discussion concerns not only how ideas get justified, but the furniture and operations of the mind. Those epistemologies which took geometry as paradigmatic of knowledge had to explain how we can be aware of self-evident truths. Are they intuited? If so, the mind must possess a faculty of intuition, an inward eye to see such truths. Are they innate? If so, the mind must be populated with innate ideas.

Empiricists require no such mental furniture. If all knowledge arises from experience, we need not populate the mind with faculties of intuition or innate ideas. In fact, empiricists claim, the mind is empty at birth. It is a blank tablet to be written on by experience. Thus "There is nothing in the mind which was not first in the senses" is not simply a claim that knowledge originates in experience; it is a claim about the furniture of the mind. The mind has no innate furniture. Anything in one's mind got there through the senses. Empiricism's dilemma is to explain how the mind, beginning with nothing, ever learns anything. Even this issue must be addressed scientifically. Suppose we take physics as the model for psychology. Perhaps, then, there are atoms of experience just as there are atoms of matter. Psychology should investigate the laws governing atoms of experience just as physics investigates the laws governing atoms of matter.

Empiricism thus sets problems to be solved by philosophers and by psychologists. The philosophical questions concern how ideas are rooted in experience. They are largely questions concerning the justification of ideas. What kind of experience is required to confirm or reject a scientific theory? How can we proceed to identify the regularities in events? These are typical of the philosophical questions of empiricists.

The psychological questions concern the operation of the mind. How does the mind learn from experience? What powers, capacities, or faculties must the mind have to learn from experience? Empiricist psychologists are concerned with the laws according to which learning results from experience. How do the atoms of experience interact?

Empiricism thus dictates some of the assumptions under which a psycologist must work in understanding learning. This is likewise the case with views of human motivation and ethics. If the mind is empty at birth, one needs to ask not only how knowledge arises, but how motives and values arise. The standard empiricist approach to these questions is that motives and values also originate in experience. Human beings not only have experiences of events in the world, but experiences arising from their own bodies. Among such experiences are sensations of pleasure and pain.

Pleasure and pain are the basis of motivation and of good and evil. People should pursue pleasure and avoid pain. Locke puts the matter simply. Pleasure and pain "like other simple ideas, cannot be described, nor their names defined; the way of knowing them is, as of the simple ideas of the senses, only by experience"[1] And: "Things are good or evil, only in reference to pleasure or pain. . . . Pleasure and pain . . . are the hinges on which our passions turn."[2] Empiricism thus extends its influence into moral psychology and ethics. Empiricists turn out to be hedonists as well. Pleasure is the good. Isn't that what experience teaches?

These ingredients of empiricism can be extrapolated into a view of rationality. It is the function of rationality to maximize pleasure and minimize pain. Success in maximizing pleasure and minimizing pain depends on identifying those regularities in experience on which pain and pleasure are contingent. For the empiricist a rational agent can manage the contingencies of experience so as to maximize the sum total of satisfaction. Indeed acting so as to maximize satisfaction is what is meant by being rational. These assumptions are at the historical center of views of political philosophy and economics, which have substantial impact on policy making in various areas, not the least of which is education.

B. LIBERALISM AND THE STATE

We can now sketch the political views of liberalism. Consider this formulation of a liberal view of the just state: *The state exists to regulate the competition among individuals for their private ends.* Let us look at its implications.

Consider the notion of private ends. While the ethics of empiricism insist that pleasure or happiness is the good, empiricism does not entail any thesis about what makes people happy. Although some liberal thinkers have suggested that a certain kind of activity is most conducive to happiness (Mill, for example, is much in favor of "the life of the mind"),[3] the general liberal theory has been "different strokes for different folks." Whatever it is that makes one happy is good because it makes one happy. Thus, while liberals recommend the pursuit of happiness, this need not lead to a recommendation of any particular mode of life. Happiness can be pursued differently by different people. This view, then, recommends little to people except that they pursue their own happiness in their own way.

It does not follow that individuals ought to do whatever they wish. Happiness as the good is not equivalent to the notion that one should act on immediate impulse. The goal is to maximize happiness over a reasonable period of time. Since the pursuit of one happiness may exclude another, one may need to defer one gratification to enjoy a superior one. Some pleasures likewise have a cost in pain. Thus some immediate gratifications should be avoided. Indeed one may need a plan. Maximizing happiness requires a rational assessment of various courses of action. One needs to choose an optimal solution given the totality of the benefits and costs.

Much the same holds at the social level. Numerous individuals seeking to maximize their happiness will generate conflict. The means of happiness (money, for example) may be scarce. Your happiness may conflict with mine. Accordingly there is a need to coordinate the plans of individuals to maximize the happiness of the largest number of individuals. Life plans, private though they may be, need to be regulated to produce maximum happiness with minimum interference with the life plans of others. This is the function of the state.

This role of the state is captured in the imagery of a state of nature and a social contract. The social condition in which people pursue their happiness without the regulation of the state (the state of nature) produces a degree of conflict such that no one is secure in his liberty or property. Hobbes describes the state of nature as a war of all against all.[4] To end the war people unite to form the state. They enter into a contract in which they agree to give up some of their natural liberty to the state in order to be more secure in pursuing their own happiness.

The state exists in order to regulate conflict in the pursuit of private goals. This view lies at the center of a number of characteristic liberal doctrines. One is the notion that the state has limited power. For example, every happiness is *per se* good; the only reason the state may legitimately interfere with an individual's pursuit of happiness is that it conflicts with someone else's pursuit of happiness. John Stuart Mill puts it best: "The sole end for which mankind are warranted, individually or collectively, in interfering with the liberty of action of any of their number is self-protection. That the only purpose for which power can be rightfully exercised over any member of a civilized community, against his will, is to prevent harm to others. . . . The only part of the conduct of anyone for which he is amenable to society is that which concerns others. In the part which merely concerns himself, his independence is, of right, absolute."[5] The liberal state thus exists to regulate conflicting patterns of action. When the person's pursuit of happiness does not conflict with someone else's pursuit of happiness, its control is beyond the legitimate authority of the state.

The liberal doctrine that values are private leads also to a doctrine of economic liberty. If values are private, individuals should be able to spend their money to realize their own conception of the good life. And if the free choices of consumers are to be meaningful, the economy must be free to provide those goods for which people are willing to pay. Liberals have, therefore, sometimes viewed attempts to regulate what may be bought and sold as equivalent to the establishment of a public concept of value. The state may, of course, regulate the economy to ensure free and fair competition and to prevent harm to others. But for the state to regulate buying and selling for other reasons is a violation of liberty. In a free society the economic system should be one in which free markets provide the goods and services which consumers choose to buy. The economic version of liberty is consumer sovereignty.

A final line of argument holds that the state may exercise only those powers extended to it in the social contract. The people, in effect, have an agreement with the state which specifies the extent of its authority. In the view of some authors this power is quite limited. The state exists primarily to protect liberty and property from crime and external agression and to enforce contracts. The state is limited to these powers and may not exceed them. When it does exceed its authority the people are justified in overthrowing it. Locke,[6] for example, claimed that the state may not confiscate a person's property without his consent. There was to be no taxation without representation. Jefferson used this doctrine to justify the American Revolution. The Declaration of Independence is an indictment of King George for breach of the social contract.

A corollary of liberal views on the limits of civil authority is that the state has no good beyond the aggregate good of its members. The state is not an end in itself. Thus, while the state may legitimately expect its citizens to sacrifice their interests to the aggregate good, it may not ask its citizens to sacrifice their interests to the well-being of the state. Moreover the state may not pursue goals which cannot be defined in terms of the aggregate interests of its citizens. It may not, for example, conceive of itself as existing to promote transcendent religious or cultural values. Therefore the state may not have or enforce a view of private morality. In the liberal state individuals may pursue their own happiness as they conceive it. The state may not interfere with an individual's conduct in order to enforce moral claims unless these moral claims concern action affecting the well being of others. Morality is otherwise a private, not a public, affair.

The liberal notion of equality holds that claims to inherited superiority are spurious. No one is entitled to preferential treatment because of family background. Everyone is entitled to equal rights.

If people are equal, then, everyone's happiness is of equal value. When adding up the aggregate happiness we cannot count anyone's happiness as worth more in the equation than anyone else's. No one has any antecedent claim to better treatment than anyone else. These doctrines commit the liberal state to policies precluding the making of decisions or the extending of benefits or opportunities in a way in which background is taken into account. Indeed many liberals would argue the stronger thesis that the state has the affirmative duty to eliminate any effects of background on a person's life chances. English liberals were, of course, interested in overturning special privileges for an inherited aristocracy. Americans have applied such doctrines to racial issues as well.

The view of equality which results is that equality is a matter of ensuring fair competition. In liberal theory the state is not a dispenser of goods or benefits. These are to be earned and should reflect the individual's merit. The state's role is to regulate the competition for goods or benefits, to make sure that how well one does reflects merit rather than family background. Success should depend on what one does, not who one is. Equality therefore does not consist in ensuring an equal division of goods, but in ensuring that people have a fair chance to compete for these goods. Liberal equality is fair competition. Indeed, on some liberal views, any distribution of goods is just so long as its results from fair competition. Liberal equality provides for equal rights, not equal outcomes.

C. LIBERALISM: OLD AND NEW, LEFT AND RIGHT

The view of the liberal state just sketched may seem dated. Perhaps it will seem more akin to the conservatism of Barry Goldwater or Milton Friedman than to the liberalism of Edward Kennedy or John Kenneth Galbraith.

The formulation thus far is a traditional one. What needs to be emphasized, however, is the extent to which these traditional liberal views endure in the contemporary political spectrum. The idea that people have equal rights is a traditional liberal theme that our time has given much attention to understanding and applying. While its specific content and what is believed about what is necessary to attain it may have much evolved, the general commitment to some concept of equal rights has been a central part of liberalism through several centuries.

But the idea of equal rights will not be the part of my description of liberalism which will seem dated. Instead the controversial point will be my characterization of the liberal state. I have suggested that the chief role of the liberal state is to regulate the competition among individuals for their private ends. Such a view of the state may seem reminiscent of the rugged individualism of the nineteenth century, suggesting a very minor role for government in human affairs. It has been a long time, however, since many Americans have taken seriously the idea that that government governs best which governs least. Liberalism is popularly identified these days with those who advocate an increased role for government.

What has changed about liberalism is not so much its basic ideals as what is believed concerning the means for pursuing these ideals. Traditionally liberals have seen the state, which is supposed to be the major vehicle for securing human rights and liberties, as the major threat to rights and liberties as well. Much in human experience tends to prove this view. The problem that liberals have had to solve is how to limit the power of the state to its central functions and prevent the accumulation of power which can allow the state to usurp human rights and restrict liberties.

Many liberals in the eighteenth and nineteenth centuries thought the key to solving this problem was a sharp restriction of the powers of the government. Contemporary liberals have had a more ambivalent view of state power. On one hand liberals have sought to restrict state power in certain areas. They have sought to defend constitutional rights such as free speech, privacy, or freedom of life-style. On the other hand liberals have also sought the expansion of state power in order to secure certain rights and liberties, especially when human rights were threatened either by local opinion or by concentrated private economic power. Thus the securing of the rights of blacks required an expansion of the power of the federal judiciary. Moreover the expanded power of the federal government generally has been seen as a balance against the economic power of great wealth and large corporate organizations. A powerful federal state is the alternative to the rule of General Motors and DuPont.

What is perhaps most important is liberals realizing that central liberal values have economic preconditions. Those values are threatened by poverty, depressions, and business cycles. Liberals have seen government regulation of economic life as a cure for such ills.

That liberals have not generally abandoned their central ideals to their tolerance of expanded state power is crucial. Liberals still believe in equal rights, they still believe that there are areas of life—one's beliefs, values, and life-style—from which state power should be excluded; and they still believe that a society comprised of self-governing citizens requires a rational citizenry. The state continues to be a means to promote each individual's pursuit of the good as the individual defines it and to adjudicate disputes which arise from the competition for such personal goods. Liberals may conceive this role more broadly, but the basic idea endures. The central values of liberalism have endured in the twentieth century well. Beliefs about how to secure these values have not.

Thus, the popular distinction between liberal and conservative is misleading. The major political parties in the United States are both liberal parties. One is simply more traditional than the other.

Marxism is in some respects an heir to the liberal's insistence that human beings are fundamentally equal and are entitled to equal rights and equal dignity. Marxists have added to these liberal views a strong sense of the extent to which human affairs are dominated by historical and economic forces, rather than by ideas or by the decisions of great men. Such ideas have contributed greatly to our understanding of human societies. Marxists have shown that there are economic prerequisites to a just society, and they have demonstrated the importance of social class in human affairs.

Marxists' strong sense of economic determinism has been corrupting, however, so far as many liberal ideals are concerned. Perhaps most important, Marxists have seen human thought as primarily the product of historical and economic forces—not of reason, argument, and evidence. "Ideology is a function of class." Marxists have also been impressed with the extent to which ideas and values play a role in perpetuating current social arrangements. One's tastes and values are not mere personal preferences. They play a role in the class struggle.

Such views have resulted in major consequences to liberal values. They have caused Marxists to have little regard for rational autonomy. To a Marxist an individual's values and beliefs are not the autonomous choices of a rational agent but are the product of an unjust social order. At best, for Marxists, rational autonomy awaits a new and just society.

Marxists also have a low opinion of the worth of such liberal institutions as freedom of speech, press, or assembly. Liberals see these rights as ways of promoting free and open debate on important social issues, thereby improving the rationality of collective decisions. Marxists tend to see them as ways of transmitting the ideology of the ruling class while at the same time creating the illusion of free choice. Consequently Marxists have engaged significantly in regulating belief and value. A just society is possible only when people believe and value the proper things. It is the responsibility of the state to ensure that they do.

Because Marxists tend to see ideas as products of social forces and instruments for the perpetuation of injustice and because they have a low regard for the capacity of individuals for rational independent thought, they tend to undervalue thought and persuasion as sources of social change and democratic institutions as its means. Instead they see change as the inexorable product of social forces. They have little regard for the ability of human beings to assume rational control over social forces and are given to entertaining the notion that people must be made to be free. Coercion, not persuasion, is the primary path to liberation. Liberals, by contrast, are more inclined to see thought, persuasion, and democratic institutions as central components of how social change should take place.

Liberals diverge from Marxists over such values as rational autonomy, personal liberty, and social change. One root of this divergence is a disagreement concerning the extent to which individuals are inevitably products of their social environment. Liberals have a higher regard for the ability of individuals to liberate themselves from social forces than do Marxists. If liberals are to be proven right, they will need to provide a coherent account of the origins of rational thought—one which accounts for the role of social forces in learning without making the individual a mere product of them.

Needless to say, such views may readily be seen in terms of schooling. Liberals perceive schools as means to create rational autonomous individuals, and they mark educational value in the free and open exchange of ideas. Marxists see schools in a capitalist society as devices to perpetuate capitalist ideology and the other interests of the ruling classes. Intellectual freedom and equal opportunity will appear as smokescreens for capitalist domination. Moreover Marxists generally use schools to transmit a "correct" point of view, and they are less willing to tolerate dissent. These tendencies are not aberrations of current Marxist societies, but are rooted in Marxist views on the social origins of ideas.

One final point: in considering the relations between liberalism and Marxism we should not identify liberalism with capitalism. Liberalism and capitalism are historically and ideologically linked. But the central liberal values at issue here do not have to be realized in a capitalist society. Perhaps they may be achieved in a society which has asserted substantial public control over the means of production. I do not regard liberal or democratic socialism as self-contradictory. I regard the form of economic life most compatible with liberal values as an open question.

D. LIBERALISM AND EDUCATION

The central values of liberalism should indicate the public function of schools in a liberal state.

Consider the obligations which flow from the concept that the citizens of a liberal state are to be autonomous—capable of running their own lives and functioning effectively in a democratic society. Such views place substantial faith in the individual's capacity to function rationally and to learn from experience. Yet the capacity for rational judgment is acquired. A society founded on liberal principles must have a substantial stake in creating institutions which ensure that the capacity for rational judgment is widely distributed. Schools are institutions which are supposed to fulfill this task.

This view entails having a sensible view of what rationality is and how it connects with autonomy and citizenship in a democratic society. A public school needs a pedagogy which does more than efficiently transmit the cultural heritage or vocational skills. It must teach students how to order their own affairs rationally, and how to function as competent citizens. In a liberal society, good pedagogy will be determined by the concept of rationality and will be oriented to the promotion of rational autonomy.

The ideas that people are entitled to equal rights and that social position should be earned, not inherited, also generate a need for public education. The idea that people have equal rights ought to be realized in institutions which provide an equal opportunity to influence collective decisions. But the ability to participate effectively in collective decisions requires more than the right to vote or the rights of free speech, assembly, and petition. It requires the capacity to understand one's own interests and to understand how to affect decisions. These capacities in turn require education. If they are to be fairly distributed, they require equal education. Furthermore it makes little sense to insist that people can advance as far as their ability can take them while allowing the opportunity to develop talents to depend on factors such as parental wealth. The public school is a place where talent can be nurtured regardless of social status. It is a device to cause social position to be earned rather than inherited.

Rational autonomy and equality suggest the basic functions of public schooling in a liberal society. The basic commodity that schooling should distribute is rationality. Equality adds the requirement that rationality must be distributed fairly. These notions can be captured in a motto for schooling: *The central public function of schooling in a liberal state is the democratic distribution of rationality.*

The final point to make about public schools is that they clash with the liberal view of a just society in one significant way. Liberal societies are not supposed to have a public concept of the good. The values that people pursue are their own business. But surely part of a reasonable education includes developing a notion of one's own good. Schools in a liberal state therefore have a difficulty to finesse. They must teach so as to allow individuals to develop their own idea of the good without making some notion of the good a matter of public policy. In a liberal society schools cannot legitimately encroach on the private sphere. They cannot be devices for forcing one person's idea of the good on another.

These areas of concern form the topics for the sections of this book which are here presented in summary.

In section I I explore the concept of rationality and its connection both with views on teaching and learning and with liberal views of autonomy and liberty. I argue that empiricism has evolved so as to undermine the liberal values it once supported. I then develop a view of empiricism more supportive of liberal values.

In section II I explore the tension between public schools and private values. I argue that public schools cannot be effective in allowing individuals to develop their own view of the good while remaining neutral concerning the good. And I claim that the school's difficulties in helping students develop a sense of their own good is increased by how it understands its economic role. Schools which train students to fill jobs that debase tastes and destroy creativity cannot expect simultaneously to help students develop creativity and refined taste.

In section III I examine the notion that equality is fair competition and consider the educational policies that attitude has generated. I argue that it is unlikely that schools can effectively promote fair competition or provide equal rights unless society is willing to reduce the extremes of wealth and poverty in direct ways. I conclude this section by attempting to develop a liberal view of justice consistent with this point and by developing some of its implications for educational policy.

The results of these inquiries should provide an enhanced sense of the role of the school in a liberal society and the obstacles to be overcome if the educational potential of public education in a liberal society is to be realized.

I

Rationality,
Pedagogy, and
Liberal Values

The liberal emphasis on the individual's right and duty to be self-directing in the private sphere and to participate competently in public affairs generates a need for a wide dispersion of competency in rational decision-making. A basic value of a liberal society is the democratic distribution of rationality. This is the central task of public education.

This view of the role of schooling requires a concept of teaching and learning which is rooted in a coherent view of the nature of rational inquiry. It also demands a view of teaching and learning which is consistent with liberal values. Section I involves the development of a view fulfilling these requirements.

The specific agenda is dominated by two concerns. I believe that the empiricist views traditionally held by liberal philosophers are substantially wrong. We therefore need a different view of rationality and a pedagogy which fits it. Also, empiricism has evolved so that its modern psychological variant, behaviorism, is at odds with liberal values. This is a problem which must be examined in detail.

Chapter 1 examines the nature of the connection between views of rationality and views of learning. Chapter 2 examines the evolution of empiricism into behaviorism and formulates the nature of behaviorist pedagogy. Chapter 3 develops a critique and provides an alternative view of rationality and pedagogy. Chapter 4 examines the conflict between behaviorism and liberal values.

A man demonstrates his rationality, not by a commitment to fixed ideas, stereotyped procedures, or immutable concepts, but by the manner in which and the occasions on which, he changes those ideas, procedures, and concepts.

—STEPHEN TOULMIN

The Idea of Rationality

Consider this definition of a rational person: *Rational persons are those whose beliefs are well ordered and are based on available evidence and who are able and willing to alter their beliefs when available evidence warrants.*

Beliefs have an organization. We do not just believe one damn thing after another. Instead we believe some things because they seem to follow from other things we believe, and we reject some things because they seem inconsistent with other things we believe.

Suppose that we are dealing with a young student who is unconvinced that the world is round. We might ask what kind of evidence would be acceptable for this claim. Let us suppose that the student agrees that if someone were to sail around the world, then the world would have to be round. We might then inform the student that Magellan sailed around the world. The student should conclude that the world is round.

Here we see a small piece of a belief system. The student recognizes that the postulate "If someone sailed around the world it must be round" and the fact "Magellan sailed around the world" require a conclusion: "The world is round." The student thus ends up with a belief structure in which the beliefs are connected as premises and conclusions.

Suppose, however, our student to be a member of the flat earth society. He is convinced that the world is not round. Such a student may respond to the identical argument by rejecting the premise that Magellan sailed around the world. Since the world is flat, one could not sail around it. Or the student might reject the claim that sailing around the world requires that the world be round. Perhaps Magellan sailed around the edge of a flat but circular world.

Here too the student's beliefs have a structure. He recognizes that the belief in a flat earth requires the rejection of incompatible beliefs. Again the beliefs have an organization which is the organization of an argument. Some beliefs stand as premises. Others follow from them.

Notice how the relations between beliefs are described in these examples. I have used words like *premise, conclusion, follows from* and *argument.* Had I expanded the examples, terms such as *infers, deduces, provides evidence for,* or *warrants* could also have been used. The conclusion to be drawn from the occurrence of such terms is that the relations between beliefs involve logical relations. Or, more accurately, the relations between beliefs are the mental representation of logical relations. *Relations among beliefs, belief structure, thus can be described by employing the vocabulary which is used to describe logical relations between propositions.*

Not all relations among beliefs can be described in this way. A student who believes that Magellan sailed around the world because he believes that his teacher will like him better if he agrees with her views about history has not inferred the first belief from the second. Therefore beliefs can also be related to one another in nonlogical ways.

The arguments which link the beliefs in a belief system need not be good ones. People make mistakes. They may incorrectly infer one belief from another, or they may make correct inferences from false or unwarranted assumptions. It follows that the structure of beliefs can be more or less logical or more or less rational. If this is the case, then we shall need some criteria for a system of rational belief.

One view of the organization of propositions holds that the set of assertions concerning a given area is optimally organized when it can be expressed as an axiomatized deductive system.[1] The view involves bodies of propositions, but it can be extended to cover the mental representation of propositions—belief systems—as well.

What is an axiomatized system? Such a system consists of a small body of propositions—axioms—from which a larger body of propositions—theorems—can be deduced. The most familiar example of such a system is geometry. Geometry consists of a small number of axioms from which an infinite number of theorems can be derived. Such axiomatized deductive systems have been constructed for many areas of mathematics and logic and have been attempted with less success for areas of the physical sciences as well.

To insist that rational agents will have all of their beliefs organized into such a deductive system is unreasonable. It is not clear to what extent such a thing is possible. History, for example, may not yield the kind of knowledge which permits axiomatization. It is even less clear that there is some kind of comprehensive set of ideas capable of subsuming history, mathematics, and physics together with other branches of knowledge. Even if these things are possible, they have not been achieved. We cannot demand that individuals succeed in doing what generations of scholars have been unable to do.

We can, however, ask what ideals about knowledge an axiomatized system captures. These can be a guide to a well-ordered belief system. Such a system is internally consistent. The theorems follow from the axioms according to recognized principles of inference. Axiomatized systems are also economical ways to represent knowledge. The axioms contain the information expressed in the theorems. That is why the theorems can be deduced from the axioms. Accordingly axioms succinctly express the information contained in what might otherwise be a vast number of theorems.

Axiomatization increases the scope and power of a set of ideas. The attempt to express what we know in general and abstract ways often allows us to generate new and unexpected results. Generating novel predictions from our general principles enables us to test these principles and to add to our store of knowledge. Axiomatized systems represent the most integrated form of knowledge. They are the kind of thing required if knowledge is not to be one damn thing after another. They allow us to see how our beliefs are related and to recognize when they are inconsistent.

These aspects of axiomatized deductive systems give us some quite plausible standards for judging a belief system. *A well-ordered belief system is one which is internally consistent, arranged in as economical and powerful a form as possible, and integrated rather than fragmented.*[2]

A belief system might succeed quite well in terms of these criteria, but nevertheless be linked inadequately to available evidence. A belief system can, for example, be internally consistent and quite at odds with the evidence. A belief system therefore must be more than well ordered: it must be related to independent evidence. In evaluating belief systems, we should be concerned with the evidence for sets of beliefs rather than each belief. We should not expect to be able to test each belief independently of the others. A well-ordered belief system should prove correct at those points where it can be checked. Other beliefs will often be evaluated by their logical connections to those which can be tested.

These intuitive ideas can be given a clearer formulation by returning to an axiomatized deductive system. How might such a system of beliefs be warranted? Philosophers have suggested two basic views. The first holds that the axioms are known to be true on grounds independent of the belief system and that other beliefs are known to be true because they follow from the axioms. Views of this sort usually hold the axioms to be intuitively self-evident (a traditional view of geometry) or true by definition (such as the basic axioms of arithmetic).

In the second view theorems are known to be true independently of other beliefs. These beliefs are known on the basis of experience. Other beliefs are held to be true because they explain and predict the facts described by these beliefs.

Let us call the beliefs which can be known to be true independent of their relations to other beliefs *basic beliefs*. Different views on how knowledge is warranted might then be distinguished according to their view on which beliefs are basic beliefs. Those epistemologies which view the axioms as basic beliefs are usually called *rationalism*. Those which consider that basic beliefs are theorems which are known by experience are usually called *empiricism*. Most contemporary views are a mixture of both.

We can formulate the concept of a warranted belief system in terms of basic beliefs. A well-warranted belief system is one which is well ordered and whose basic beliefs are confirmed. If a belief system is to be considered reasonable, an individual must have plausible grounds to consider the basic beliefs of the system to be true. A rational person is thus one whose beliefs are well ordered and are rooted in available evidence.

This formulation does not require rational beliefs to be true. A belief system can be reasonable, given the evidence available, but nevertheless be incorrect. The evidence available is often incomplete and can be misleading. One need merely contemplate the history of ideas to find numerous cases of individuals who constructed eloquent and brilliant intellectual edifices on the basis of available evidence and who were subsequently shown wrong. One should not conclude that Plato, Newton, and Kant were not rational because much of what they believed was mistaken. A rational person, then, is one whose beliefs are plausibly based on the evidence he has, not a person who is right.

We can now turn to the last part of the definition of a rational person. *Rational persons are those who are able and willing to change their belief structures when the evidence warrants.* Consider an individual who appears to have a well-ordered belief system. Imagine a scientist who accepts the current theory in his discipline and who is aware of all of the experiments and arguments which support that theory. Suppose now that some new piece of evidence turns up which is at odds with current theory. At first everyone in the field is skeptical. The experiment is replicated with the same results. Theoretical attempts to fit the new data into the old framework fail. New theories are proposed, one of which ultimately triumphs in the field. Our scientist, while aware of this, continues to hold to the old theory in the face of mounting evidence that it is false.

What might we say of such a case? At the beginning we might easily think that the scientist is a model of rationality. However, as the scientist continues to hold to the old theory against mounting evidence, we begin to suspect that he is not as rational as we had supposed. We begin to suspect that he is attached to the old theory in some way having little to do with the evidence. Perhaps he regards this theory as supporting some other cherished belief. Perhaps he has some personal grudge against the person who made the new discovery. All of these speculations suggest that his commitment to the theory is irrational.

Indeed they suggest that the commitment was irrational all along. When people refuse to alter their beliefs when they become implausible we begin to wonder whether their beliefs were ever firmly rooted in the evidence. Perhaps they were always irrationally held, but by chance the persons's irrational commitments happened to coincide with plausible views. The irrational character of the commitment becomes apparent when the beliefs continue to be held even when they have been refuted.

What enables a person to alter beliefs on the basis of new or changing evidence? There are two conditions which I shall call the *skill condition* and the *mental health condition.*[3]

If people are to be persuaded to alter their belief structures by new evidence, they must possess those skills necessary for the evaluation of evidence. Facts do not wear their implications on their sleeves. To treat a fact as a piece of evidence one must be able to apply appropriate standards of judgment and evaluation to its assessment. A person who has not acquired an appropriate range of evaluative skills is not in a position to respond to evidence.

The mental health condition is required because people who are unable to change their minds on the basis of evidence are often incapacitated because they have a heavy emotional investment in believing certain things. A belief which is overloaded with psychic freight will not easily be moved along the track of rationality. Mentally healthy people should not be expected to shed their beliefs with cold detachment, but they are more likely to be able to face the truth when they see it even when it requires the abandonment of cherished beliefs. Mental health is thus a feature of a rational person.

This rough-hewn discussion of rationality has implications for how learning should be described and thought about. A certain language is required for describing the structure and changes in belief systems. Relations between beliefs were often described by means of language used by philosophers to describe logical relations between propositions. Such terms as *deduce, infer,* and *follows from* are typical. Similar concepts were used to describe how beliefs change. Concepts such as *warrants, evidence, entail,* and *evaluate* were employed. These terms are the stock-in-trade of logic and epistemology. They are among the more general terms used for the purpose of discussion of the nature of evidence, rational inquiry, or valid argumentation. The language is normative since it specifies what kinds of arguments are acceptable or reasonable and what kinds aren't. The more precise terms of this language often refer to particular forms of argument or rules of inference.

The discussion of what counts as a rational person thus implies something about the language in which mental states and mental processes should be described. *If we are to think of persons as rational agents, we must use a logical or epistemological language in characterizing belief structures and ways of changing beliefs. If we do not describe people in this way, our concepts about rationality cannot be applied to individuals.* We cannot use the standards of logic and epistemology to evaluate the rationality of belief and thought unless we regard belief and thought as governed by these standards. But to view belief and thought as governed by such rules is to see the relations among beliefs as embodying logical relations and thus as correctly described by a logical language.

A similar point can be made concerning the explanation of rational belief, change of belief, or rational action. *To the extent that we can consider some belief rational, it must be explained by what I shall call a reason-explanation.*[4] Consider two explanations of someone's belief that the world is round. 1. John believes the world is round because he believes that Magellan sailed around the world and that if someone sailed around the world it must be round. 2. John believes the world is round because his teacher praised him for that belief.

The first explanation is a *reason-explanation*. The second is a *causal explanation*.

Explanation 1 contains not merely an explanation of John's belief that the world is round but an argument for it. John believes the world is round because he believes that Magellan sailed around it, and he believes that if someone sailed around the world it must be round. The fact that a reason-explanation contains an argument provides several ways to distinguish a reason-explanation from a causal one. One such way is to note that a reason-explanation contains both an explanation of belief and a justification of it. Explanation 1 not only explains John's belief but it provides evidence which, if adequate, entitles John to the belief. Causal explanations explain, not justify. That John will be praised for his belief is not evidence that the belief is true.

This suggests a second way to distinguish reason-explanations from causal explanations. A reason-explanation can be evaluated in two ways whereas a causal explanation can be evaluated in only one. We can ask of a reason-explanation both if the explanation is true *and* if the justification it contains is successful. These questions are independent of each other. A reason-explanation can be true even if its justification fails. Not all reasons are good ones. Moreover the justification can be successful even though the explanation fails. (One then concludes that if these reasons had been the ones which explained a belief, the belief would have been justified.)

Questions about justification cannot be asked of causal explanations since such explanations do not involve an attempt to justify anything. It does not make sense for us to ask whether a teacher's praise is adequate evidence for believing the world to be round because such praise is not evidence. We may, of course, conclude that John is not justified in his belief because he has no reason for believing it, but this is quite different than saying that his reasons fail to justify his belief. A causal account contains no argument for what it explains. One cannot, therefore, evaluate the argument.

I believe the discussion of the nature of a rational person is of the greatest importance in understanding the nature of learning and the nature of schooling in a liberal society. I hope the reader will agree that if we are interested in having schools produce rational individuals, we need to know what one is. But this account of rationality has implications for understanding not only the ends of education but its means. The account of rationality assumes that a rational person is one whose beliefs are properly acquired and modified. A rational person is one who reasonably changes or acquires beliefs. The beliefs of a rational person must have reason-explanations, not just causal explanations.

This means that *if we wish to think of individuals as rational agents, epistemology must be regarded as at the center of learning theory.* To change beliefs is among the paradigm cases of learning. If we are to think of these changes as rational, we must describe not just the results of learning but the *process* of learning in epistemological concepts. We must give reason-explanations of learning if we are to view learning as a rational endeavor.

If this view seems wrong, perhaps that is because we are used to thinking of learning as the province of psychologists, not philosophers. We have in mind a kind of division of labor between philosophy and psychology which views philosophy as properly concerned with justifying or clarifying the ends of education and views psychology as concerned with the discovery of the means whereby these ends can be achieved. My view upsets this division of labor by involving epistemology in the understanding of the means as well as the ends of learning.

Perhaps then we might be clearer about what it would mean for epistemology to be at the heart of learning theory by contrasting the ideas about teaching and learning which result from this view with the ones which often seem implicit in psychology texts. My view requires us to treat learning as a rational activity. Learning is not primarily considered as remembering or skill acquisition. Instead it is inquiry, a kind of thinking. The student should be viewed as analogous to the scientist on the forefront of knowledge in the sense that learning is viewed as finding out something one does not know and finding out is not a matter primarily of asking someone or looking something up, but rather of comprehending a new idea and obtaining evidence to determine whether it is true.

This does not mean that the student must discover everything without the assistance of books or teachers. But it does require that the student believe for reasons. If we are to view students as rational agents, we will want them to comprehend ideas because we have shown how those ideas make sense and how they can be justified.

This view of learning has a complementary view of teaching. If we want students to believe for reasons, then we should view teaching as the act of reason-giving. We must think of teaching as an activity which arranges experiences and resources so that reasons and evidence for reasonable beliefs are made accessible to students.

Such a view of teaching and learning requires a theory of how rational intellectual change and development occur. When we want to teach something we will have to ask questions concerning what reasons there are for someone to believe the idea we are trying to communicate and concerning how to construct a rational path from the student's current ideas to a more adequate set. These are primarily epistemological questions. They concern the nature of evidence and warranted belief. Thus epistemology, the theory of reasonable belief, is at the center of learning theory.

This view of learning is at odds with what has been the orthodox view of psychology for much of this century. Many psychologists have wished to study learning scientifically and have tried to understand science as they believe it is understood in the natural sciences. They have wished to view the study of learning as the empirical identification of the conditions under which learning occurs and have thought of a learning theory as the discovery of the causes of learning and the laws which govern learning.

This traditional psychologist's view of learning theory differs from my view in that it attempts to provide causal explanations of learning rather than reason-explanations. It has not seen learning as a kind of inquiry or rational activity and has not been much interested in looking at the contribution of epistemology to the study of learning or teaching. Behaviorist theories are paradigmatic of this approach. Here epistemological concepts disappear from the account of learning to be replaced with causal notions such as reinforcement. Anyone with such views thus has great difficulty in seeing learning as a rational enterprise and indeed as seeing persons as rational agents.

It does not follow from my view that psychology should be replaced by epistemology. There are, after all, a host of legitimate questions concerning the empirical circumstances under which learning occurs, and there are causal aspects of learning as well as epistemological ones. The empirical study of learning needs to incorporate, and be informed by, a reasonable epistemology; and the study of learning cannot be regarded as simply the empirical study of the laws of learning. Learning might be seen as an Alsace-Lorraine between philosophy and psychology. It seems to be much fought-over, but it might be more sensibly cohabited.

If we are to think of individuals as rational agents, we must view learning as a rational activity; and if we are to view learning as a rational activity, we must make epistemology a part of learning theory. If these claims are true they suggest three questions which should be taken up in later chapters. 1. *If epistemology should be part of learning theory why is it not taken seriously by so many learning theories?* The thesis I have developed about learning is hardly the prevalent view. We should therefore look at an alternative conception to see what can be said for it. 2. *What epistemology happens to be true?* If we want a learning theory based on an acceptable epistemology we will have to look at some substantive epistemological views. 3. *What are the consequences of failing to take epistemology seriously?* Our interest in epistemology originates in the importance attached to rationality in liberal theory and liberal views of schooling. What happens to these views if we accept a notion of learning which alters or denies the concept of rationality? These questions are topics of the next three chapters. We can begin with the first.

CHAPTER 2

*Any field of inquiry which for fifty years has en-
forced mis-phrasings, and even denials, of subject
matter will have so corrupted most concepts in the
public domain, the thought-schemas of those who
teach the young, and thus the sensibilities of the
young, that the past can somehow survive every
proclamation of its demise.*

—SIGMUND KOCH

Empiricist Views of Learning

Consider this claim about learning. *Reinforce-
ment increases the probability that the behavior reinforced will recur.*
What this says is that if you do something and the consequences of doing
it are favorable, you will probably do it again. Nothing very troublesome
here. But add this claim to it: *All learning can be accounted for in this
way.* Now this idea may be excessive. The first claim may explain how my
cat learned the location of her supper dish or how I learned to play tennis.
But what does it have to do with how I learned astronomy or learned to
talk? Learning astronomy seems to be a matter of acquiring some beliefs
or ideas. They should be described in terms of the belief structures just
sketched. What does acquiring a belief system have to do with one's
behavior having desirable consequences? Shouldn't a belief system reflect
the available evidence, not whether the consequences of holding it are desirable?

How might such a view of learning be expanded to account for
varieties of human learning? Let us imagine a hypothetical course on
astronomy and ask how we might proceed to teach it if we believed the
two claims about learning just asserted.

The first question to address is Can all learning be treated as the
learning of behavior rather than the acquiring of ideas or beliefs? The
behaviorist (as the person subscribing to the two claims is usually called)
may respond as follows. When anyone claims that a person has acquired a
given idea, he assumes that this idea will cause the person to behave in certain ways under specified conditions. Suppose, for example, that the individual has learned that Pluto is the most distant planet from the sun.
Such a person will, when asked What is the most distant planet from the
sun, respond that Pluto is the most distant planet from the sun. In such a

view there is a "causal path" assumed between the external conditions, the idea, and the verbal behavior of the following sort:

$$C + \boxed{I} \rightarrow B$$

This can be read *Conditions plus Ideas cause Behavior.* The box around the letter I indicates that the idea is in the mind. The external conditions and the behavior are, however, observable to everyone.

In this equation what is the point of talking about the mind? Suppose we say that to have learned that Pluto is the most distant planet from the sun is to have learned to emit the verbal behavior "Pluto is the most distant planet from the sun" under the conditions that one is asked: What is the most distant planet from the sun? Why not treat learning as having acquired the propensity to exhibit behavior B under condition C? The behaviorist thus wishes to reject a view of learning in which learning is a matter of acquiring an idea and to replace it with a view of learning where learning is acquiring a propensity to behave.

Why hold such a view? The behaviorists' response is that when learning is discussed, any reference to mental states is at best pointless and at worst meaningless. Once we know about the external conditions under which an act will be performed, what does it add to our ability to produce the act to know that there is an idea involved? Moreover how can we rationally investigate or meaningfully discuss events such as ideas which are unobservable? Events which cannot be publicly observed cannot be the topic of scientific observation. Thus, if we want to think scientifically about learning, we must understand it as involving a propensity to behave predictably under specified circumstances.

If the behaviorists' argument has been accepted, two things have been shown. It has been shown that all learning can be understood as acquiring a behavioral repertoire (subject matter is a repertoire of verbal behavior), rather than as acquiring a belief system. And it has been shown that, for purposes of the scientific investigation of learning, it is preferable to think of learning in this way.

Allowing the behaviorist the claim that all learning can be adequately stated as a behavioral repertoire, how does one proceed to teach a behavioral repertoire? A behaviorist response can be expressed in terms of these four tasks: 1. The basic objectives to be achieved have to be expressed as behaviors to be acquired. 2. These basic behaviors have to be analyzed into their behavioral components which are taught by moving from simple to complex. 3. A strategy for eliciting the first instance of a simple behavior must be devised. 4. The desired behavior must be reinforced when it occurs.

Suppose, then, that our objective in our astronomy course is to teach these two ideas: Pluto is the most distant planet from the sun, and intergalactic distances are measured by the red shift. We now have to treat each of these "ideas" as a form of behavior to be acquired. We can assume that the behaviors will be verbal behaviors emitted (perhaps) in response to a proper question. Next we will have to ask if any of these behaviors are complex. The assumption here is that complex patterns of behavior are built from simple "atoms" of behavior. Clearly one complex part of our curriculum is the claim concerning the red shift. Here we might proceed by identifying the simple ideas necessary to understand the red-shift phenomenon and state each of these as behaviors to be acquired. The student will need to acquire verbal behaviors about white light being complex, about colors being manifestations of the wavelength of light, about red light having a long wavelength, and about wavelength increasing in proportion to the speed at which two objects move away from one another. Verbal behavior about such complex phenomena as the red shift can be constructed out of these simpler verbal behaviors. Ultimately our curriculum will resemble a pyramid with numerous simple behaviors at the bottom and a few complex ones at the top.

To reinforce these behaviors, beginning with the most simple, we will have to elicit them. We cannot simply wait for the student to say "Pluto is the most distant planet from the sun." This piece of verbal behavior might be elicted by the teacher saying it and asking the student to repeat it.

When the proper behavior is emitted, it must be reinforced. Behaviorists are fond of such reinforcements as candies, stars, praise, and grades. If the student is properly reinforced, it is assumed that the behavior will be acquired.

Here we have a behaviorist's program for teaching. We must identify, elicit, and reinforce a collection of behaviors. Now we must ask why anyone would believe such ideas, I shall approach this question by looking at the conceptual history of behaviorism, locating its logical and historical roots in the empiricist epistemology developed by liberal philosophers.

A. HUME AND THE PHILOSOPHICAL ROOTS OF BEHAVIORISM

The works of eighteenth-century Scottish philosopher David Hume[1] represent the purest expression of empiricism. The mind, Hume holds, is a blank tablet, empty at birth. All knowledge arises from experience. There is nothing in the mind that was not first in the senses.

The beginnings of knowledge are found in the impressions on the mind made by experience. Impressions are the atoms of experience. Impressions are momentary and fleeting, but they leave a mental residue which Hume terms ideas. Ideas are copies of impressions. They differ from impressions in being fainter. Ideas, the mental copies of experience, are the base on which knowledge must be built.

Knowledge is created by linking or associating ideas. According to Hume there are three principles through which ideas become associated. These are resemblance, contiguity of time or place, and cause and effect. Thus we connect one tree with another because they resemble one another; we connect fish with water because they are spatially contiguous; and we connect smoke with fire because they are related by cause and effect. Such processes account for our concepts and our scientific knowledge. Our concept of a man results from the contiguity of certain ideas—certain shapes, colors, and configurations. Likewise scientific knowledge represents connections among observed events. Scientific claims are elaborate ways of reporting that one experience is constantly conjoined with another. For Hume the sole power of the mind is the power to associate ideas. The whole of knowledge must therefore consist of such associations.

Impressions and ideas include not only colors and smells but inner sensations as well. Thus the associations among ideas include connections with the sources of motivation, pleasure and pain. Fire may be connected not only with smoke but with the pain of a burn or the pleasure of warmth. Hume's views contain both an account of knowledge and an explanation of how knowledge is connected with motivation and action.

Hume's views can be expressed by means of eight distinct doctrines.

1. *Atomism:* Experience, the basis of knowledge, can be broken down into discrete units.

2. *Sensationalism:* The units of experience are the reports of various senses and one's inner sense. The atoms of experience are the mental representation of colors, sounds, and tastes as well as tactile sensations and pleasure and pain.

3. *Experience is unproblematic:* Impressions and ideas are directly given to the mind. They are unmediated—i.e., we do not need concepts or inferences to grasp them. Hence they are indubitable. Because impressions and ideas have these features, our knowledge of them is unproblematic. Thus they can serve as the base on which other knowledge is constructed.

4. *Associationism:* Knowledge, other than direct knowledge of impressions and ideas, results from associating or connecting the basic units of experience.

5. *Constructionism:* Because knowledge is built on a base of associations between ideas, more abstract or general ideas must be constructed from simpler ideas. The growth of knowledge thus proceeds

from the particular and concrete to the general and abstract. General ideas and abstract theories are constructions from the basic units of experience.

6. *Reductionism:* If knowledge is a construction of connections among ideas, it should be possible to analyze knowledge into its components. For instance laws of science should be reducible to statements concerning the relations among basic units of experience. This reduction should exhaust the meaning of the reduced conception.

7. *Hedonism:* Included among our experiences are impressions and ideas of pleasure and pain. The fact that ideas of pleasure and pain are connected with other ideas and the fact that persons act to pursue pleasure and avoid pain accounts for the connection between knowledge and action. We pursue those impressions which are associated with pleasure and avoid those associated with pain. The human being is a pleasure maximizer.

8. *Mechanism:* Hume's view is mechanistic in the sense that the principles of association are understood as laws of mental operation rather than as logical standards for judging the validity of arguments.

These commitments lead to a view of science which regards scientific inquiry as atheoretical, observation-oriented, cumulative, and "bottom-up." Empiricists were inclined to treat ideas inherited from the past as sources of prejudice and error. What is needed, they argue, is a method which takes an unbiased but careful and systematic look at experience. Experience will teach us most if we come to it without any preconceptions, without any theories about what the phenomena are supposed to be like. Knowledge begins in careful and systematic observation, not in theoretical construction.

Scientific knowledge grows by the accumulation of those observed regularities among experience, by the discovery of simple laws, and by finding ways to express lower-level laws as instances of more general laws.

Of greater interest is the psychological program to which Hume's views lead. The mind begins with elementary units of experience and constructs on this base a substantial edifice of knowledge. How? To address such questions within a Humean framework requires concepts and techniques for analyzing, describing, and identifying the basic elements of experience. What are they? How can they be studied? It is also necessary to investigate the mechanisms whereby basic units are combined into more complex mental entities. What are the laws of association? How can they be investigated?

By the early twentieth century Hume's program had developed into introspectionist psychology, an approach which pursued Hume's basic program through experimental and observational techniques designed to elicit the nuances of consciousness and investigate the principles according to which conscious elements combined.

Richard Peters has described the outcome of introspectionist psycology.

The main theoretical importance of the innumerable experiments done by the Introspectionist School was to exhibit the inadequacy of the assumption of the observationalist tradition that all mental events were either sensations or images; for queer goings on were revealed which could not easily be fitted into either category. . . . These introspective findings were particularly interesting in that . . . they nevertheless undermined the observationalist epistemology. No longer could the mind be regarded as a receptacle for or collection of sense-data and images; no longer could the acquisition of knowledge be described as the passive colligation of these elements by laws of association.[2]

By the early twentieth century the Humean program in psychology apparently had failed. What was wrong? Why did the careful observation and experimentation of a century and a half fail to produce the results in psychology which they had produced in the physical sciences?

An answer to this question was provided by behaviorist psychologists. The behaviorist critique is directed against the introspectionist's attempt to describe conscious events rather than observable behavior. Part of this critique is practical. Introspectionist psychologists discovered little in their attempts to describe consciousness other than how elusive mental content is. Perhaps psychology would progress if it would direct itself to something more substantial. Why not focus directly on behavior and the experimental conditions under which it occurs?

This practical critique was supplemented by a set of philosophical doctrines which had the force of suggesting that mental events were not legitimate objects of scientific investigation. These arguments attempt to show that something is to count as observable only if it is *intersubjectively* observable. An observation is something that is public. The problem with conscious events is that they are inherently private. Only I can be directly aware of what is going on in my mind. To anyone else the content of another's mind must always be a matter of inference and conjecture. But behavior is intersubjectively observable. It is therefore a proper object of scientific study.[3]

These views on the nature of scientific investigation and observation exclude private mental events as objects of inquiry. Overt behavior, however, and the conditions under which it occurs fulfill the requirements of these views. The behaviorist's program accordingly involves a change from a study of consciousness to a study of behavior. These arguments, however, require the rejection of only one part of Hume's program, sensationalism, but the other aspects of Humean epistemology are retained.

The following principles represent a behaviorist epistemology.

1. *Atomism:* Behaviorism seeks to identify units of basic or elementary input—stimuli—and units of basic output—behavior.

2. *Physicalism:* Here is the basic modification of Hume's program. For Hume the basic units of experience are mental events, impressions, and ideas. For the behaviorist the basic units of experience are physical objects or events. Behaviorists insist on a "physical thing" language.

3. *Experience is unproblematic:* Our knowledge of physical objects is treated as direct and unproblematic. This provides the foundation on which knowledge is constructed.

4. *Associationism:* The explanation of behavior consists in discovering the laws of association acording to which stimuli become linked to behavior or responses.

5. *Constructionism:* Complex patterns of behavior are constructed from simple S–R units.

6. *Reductionism:* Since complex behavior is built from simple behavior it should be possible to analyze any complex behavioral pattern into the simple units which comprise it.

7. *Hedonism:* In most behaviorist theories pleasure and pain have been replaced by positive and negative reinforcement. These notions play the same explanatory and normative roles in behaviorist psychology as pleasure and pain play in traditional empiricist psychology and ethics.

8. *Mechanism:* Behaviorism has become explicitly mechanistic. It provides an account of learning and explanations of learned behavior which exclude reason-explanation. It is concerned with laws of association rather than reasons for believing.

The empiricist motto, "There is nothing in the mind which was not first in the sense," reappears in behaviorism as a theory of meaning. In its traditional form the view required complex ideas to be reducible to the simple ideas from which they derive. In its modern form the view requires that all meaningful terms be capable of exhaustive definition by means of terms which refer to observable objects or events or which refer to operations. In more technical language, all meaningful terms can be defined in a data language with no residue of meaning. Some behaviorists apply this view so as to eliminate the possibility of any theoretical language for psychology. Skinner suggests a rigorous version. "Operationalism may be defined as the practice of talking about (1) one's observations, (2) the manipulational and calculational procedures involved in making them, (3) the logical and mathematical steps which intervene between earlier and later statements, and (4) nothing else."[4]

In the introduction to this chapter I described a behaviorist program of instruction. Let us return to that account by looking at a behaviorist program from the perspective of the eight features of behaviorist metatheory. I said that a behaviorist program of teaching involved four tasks: 1. The basic objectives to be achieved have to be expressed as behaviors to be acquired. 2. These behaviors have to be analyzed into their behavioral components which are taught from simple to complex. 3. A strategy for eliciting the first instance of a simple behavior must be devised. 4. The desired behavior must be reinforced when it is emitted.

Points 1, 2, and 4 of this list reflect the epistemological commitments of behaviorist metatheory. The need to state objectives as a list of behaviors to be acquired stems from those arguments in which the proper objects of science are viewed as intersubjective, not private, happenings.[5] Such arguments lead to the rejection of a mental-state language for the description of educational goals and to a demand for a behavioral language. The demand that behaviors to be taught be reduced to their basic behavioral components reflects the commitment to atomism and reductionism. It is assumed that complex behavior consists of, and can be reduced to, a set of simple behavioral units. The claim that learning moves from the simple to the complex reflects the constructionist assumption. In teaching, what one is doing is constructing complex behaviors from simple ones.

The final part of the program—the reinforcement of desired behavior—reflects behaviorism's hedonism: it is pleasure and pain or, in the language of physical things, positive and negative reinforcement, which are the springs of action. In evidence also is associationism. The laws of association determine that learning is governed by the contingencies of reinforcement.

We can now look at programs which reflect various behaviorist assumptions. The enterprise can be divided into three subprograms—the program of analysis, the program of organization, and the program of instruction. The first involves the demand that educational goals be stated as behaviors; the second concerns the organization of curriculum from the simple to the complex; and the third deals with the theory of instruction as exhibited in operant conditioning.

B. THE PROGRAM OF ANALYSIS: BEHAVIORAL OBJECTIVES

Any educational endeavor must face questions concerning its goals. Such questions concern not only what is worth learning but how goals are to be analyzed for purposes of instruction. We may wish to teach physics. But one cannot teach physics in general without teaching something in particular. How do we proceed to identify these particulars?

It will be useful to capture these problems in two questions: What is the proper language for stating educational goals, and what characterizes the nature of goal units? How would we expect our two questions to be answered on behaviorist terms? The answer to the question of language is that educational goals are to be stated in a language of physical things. Educational goals will entail descriptions of behavior. The answer to the question concerning goal units is that we must seek out behavioral atoms. We must look for the elementary units of which more complex behaviors are constructed.

These responses can be expanded into five points which characterize a behaviorist program of analysis. 1. A behaviorist view assumes that the meaning of any goal statement is problematic unless stated in a behavioral language. 2. A behaviorist view assumes that objectives stated in a cognitive or mental language are either meaningless or can be translated into a behavioral language. 3. A behaviorist view will not distinguish between behavioral objectives and behavioral evidence that an objective has been achieved. Since objectives are behavior no such distinction is possible. 4. A behaviorist view tries to separate behavior into its atomic components. The goals of any given endeavor will be highly specific and numerous. 5. A behaviorist view assumes each objective to be discrete and independent of every other objective.

To assess these views it is crucial to distinguish between educational goals and the behavioral evidence that they have been achieved. No rational epistemology will deny that what people do is relevant to deciding if educational goals have been achieved. But only a behaviorist view will assume that goals *are* behaviors. The failure to distinguish behavioral objectives and behavioral evidence is thus the most telling sign of a behaviorist view.

Consider now the arguments for behavioral objectives. I will discuss here the argument as stated in Robert Mager's *Preparing Instructional Objectives* since that has become a kind of classic in the enterprise. Consider the first paragraph, "Why We Care About Objectives":

An objective is an *intent* communicated by a statement describing a proposed change in a learner—a statement of what the learner is to be like when he has successfully completed a learning experience. It is a description of a pattern of behavior (performance) we want the learner to be able to demonstrate. As Dr. Paul Whitmore once put it, "The statement of objectives of a training program must denote *measurable* attributes *observable* in the graduate of the program, or otherwise it is impossible to determine whether or not the program is meeting the objectives."[6]

Here we see a clear instance of a central feature of behaviorist viewpoint. The educational objective and the behavioral evidence that it has been achieved are not distinguished.

This is followed by an expression of the dubiousness of objectives stated in a cognitive language.

Though it is all right to include such words as "understand" and "appreciate" in a statement of an objective, the statement is not explicit enough to be useful until it indicates how you intend to sample the "understanding" and "appreciating." Until you describe what the learner will be DOING when demonstrating that he "understands" or "appreciates," you have described very little at all. Thus, the statement that communicates best will be one that describes the terminal behavior of the learner well enough to preclude misinterpretation.[7]

It is odd that cognitive terms such as *understand* or *appreciate* are all right since they seem not to be the educational objective and indeed describe little. Presumably Mager is willing to exhibit a little largesse to people with cognitive problems. The crucial point, however, is that Mager exhibits the characteristic appeal to a physical-thing language as the standard of clarity. A cognitive language is salvageable only if it can be attached to a physical-thing language.

This discussion of music appreciation is most interesting.

Though I can understand how you might say that "To develop an appreciation for music" is stated in performance terms, you are *not* correct.

Let's ask the key question of this objective. What is the learner DOING when he is demonstrating that he has achieved this objective? What is he doing when he is "appreciating" music? You can surely see that, as now stated, the objective does not give the answer. Since the objective neither precludes nor defines any behavior, it would be necessary to accept *any* of the following behavior as evidence that the learner appreciates music:
1. The learner sighs in ecstasy when listening to Bach.
2. The learner buys a hi-fi system and $500 worth of records.
3. The learner correctly answers 95 multiple-choice questions on the history of music.
4. The learner writes an eloquent essay on the meanings of 37 operas.
5. The learner says, "Oh, man, this is the most. It's just *too* much."[8]

No doubt the example is not meant altogether seriously. Its features are nevertheless revealing. It is not clear whether Mager is providing a behavioral repertoire to be substituted for the meaningless term *appreciation* or whether he is suggesting the sort of empirical evidence we ought to look for if we are to identify an instance of appreciation. Suppose for the moment that he is doing the former. Then our objectives are to get the learner to sigh, buy, answer, write, and say in the ways specified. We then have a classical example of the kind of atomism to which the application of a behaviorist interpretation of behavioral objectives leads. The substitution is objectionable. Sighing and buying and so on are not what is meant by appreciating. Appreciating is more than sighing and buying. One could easily imagine that students could be gotten to sigh and buy without getting them to appreciate. Indeed it is arguable that to aim at sighing and buying makes this probable.

Let us try a nonbehaviorist interpretation of Mager's illustration. Let us treat sighing and buying as evidence that our objective of getting the child to appreciate music has been accomplished. Such an interpretation seems difficult to reconcile with the earlier passages. It requires a distinction between behavioral objectives and the behavioral evidence that these objectives have been achieved, a distinction that Mager apparently rejects. Nor can this interpretation be reconciled with the view that cognitive terms are meaningless. If we accept a nonbehaviorist reading of the example, then Mager will have to explain how it is that sighing and buying clarify appreciating. No doubt sighing and buying are under proper conditions reasonable evidence that someone has learned to appreciate music, but how do they clarify the concept? It is doubtful that, having noted the things which Mager treats as evidence for appreciation, the normal person would better understand what was meant by appreciating. That these pieces of evidence should breathe meaning into an otherwise meaningless phrase is absurd. Indeed it is puzzling to ask how we could decide what counted as evidence for appreciation unless we had some prior understanding of what is meant. The very attempt to operationalize a concept presupposes that it is meaningful.

Thus this example places Mager on the horns of a dilemma. If he accepts a behaviorist interpretation of it, it provides an excellent case against his program. If he accepts a nonbehaviorist reading, then a good deal of what he has said concerning behavioral objectives and nonbehavioral objectives (claims which have become the stock-in-trade of the movement) is nonsense.

Can these conflicting passages by reconciled? Mager seems to accept some of the tenets of a behaviorist program of analysis. Only a physical-thing language is unproblematic. Cognitive terms are suspect. Objectives are behavior. Objectives need to be analyzed into their basic components. When constructing examples, however, Mager tends to undercut his position on these behaviorist commitments. Then it begins to sound as though behavior is only evidence that some cognitive goal has been achieved.

The reasons for this shift are obvious. It is absurd to treat music appreciation as though it were composed of behaviors like sighing and buying, and it is absurd to direct instruction at producing sighing-and-buying behavior. When one wants to teach music appreciation, one wants students to appreciate music. Sighing and buying may be evidence that a student appreciates music. But not even Mager can digest the absurdity of identifying the goal and its evidence in a concrete case.

This confusion seems to characterize most enterprises in which behavioral objectives are important. It is rampant in discussions of competency-based education (CBE), competency-based teacher education (CBTE), and accountability. It is desirable that students and teachers be competent and that educators be asked to provide empirical evidence that they are doing something worthwhile. These laudable goals are so frequently described in terms of a behaviorist program of analysis that it has become difficult to separate the two. Fortunately, however, those who preach a behaviorist program often do not practice it. (I have recently been shown a program in career education which contained the objective *Student will exhibit dignity behavior.* Perhaps there is more humor than harm in such nonsense.) How is one to view sensible goals described in noxious ways? Perhaps with tolerance. It is, however, no virtue to be less absurd than one would be if one acted in ways consistent with professed belief.

This discussion should suggest the difficulties of a behaviorist program of analysis. If taken seriously, it tends to dissolve educational goals into lists of trivial behaviors which turn out not to add up to what they replaced. If not taken seriously, it clutters thought by describing reasonable procedures with behaviorist jargon.

C. THE PROGRAM OF ORGANIZATION

Once we have our behavioral objectives, how do we organize them into a coherent curriculum? The response of a behaviorist program of organization is that learning is from the bottom up. The assumption is that complex skills are constructed out of their parts. We must order the parts so as to facilitate their combination into more complex skills.

The most prominent instance of such an approach is represented by Robert Gagne's concept of a learning hicrarchy. A learning hierarchy "identifies a set of intellectual skills that are ordered in a manner indicating substantial amounts of transfer from those skills of lower position to connected ones of higher position."[9] Here the notion of upward transfer reflects Gagne's view that the order of learning moves from the particular to the general. Thus the empirical condition of learning a general skill is to learn a set of lower-order skills. The reason for the bottom-up approach is that general skills are comprised of their instances.

Some of the features of this notion of a learning hierarchy are specified by R.T. White. White states nine steps for generating and validating a learning hierarchy. Stages 1 through 4 are relevant to our concerns:

Stage 1: Define in behavioral terms the element that is to be the pinnacle of the hierarchy; Stage 2: Derive the hierarchy by asking Gagne's question, "What must the learner be able to do in order to learn this new element, given only instructions?" of each element in turn, from the pinnacle element downwards; Stage 3: Check the reasonableness of the postulated hierarchy with experienced teachers and subject matter experts; Stage 4: Invent possible divisions of the elements of the hierarchy so that very precise definitions are obtained.[10]

These steps reveal the complementary nature of constructionism and reductionism. The order of learning reflects the constructionist assumption that complex behaviors are composed of simple behaviors. The identification of the hierarchy requires the reduction of the complex to the simple. The order of analysis for discovering a hierarchy is the reverse of the order of learning. One has to reduce complex or general behavior to its components.

Gagne and White see the unpacking of a skill into its parts as a matter of identifying those skills which are prerequisites to acquiring more complex skills. Judgments about learning prerequisites should be made on the basis of observation rather than in terms of any analysis of the concepts of the subject matter. Gagne regards learning hierarchies as expressions of the psychological organization of knowledge rather than the logical organization of knowledge. He suggests that it is possible that there is a relationship between the two but seems not to find the problem of interest.[11] White's step 3 may be inconsistent with this view of hierarchies, however, since it is tempting to see appeals to the experience of subject-matter experts as a way of discovering if the hierarchy adequately captures the logical relations of the subject.

The behaviorists' program of organization can be stated in five assumptions. 1. General skills are viewed as constructs of simple skills. 2. The order of learning is from the simple to the complex. 3. The simple skills which constitute complex skills are discovered by a procedure for reducing the complex to the simple. 4. This reduction is accomplished by identifying skills which are prerequisite to more complex skills. 5. The order of analysis of hierarchies is the reverse of the order of learning.

D. THE PROGRAM OF INSTRUCTION

Having succeeded in discovering a hierarchy of skills to be taught, how does a behaviorist proceed to teach them? The dominant view is an extension of empricism's traditional commitments to hedonism.

According to modern behaviorists, positive reinforcement is the key to learning. The difficulty with negative reinforcement is that although it results in a momentary reduction of the undesired behavior, as B.F. Skinner has said, "punishment does not actually eliminate behavior from a repertoire, and its temporary achievement is obtained at tremendous cost in reducing the over-all efficiency and happiness of the group."[12] Negative reinforcement may have the virtue of getting a student to stop something long enough so that you can teach him something better, but its use in teaching is limited. Positive reinforcement, however, produces learning. Behaviorism's fundamental claim is that positive reinforcement of a behavior increases the probability of its recurrence.

This means that once a teacher has identified the behaviors to be learned, there are two tasks to perform. One must elicit the desired behavior, and one must reinforce it. Behaviorists have little to say concerning eliciting behavior. The theory does not require or forbid much here. The concern is with reinforcement. How then are reinforcements identified?

We can approach this question by an objection. It is alleged that the law of effect is not an empirical law; instead it is a tautology. It is true by definition. The law of effect asserts *Positive reinforcement increases the probability of behavior.* If, however, positive reinforcement is not a mental event such as pleasure or satisfaction, what is it? The behaviorist's answer is that positive reinforcement is defined as that which increases the probability that behavior will occur. But by substitution the law of effect thus becomes *Whatever increases the probability of behavior increases the probability of behavior.* This is surely true; however, its informativeness is in doubt. Moreover it appears to violate a basic tenet of empiricism that scientific claims should be confirmable or falsifiable by experience. What experience can confirm or reject a tautology?

I do not, however, believe that this is as problematic as it seems.[13] The significance of the law of effect is to tell us what sorts of variables to look for. We need to find reinforcers. Moreover the connection between any given reinforcer and any given behavior is clearly not tautological. *Money reinforces work* is not a tautology. If there is a problem, it is that we only know how to look for reinforcers by giving the concept of reinforcement a mentalistic interpretation. Look for something people like.

What the teacher must do is identify some contingency which in fact increases the probability of behavior. Two other things must be done as well. The teacher must introduce these contingencies in a way reflecting the behaviorists' views on the temporal features of reinforcement. Reinforcement must be timed properly. When teaching a group one must design a consistent system of reinforcement for the entire group. Since what reinforces one person may not reinforce another, this may not be easy. It is possible for something (cigarette smoke, for example) to be positively reinforcing for one person and negatively reinforcing for another. The most distressing aspect of this problem is envy where one person treats any reward to another as a negative reinforcement. (Consider the effect of grades on low achievers.) Thus designing a consistent set of reinforcements for a group can be difficult.

The behaviorists' program of instruction can be expressed in four

parts: 1. The behavior must be elicited. 2. Reinforcements must be discovered. 3. Reinforcements must be properly timed. 4. A consistent
system of reinforcements must be developed.

The reader should note that these aspects of a behaviorist program—the program of analysis, the program of organization, and the
program of instruction—faithfully capture the epistemological assumptions of the behaviorist variant of traditional empiricism. The fact that
these assumptions are represented in popular and widespread educational
enterprises should be sufficient motivation for investigating their adequacy.

CHAPTER 3

An Epistemology
for a New Theory of Learning

A. A CRITIQUE OF BEHAVIORISM

A distinctive feature of behaviorism is its insistence on speaking a physical-thing language. A science, it insists, must deal with what is publicly observable. Behavior and external stimuli are in; minds and their contents are out. Unhappily *the concepts of stimulus and behavior turn out to be implicitly mentalistic. Behaviorists cannot consistently speak a physical-thing language.*

Let's start with the stimulus. What is it? Consider some options. I shall focus on visual stimuli for simplicity. Here a stimulus might be (1) an external object or event, (2) a condition of the retina, (3) a message on the optic nerve.

But none of these will serve. Suppose you hand a friend a one-thousand-dollar bill and the friend responds, "Wow, I'm rich!" What is the stimulus? Not any external event will do. One must be looking at it. External happenings are not stimuli when one's eyes are shut or when the event occurs behind one's back. This problem can be solved by treating the stimuli as either a retinal image or an optic-nerve message. There are, however, difficulties which are not thereby solved. Not every event in the visual field is a stimulus. The bill was presumably held in hand, a hand attached to an arm which was attached to a body which was situated in a setting. Yet it is the bill which is responded to. This implies that the person performs an act of selection on the input. The individual attends to some features and not others. Therefore the stimulus cannot simply be an external event, a retinal image or a happening on the optic nerve. It is a selected feature of the situation. This selection requires knowledge of the economic system and the intentions of the other person. In short the element responded to is not any external event, but something focused on in terms of what it signifies. To recognize this is to see that the stimulus is a mental object, the construction of an active intellect.[1]

Another feature needs attention. What about the bill is being responded to? A bill has certain observable properties. It is rectangular, green, and a certain size and shape. But none of those properties is what is responded to. Instead the bill must be seen *as* money. It is responded to in terms of its economic significance. What is being responded to is not some external intersubjectively observable empirical property. What is being responded to is the *meaning* of the object. It is impossible to make sense of the stimulus, the element responded to, without introducing mental concepts into the account.

A similar line can be taken with respect to behavior. For the notion of behavior to be introduced into a physical-thing language, it must be specified in terms of changes in the spatial and temporal coordinates of bodily parts. Behavior to Hull is "colorless movement." But clearly what we account for when we consider what a person does is not colorless movements. In about an hour I shall stop writing, get up, put on my coat, walk to my car, and go home. What am I doing? On the behaviorist account I am producing a complex set of movements. In any sensible description I am going home. The interesting thing is that it is only the latter description which will have any predictable connection with a given stimulus. Let us say in an hour I get up and go home. One who was aware of my habits could easily predict my going home. Could he predict my movements? Perhaps in broad terms, but only by recognizing them as required in order to go home.

In short the kind of behavior which correlates with something else is not colorless movement but purposeful action. Actions such as going home are described by the result they are intended to achieve. Actions are inherently teleological and mentalistic. Behavior, what one is doing, is usually described in terms of what one intends to do.[2]

Thus the behaviorist has a difficult choice. Insofar as one can identify stimuli or responses which fulfill the standards for behaviorist language, it becomes impossible to relate them in an account of what people do. If, however, we choose concepts of the stimulus or response which facilitate our explaining behavior, these concepts turn out to be implicitly mental.

These examples refute several basic doctrines of behaviorist metatheory. What is at stake is both *atomism* and its associated doctrines *constructionism* and *reductionism* and the notion that a physical-thing language is objective and unproblematic.

To see the force of these claims, I shall focus on the stimulus by means of one more example. Consider the famous duck-rabbit illustration.[3]

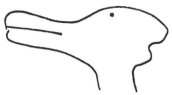

One can see the diagram as a duck or a rabbit. It all depends on what concept is employed in the seeing. But this makes it very difficult to see the stimulus as simply the result of a combination of observable properties. How could seeing the duck or seeing the rabbit depend on a combination of elements when both the duck and the rabbit contain the same elements? Thus something is wrong with the doctrines involved in atomism, constructivism, and reductionism. Here is a case in which *the perceptual whole is not the sum of its parts.*

The same illustration suggests the difficulty of assuming that our observation of external objects and events provides us with an unproblematic base of evidence on which knowledge can be constructed. We can have a problem-free data base only if what we observe is independent of what we think. But if sometimes what we see depends on the concepts we bring to the world, we cannot uncritically assume the objectivity and intersubjectivity of our observations merely because we are observing physical objects or events.

These points could also be made concerning behavior. These arguments show that human actions are not constructions of bodily movements and that we cannot assume that our observations of behavior are unproblematic simply because we are observing physical events. This argument against behaviorism refutes a good part of the background meta-theory derived from traditional empiricism.

The next argument to be considered shows that one cannot construct a viable concept of reasoning in behaviorist terms. *The concept of a reason-explanation cannot be constructed on behaviorist assumptions.*

Consider the following examples of explanations of someone's belief in God. 1. Jones believes in God because his parents reinforced "God-believing" behavior. 2. Jones believes in God because he accepts this syllogism: If anything exists, God must also exist. Something exists. Therefore, God exists.

Case (1) is a causal account of the sort one would expect to be provided by a behaviorist. Case (2) is a reason-explanation. It accounts for the belief in God by means of an argument for God's existence. The reason-explanation, but not the causal explanation, incorporates reasons for believing in God.

The reason-explanation differs from the causal account in being a rule-following act. One belief follows from others according to the ap-

propriate rules of inference. This is a general account of the act of thinking or reasoning. Thinking is inferring one thing from another according
to some rule of logic or standard of judgment.

Why would a behaviorist have difficulty in incorporating such a notion? Consider how the rule works. The rule allows the individual to see a
highly diverse set of assertions as instances of the same principle. The rule
states the form that a class of valid arguments have in common. To know
the rule is to know that a large and otherwise diverse class of assertions
constitute valid arguments. Two additional arguments of the same form
will illustrate:

> If the moon is green, it is made of green cheese.
> The moon is green.
> Therefore it is made out of green cheese.
>
> If glonderells are sarbonic, they are clefel.
> Glonderells are sarbonic.
> Therefore, they are clefel.

Both arguments are valid. Their conclusions follow from their
premises. The latter case is perhaps the most forceful. One can recognize a
valid argument by its form (the rule involved) even if its nonlogical
vocabulary is comprised of nonsense words.

These examples suggest that in reasoning a person must recognize the
input as an instance of a set of premises with a common form. Then one
must follow the rule in that one must recognize that premises with that
form entail a conclusion in a sentence of the proper form and with
nonlogical vocabulary appropriate to the nonlogical vocabulary of the
premises.

The following diagram illustrates the process.

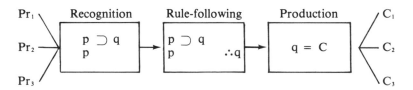

Here 'Pr' stands for premises of the form $p \supset q$, p. (The argument reads:
Proposition p implies proposition q. P is true. Therefore q is true.) 'C'
stands for conclusions of the form q. The diagram is primarily meant to
suggest that reasoning depends on our ability to see diverse inputs as
members of a class determined by a given rule.

What would a behaviorist account look like? Presumably the
premises would be treated as a verbal stimuli while the conclusions would

be treated as verbal behavior. We would then view the premises as associated with the appropriate response.

But what exactly is associated with what? Suppose it is held that each set of premises is associated with its own conclusion. It follows that each argument must be captured in a separate and distinct association and must be learned separately. Pr_1 is linked to C_1, Pr_2 to C_2, etc. This would be diagrammed:

$$Pr_1 \text{———} C_1$$
$$Pr_2 \text{———} C_2$$
$$Pr_3 \text{———} C_3$$

This account, however, is clearly impossible. It does not explain our capacity to recognize the validity of novel instances. How is it that we can provide the correct response when we have never seen the premises—even when the premises contain nonsense terms? It cannot be that we have learned the correct response. Nevertheless we know what it is. It seems then that the rule which unifies these diverse premises and conclusions into a single argument form must provide part of the account of what we do.

But how can a behaviorist incorporate the notion of a rule into the account? The difficulties are formidable. The connection between the premises and the conclusion is mediated by the rule. The connection is not, therefore, an association. Rule-following accounts and associationist accounts obviously seem incompatible. Moreover my account was explicitly mentalistic. It involves mental processes such as recognition, rule-following, and sentence production. To succeed in incorporating the concept of a rule into the account, the behaviorist must include it in a way which is not mentalistic and which does not disregard the concept of an association. Not an easy task.

One strategy which has been attempted[4] is to try to incorporate the logical form of the argument into the notion of a stimulus and a response. Thus a diverse set of premises becomes a single S—a *Modus Ponens* (the name of the rule) stimulus. And a diverse set of conclusions becomes a single R—a *Modus Ponens* response. The relation can be diagrammed as follows:

$$
\begin{array}{cccccc}
Pr_1 & \diagdown & S & & R & \diagup C_1 \\
Pr_2 & \rightarrow & p \supset q & \text{association} & q & \diagdown C_2 \\
Pr_3 & \diagup & p & & & \diagdown C_3 \\
\end{array}
$$

Skinner has suggested such an account. The following statements are illustrative:

The logical syllogism is a way of arranging stimuli. The logician possesses a verbal repertoire in which certain conclusions are likely to be made upon the statement of certain premises.[5]

The logical and scientific community also sharpens and restricts verbal behavior in response to *verbal* stimuli.[6]

In engaging in verbal behavior which is logical and scientific the speaker slowly acquires skeletal intraverbal sequences which combine with responses appropriate to a given occasion.[7]

The view has a superficial plausibility. The idea of a rule is incorporated on behaviorist terms by treating it as part of the stimulus and part of the response. These are then linked by association. But the account does not succeed. Mentalism is not avoided. To see this one needs to ask what physical properties comprise a *Modus Ponens* stimulus. Is it red or green, tall or short, square or round? *Modus Ponens* stimuli may be written or spoken. *Modus Ponens* premises are therefore not empirical properties of physical objects. One needs to learn to see squiggles on a page or patterns of sound as instances of *Modus Ponens*. In short anything which can count as a *Modus Ponens* stimulus will be a mental object. Calling *Modus Ponens* premises stimuli does not eliminate the mentalism of an account of rule-following; it simply disguises it.

The claim to have provided an associationist account will not do, either. Assertions about associating *Modus Ponens* stimuli with *Modus Ponens* responses are hardly more than euphemisms for the notion that the person has learned to follow the rule. Calling such rule-following behavior associationist is roughly on a par with considering mammals to be furry, mobile, nonchlorophyll possessing plants with warm red sap. Perhaps the concepts of plant and sap are qualified enough or made vacuous enough by the rest of the description such that the description has a perverse accuracy. But numerous questions arise. Is there any theoretical justification for seeing mammals as a kind of plant? Can a theory which obscures obvious differences be a reasonable one? Do the concepts plant and sap mean anything here? The answer is that such an odd definition must be motivated by a bizzare theory, and that the concepts of plant and sap are stretched to cover mammals and blood only by rendering them vacuous.

A similar judgment is called for when rule-following behavior is classified as an association between logical stimuli. Only a powerful well-confirmed theory could justify collapsing such a compelling distinction. In this case, however, the attempt merely reveals the poverty of the basic theory and the fact that the theory is extended to rule-following behavior largely by rendering concepts such as stimulus and association devoid of meaning. We are therefore entitled to conclude that behaviorism cannot construct a coherent account of reasoning. Attempts to do so are incipiently mentalistic and appear successful only when behaviorist concepts are stretched so as to be virtually meaningless.

That behaviorism has difficulty formulating a cogent view of rationality suggests that the evolution of empiricist epistemology into behaviorist psychology has an element of paradox. Empiricist views of rationality lead to a view of learning which cannot incorporate a view of rationality. The paradox can be put cryptically as the claim that *the epistemological commitments of behaviorism lead to a view of learning which does not take epistemology seriously*. The point of this remark can be seen when one distinguishes two questions which can be asked about a given theory of learning. They are: What epistemology governs the research program of psychology P? What epistemology is incorporated into the theory of psychology P?.

The first question assumes that epistemological commitments will influence the way in which research in psychology is conducted. The eight commitments of behaviorism noted in chapter 3 function for behaviorists to answer such questions as "What terms are permissible in a science of behavior?" "What form must a successful explanation take?" What variables should be investigated?" Thus epistemology often functions as what philosophers call metatheory. The theories of psychology are intended to explain the relevant data. Metatheory is theory about theories. The metatheory of psychology thus specifies what is to count as a good, properly organized psychological inquiry or theory. The first question assumes that epistemology is an important component of the metatheory of psychology.

The second question reflects my claim that learning is a rational activity. If this is the case, any theory which attempts to describe how people learn will need to incorporate a set of epistemological concepts into its description of learning, since such concepts are necessary to describe rational activity. The failure to incorporate an epistemology into one's psychological theory thus leads to the conclusion that people are not rational. It is a variant of the claim that there are no true reason-explanations. A psychological theory, by contrast, which views people as rational will have to use epistemological concepts—concepts which characterize what counts as rational—in explaining rational behavior.

The distinction between these two questions can be succinctly put by noting that the first concerns the metatheory of a psychology while the second concerns the theory of a psychology. My claim that the epistemological commitments of behaviorism lead to a view of learning which does not take epistemology seriously can be stated as the claim that *the epistemological commitments of the metatheory of behaviorism lead to a psychological theory which fails to incorporate an epistemology.*

Consider a central piece of behaviorist theory, the law of effect: reinforcement increases the probability of the recurrence of the behavior reinforced. The metatheory which organizes the research of behaviorists is a variant of empiricism, classical empiricism. Knowledge is rooted in experience, psychological terms need to be firmly grounded in observations —such claims govern the questions asked and the phenomena investigated.

Suppose, however, we ask why someone believes some proposition, p. An empiricist account of "A believes that p" might hold that the concepts of p are suitably defined in terms of experience and that A has made the observations necessary to establish the truth of p. This is not, however, the account of A's belief that p which is provided by behaviorist theory. Instead the law of effect suggests that the belief that p must be understood as a tendency to exhibit utterance p, given the proper stimulus conditions. The fact that A tends to exhibit p rather than q is explained by the history of reinforcement of p. P–utterances have been reinforced while q–utterances have not been reinforced.

Beliefs, then, are explained by behaviorists not by talking about the empirical evidence and the reasoning which led to them but in terms of the history of reinforcement of utterances. What follows is that behaviorists give incompatible answers to our two questions. The answer to What epistemology governs the research program of behaviorism? is that empiricism governs it. The answer to the question What epistemology is incorporated into the theory of behaviorism? is that none is. Behaviorism's metatheory, therefore, is inconsistent with its theory. Its metatheory assumes that people reason in empiricist ways while the theory denies that. Unless we assume that psychologists are somehow exempt from the laws of learning, behaviorism is self-refuting.

This discussion suggests some notable things concerning how basic programs in psychology can be evaluated. For one, it suggests that the epistemological assumptions of the metatheory of a psychology must be consistent with the epistemological views incorporated into the theory of psychology. Inconsistency here quickly leads to absurdity. The psychologists' metatheory will require the performance of acts of reasoning which the theory indicates cannot be performed. The discussion also indicates that psychologies are susceptible to philosophical refutation. If the foregoing discussion shows anything, it is that psychologies must make epistemological sense. Neither the theory nor the metatheory of psychology can coherently deny what we know to be true about how knowledge is achieved. The reverse is also the case. Epistemologists cannot reasonably deny the epistemological claims embedded in well-established psychologies.

Behaviorism fails both of these tests. The theory and the metatheory are inconsistent, and the epistemological commitments of the metatheory are largely false. Behaviorists have thought that the rejection of introspection and the focus on behavior exclude the use of mental terms. Mental terms refer to private mental entities, not observable behavior. They are therefore not permissible in a science of behavior. But, such concepts are required if we are to incorporate epistemology into learning theory.

The concept of an association has been interpreted by behaviorists to exclude incorporating epistemological concepts into learning theory. This point requires a distinction between a rule and a law of nature. Rules are norms or standards. They specify what ought to take place. Laws, however, state invariances among events. When a rule is violated the violator has made a mistake. When a law is violated it is falsified.

Hume's notion of an association obscures this distinction. It is not clear that notions such as similarity or contiguity describe laws of association or criteria of judgment concerning when an association is warranted. *Behaviorists, however, regard the laws of association as laws , not rules. These laws describe mechanisms according to which associations are formed, not rules according to which they are evaluated.* Epistemology, however, is concerned with rules, not laws. It specifies the criteria or standards for rational belief. Thus the behaviorist conception of laws of association tends to preclude incorporating epistemology, even empiricist epistemology, into behaviorist theory. Behaviorists are committed to looking for causes, not reasons.

Such considerations have led behaviorists to view learning as something other than as a rational activity. Hence the paradox: Behaviorists have interpreted traditional empiricism in such a way that epistemology is seen as unrelated to learning. Learning in turn is not seen as a rational activity. It is something that happens to people under the proper empirical conditions.

These arguments destroy what remains of the behaviorist program. They undermine associationism and mechanism. What remains of the basic eight commitments is hedonism. I shall save that for a later chapter. Our critique, however, is complete. Empiricist epistemology is inadequate at every point. Moreover it leads to a view of education which separates learning and thinking because it is unable to formulate the concepts necessary to make sense of thinking. This seems its ultimate absurdity. Thus neither traditional empiricism nor its modern successor, behaviorism, is a rational basis for constructing a theory of learning. We shall have to look elsewhere.

B. EPISTEMOLOGICAL COMMITMENTS FOR A NEW VIEW OF LEARNING

One place to look for new assumptions for a theory of learning is recent philosophy of science. Here one can find not merely a critique of traditional empiricism but a new set of views which provide a plausible alternative to it.

Consider Karl Popper's[8] critique of the view of science which flows from classical empiricism. Classical empiricism views science as an atheoretical process in which basic connections in experience are constructed into ever higher order generalizations. Popper suggests that such a view fails to reconstruct what scientists actually do. It fails in that classical empiricism has an inadequate view of the role of theory in inquiry. Theory is more than just an encumbering set of prejudices, and scientists do not and cannot simply observe experience independent of any antecedent theory. Instead theories play a constructive role in guiding research. Theories suggest which among the almost infinite aspects of experience is worth investigating. Consider, for example, a twentieth-century experiment in astronomy. One reason that modern astronomers are interested in solar eclipses is that they are able to view light from stars whose light passes close to the solar circumference. The point of such observations is to see whether light from these stars is affected by the gravitational field of the sun. This is significant because Einstein's theory of relativity predicts that light is influenced by gravity. The current interest among astronomers in looking for black holes—bodies so massive and dense that not even light can escape their gravitational field—is likewise a result of this aspect of Einstein's theory.

Is it conceivable that these phenomena would have been investigated had it not been that they were the predicted consequences of some theory? *Theories have an indispensable role in inquiry. They indicate what is relevant to investigate. Inquiry, far from being impeded by theory, is impossible without it.*

Popper's second objection to classical empiricism is that it contains an incorrect view of the role of experience in science. Experience is neither the material from which theories are constructed, nor is its primary role to confirm theories. Theories are instead free creations of the mind whose origins Popper tends to view as a question for psychologists. Experience functions not to confirm them but to reject them. After all, Popper reasons, even the weakest theory has numerous confirming instances. What is the point in acquiring more? But to be adequate a theory must not account for some of the relevant phenomena but all of them. Thus it makes sense in scientific research to focus on the problematic consequences of a theory—to seek to refute it, not confirm it. Experience serves to falsify scientific theories.

Popper views science as a matter of what he terms conjecture and refutation. Scientists propose bold and imaginative theories and deduce their empirical consequences. Theories are then checked against experience by testing their most unlikely consequences. When one of these predictions fails, the theory is falsified. The scientist must then invent another and begin the process again. This view of science has been called the hypothetical deductive method.

Popper's view of science has itself been the object of severe criticism in recent years.[9] One objection is that Popper's view of falsification assumes a naive view of the relations between theory and experience. It assumes that each theory entails a clear, determinate, and unproblematic set of predictions, the truth or falsity of which can be straightforward checked by comparison of the prediction with actual experience. This is not the case.

Abstract theories do not directly entail anything about experience. Instead predictions are derived from abstract theories by augmenting them with additional theories and hypotheses. Predictions flow from a complex set of assertions rather than a single theoretical claim. The consequence of this, given a falsified prediction, is that we know that one of the assumptions made in generating the noxious prediction is false, but we do not know which one. The scientist is under no logical obligation to give up anything in particular. In fact the scientist will give up some assumption which is not crucial to the basic line of research. *Theories therefore are not directly refutable by experience. Instead they tend to generate research programs designed to discover ways of augmenting them such that they can be gotten to generate observed results. Theories themselves rarely succumb to single failures, but to histories of failure.*[10]

Popper's notion of falsification also assumes that experience is unproblematic. *Experience, however, is not unproblematic. The duck-rabbit example shows that what we see depends partly on the concepts we bring to the experience.* In philosophy of science what this suggests is that experience is theory dependent. What one sees depends to some extent on the theory brought to the experience. People with different theories can see different things. It is important not to overstate or understate the import of the theory dependence of observation. Experience is not infinitely malleable. Neither, however, is it always possible to settle conflicts between theories by a crucial experiment. Scientists with different theories may see the results differently. The theory dependence of observation suggests that theories are not falsifiable because experience is problematic.

A further objection to hypothetical deductive views of science is that they tend to see scientific method as exclusively a matter of formal logic. Theories are simply interpreted logical calculi. The inferences involved in scientific reasoning are the formal rules required to manipulate such calculi.

Formal logic does not adequately characterize scientific reasoning. Instead scientists are guided by what Toulmin calls explanatory ideals.[11]

Explanatory ideals are substantive claims which specify what is to count as an adequate explanation or a permissible inference in a given discipline. For example in particle physics it is assumed that explanations must be stated in terms of relations between simple, uniform, and indivisible entities. If (as is the case with hadrons) "elementary particles" come in excessive complexity or variety, it must be because they are actually composed of a few simple uniform particles such as quarks. Thus the origins of modern theory about quarks can be traced to the conflict between the proliferation and complexity of a class of particles and the dominant explanatory ideal. *An adequate account of scientific method must involve substantive as well as formal principles of inference.*

Finally hypothetical deductive accounts do not contain an adequate account of conceptual change. Popper provides an account of the process whereby theories are rejected, but he gives no account of where theories come from. Indeed he regards the topic as nonphilosophic, as something for psychologists, as though the origin of theories like the origin of dreams is best accounted for by the unconscious or by what one had for dinner. Surely this is inadequate. *There are rational constraints and criteria which pertain to the generation and initial selection of theories as well as criteria for their rejection. For one a new theory must solve the problems generated by its predecessors.* Theories become problematic for particular reasons. These reasons function as a guide to what would count as a plausible successor. The scientist may have available a set of models, analogies, or metaphors which lend intelligibility and plausibility to new theories as the solar system served as a model for the atom. The initial selection and plausibility of a theory is also influenced by what is known in other areas. Finally, the explanatory ideals of a discipline influence the antecedent plausibility of an hypothesis. Toulmin[12] summarizes such ideas with the suggestion that *conceptual variation occurs in a conceptual ecology. An adequate account of science must not just explain why claims are accepted or rejected, but how they are changed. Epistemology on this view is the theory of conceptual change.*

Such objections to hypothetical deductive views are rooted in alternative accounts of science. The most widely known is that of Thomas Kuhn in *The Structure of Scientific Revolutions.*[13] Kuhn's account is based on a distinction between what he terms normal and revolutionary science. Normal science is dominated by a paradigm. A paradigm is a complex integrated conceptual entity which determines the nature of scientific research done under its sway. The paradigm under which an enterprise functions contains the standards of rationality of the enterprise, and it comprises the conceptual glasses through which the scientist views the world. Normal science, according to Kuhn, is puzzle-solving. The paradigm at any given moment will determine a number of unanswered questions, unsolved problems, and outstanding anomalies. Most scientific work consists in the solution of such puzzles.

Occasionally, however, a paradigm will be swamped by a sea of anomalies. The process of normal science usually will produce an agenda of recalcitrant anomalies, puzzles which resist solution. When a paradigm is beset by anomalies and faced with a rival, the stage is set for a scientific revolution where one paradigm is overthrown and replaced by a competitor. Now a scientific revolution cannot be a fully rational enterprise. The theory-laden character of observation prevents settling the issue between rival paradigms by experiment. Scientists of different persuasions see the world differently. Even worse, Kuhn regards the very standards of rationality as internal to a paradigm. That being the case, there are no standards available for rational choice between paradigms. Thus Kuhn likens a paradigm change to a gestalt shift or a conversion experience. Scientists come to see it all differently. A new paradigm gets certified because it has achieved sufficient dominance among the appropriate scientific group to have its standards become the standards of rationality for the groups. Dissidents then become viewed as incompetent. In Kuhn's account revolutionary science appears as a mixture of conversion and coup.[14]

Kuhn's emphasis on the nonrational aspects of revolutionary science has received a great deal of criticism. Toulmin[15] suggests that the difficulty arises from Kuhn's tendency to see a paradigm as something which must be either accepted or rejected all of a piece. Suppose, however, our scientific concepts occur not in tightly packaged paradigms but in loosely linked populations. Perhaps then we can examine one of our concepts while the remainder provide the intellectual ecology which makes a rational conceptual shift possible. If scientific change is evolutionary rather than revolutionary, we need not regard major conceptual shifts as akin to leaps of faith.

This characterization of some recent views and debates in philosophy of science should provide a sense of the perspectives which distinguish modern empiricist views from their classical predecessors. We need now to see if we can distill a set of agreed-upon points which will serve to sharpen the distinction between my views and those of classical empiricism and which will set the stage for further reflection on a more adequate view of pedagogy. I think that something of a consensus can be expressed in eight interrelated doctrines which will represent an alternative to the eight points which I employed to characterize classical empiricism.

1. *The primacy of the conceptual:* Traditional empiricism treated theories and concepts as solely a product of inquiry. More recent views have assigned a much broader role for concepts. Concepts organize expe-

rience and generate the questions for inquiry. Concepts are not therefore mere products of thought. They are preconditions of it.

2. *Coming to know is conceptual change:* The growth of knowledge is not the accumulation of empirical facts. It is the elaboration of our current conceptual structures and their alteration and replacement by more adequate structures.

3. *Experience is theory-laden:* Traditional empiricism attempted to ground knowledge on a class of basic beliefs. These beliefs are directly confirmable by experience. Experience itself is unproblematic. Experience, however, is not unproblematic. People with different concepts sometimes see different things. Experience is not infinitely mutable by theory. If it were it is hard to see how knowledge would be possible. But neither is it unproblematic—simply given—as traditional empiricism supposes.

4. *Nonexperiential criteria are important in knowing:* Traditional empiricism gave almost exclusive weight to experience in certifying knowledge. That experience is theory-laden suggests that experience cannot bear this weight. The discussion of the importance of a conceptual ecology in judging the adequacy of new concepts suggests the importance of other criteria. The notion of an explanatory ideal is one such nonempirical criterion.

5. *Knowing is a process of assimilation and accommodation:* Kuhn's distinction between normal and revolutionary science, while overstated, indicates a need to distinguish between processes in which current conceptual systems are extended to cover new phenomena and processes wherein current concepts are modified to manage phenomena which proved anomalous for prior concepts. I shall employ Piaget's terms *assimilation* and *accommodation* to label these processes.[16] The idea is this. People will usually try to assimilate new phenomena to old concepts in a way so as to require minimum dislocation of central beliefs. Accommodation, the alteration of central commitments, occurs when assimilation of phenomena to current concepts is unsuccessful and new central concepts must be adopted.

6. *Conceptual ecologies have an important role in conceptual change:* The process of selecting new concepts is neither a random happening, nor a psychological phenomenon. Instead anomalies, explanatory ideals, knowledge in other areas, and various models, metaphors and exemplars function to bring plausibility and intelligibility to new ideas. New ideas thus occur in an ecology which provides a logic of discovery.

7. *Reason-explanations are important in explaining human action:* Mechanistic accounts of knowing and learning have proven unworkable and self-refuting. Thus reason-explanations are required in accounting for knowing and learning. Knowing is a rational activity.

8. *Intrinsic motivation is important in learning:* Traditional empiricism views knowledge as the servant of the passions. Learning is pursued because of its capacity to create conditions maximizing pleasure over pain. It seems clear, however, that the elaborate and careful effort people put into inquiry and theory construction cannot be accounted for in such terms. People have an intrinsic need to overcome cognitive dissonance and establish reflective equilibrium. Such concepts are not simply pleasure and pain as they relate to knowledge.

C. THE EDUCATIONAL PROGRAM

These claims form the basic ingredients of a much modified empiricism. If we are to take seriously the view that learning is thinking, these claims should form the basis of views on learning and teaching. They are not, of course, self-applying. A good deal of research and experience will be necessary in order to realize these ideas in actual educational programs. These notions do form a more practicable metatheory for developing educational programs than does classical empiricism or its behaviorist progeny.

The approach required by this theory is viewing learning as a process of conceptual change. The student must either elaborate current concepts to assimilate new ideas or information or must accommodate concepts when they prove inadequate. The art of pedagogy is the art of organizing and providing the resources which bring about a rational process of conceptual change. The student, then, is like the scientist investigating an unknown phenomenon. Ways must be found to extend current concepts to cover the phenomenon or to adapt new concepts to it. The educator's role is to make the process as efficient and as rational as possible.

I shall expound this view as I did the behaviorist account of pedagogy. We will first look at the program of analysis, the program of organization, and finally at the program of instruction.

The Program of Analysis

Behaviorism generates a clear answer to the question concerning the form and organization of educational goals. Educational objectives should be behaviors. To organize an educational situation one must identify basic units of behavior of which more complex behaviors are constructed. I have rejected all of the assumptions on which this program of analysis depends. Educational goals are not behaviors. Nor are there any basic atoms of learning. But do we have a program of analysis to replace this one, and on what assumptions does it depend?

Part of the response is that instead of a behavioral language we will speak a cognitive language. But it is less obvious that we can identify anything like a fundamental or basic unit of instruction. Even if we can, we will mean something different by *basic*. We will not be seeking to analyze subject matter into its atomic parts. What we need to look for instead are reasonable conceptual units.

What would such a basic unit be? Consider again the notions of assimilation and accommodation. This distinction depends on the notion that some concepts are more important to our understanding a given range of phenomena than others. *Some concepts, like Kuhn's paradigms, organize inquiry, generate the puzzles to be overcome, and provide the framework in which phenomena are to be understood. Such concepts provide the structures into which new phenomena are assimilated and which change when new phenomena prove unassimilable.*

Let us call such concepts *basic*. A basic concept would be identified by the criteria (a) of being what other concepts are assimilated to, and (b) of being what changes when accommodation is required. We might, then, consider a basic unit of instruction to be a basic concept (or a related group of basic concepts) plus the other concepts and phenomena which have been assimilated.

This notion of a basic unit has several advantages. It allows us to slice up our instructional pie into pedagogically manageable units without lapsing into atomistic assumptions. The notions of a basic concept and a basic unit recognize the primacy of the conceptual in inquiry and experience. They help to identify concepts which are important in thinking and to recognize that other concepts are not just independent facts, but fit into a conceptual structure. These notions recognize that concepts have an organization and that the organization of instruction should reflect this organization.

The ideas of a basic concept and a basic unit are not problem-free. The distinction between assimilation and accommodation can be relative. Often we alter one concept in the interest of assimilating a new phenomenon to another more important one. The logical relations between concepts are often sufficiently complex such that the application of the criteria for picking our basic concepts will not produce clear results.

It does not, however, follow that these criteria cannot be usefully employed in selecting and organizing what is to be taught. People with a reasonable sensitivity to their subject can usually identify those concepts which are crucial for understanding subject matter. The epistemological assumptions I have sketched in this chapter thus suggest that the first task in analyzing a subject matter for instructional purposes is to identify its basic concepts and its basic conceptual units.

The Program of Organization

Teaching can be formulated as the task of communicating basic concepts and the conceptual units which basic concepts underlie. One phase, accommodation, consists in teaching the basic concept. The other, assimilation, consists in extending the basic concept to its range of application.

Consider assimilation first. Any advanced intellectual enterprise will have developed a set of subordinate concepts and strategies through which its basic concepts are applied to relevant phenomena. Suppose that we are teaching a unit in psychoanalysis and abnormal behavior. The most important basic concepts to be introduced involve the unconscious mind and the idea that abnormal behavior reflects the workings of the unconscious. At the point where we can assume a reasonable grasp of the notion of the unconscious, we are faced with the task of showing students how psychoanalysis applies this central concept to its range of phenomena. Thus students must learn such things as how to interpret dreams and techniques for discovering the meaning of psychic symbolism. They must learn that the unconscious hides itself from consciousness while expressing itself by disguising real meaning through symbolism. They must learn such distinctions as that between the id, the ego, and the superego. In short, having grasped the basic concepts of psychoanalysis, students will have to grasp a range of other techniques and concepts whereby the basic concepts are applied.

The basic components of the mechanisms of assimilation include:

1. *Additional hypotheses and concepts:* These are lower-order beliefs or concepts which help apply basic concepts to phenomena. Concepts such as the id are illustrative in psychoanalysis.

2. *Standard argument styles:* Most rational enterprises have some basic strategies for showing the need for their basic concepts and defending the basic concepts against objections. Freud's discussion of "mistakes" in *The Psychopathology of Everyday Life*[17] can be treated as a defense of the need for the concept of the unconscious.

3. *Exemplars:* These are standard cases which function to show the initiate how the concepts of an enterprise are related to concrete cases. Freud's discussion of dreams in *An Introduction to Psychoanalysis*[18] is illustrative.

4. *The mathematics of application:* For many enterprises there are mathematical techniques which are important in applying basic concepts to phenomena. (Psychoanalysis is not one of them. Consider, however, the use of geometry in astronomy or architecture.)

5. *Measurement techniques:* Rational enterprises have standard ways of collecting data and documenting their claims. Psychoanalysis depends largely on the case study.

6. *Strategies for resolving puzzles or dealing with apparent anomalies:* Rational enterprises usually contain standard approaches for investigating new or recalcitrant phenomena. The patient who rejects an

analyst's interpretation is inclined to find objections being assimilated to psychoanalytic concepts as a species of defensiveness.

7. *Range of application:* Rational enterprises will have ways of distinguishing between phenomena to which their concepts apply and those to which they do not apply. The boundaries of psychoanalysis are often controversial concerning the extent to which the concepts apply to other than abnormal behavior.

An educator who is faced with a problem of assimilation will have to identify and communicate those conceptual artifacts which mediate between basic concepts and the phenomena.

But how do we approach teaching basic concepts? Here the problem is one of accommodation. The student's current concepts are inadequate for managing the phenomena. We must devise ways to bring about a conceptual change.

The task of an educator in bringing about a rational conceptual change is to organize the conceptual ecology. Organizing an ecology will be a matter of generating the anomalies which indicate the inadequacy of a current set of concepts and adding to the anomalies the background knowledge, explanatory ideals, and models and metaphors which render new concepts initially plausible and comprehensible.

The following list suggests some of the components of an ecology which should help in bringing about an accommodation.

1. *Anomalies:* Anomalies are more than recalcitrant phenomena which help to overthrow some prior set of concepts. Since new ideas must solve the problem generated by their predecessors, anomalies are the central component of the ecology which will select a new concept.

2. *Background knowledge:* New concepts must be consistent with what else we know in relevant related areas.

3. *Explanatory ideals:* New concepts in a given area must be in accord with what counts as a good explanation in that area.

4. *Exemplars:* Exemplars are paradigm instances of a new concept. They are useful in clarifying the application of a new concept.

5. *Models:* A model is a familiar instance which has some structural isomorphism with the referents of a new set of concepts. The solar system is a model of the atom. Models can lend intelligibility to new concepts and suggest plausible lines of inquiry concerning them. In what ways, for example, are the forces holding together the atom similar to or different from gravity?

This illustration may suggest something of what is involved in organizing an ecology. Several years ago my young son discovered stars. "What are they?" he asked. The explanation was that stars are suns which are much farther from the earth than the sun. It was not a success. Later questions revealed reasons for the failure. He lacked the basic idea of heavenly bodies. We spent a couple of sessions puzzling (with dubious results) over how a small bright point in the sky could really be a large bright ball. Further on into the summer he announced his own solution. Stars were holes in the sky that the light comes through. This account persisted about a week until one night I found him watching a high flying airplane making its slow way across the night sky. After a few moments he informed me that stars could not be holes in the sky since they moved. An anomaly (incorrect though it was) had overturned his brief journey into ancient cosmologies. Subsequently, with the acquisition of concepts connecting distance and apparent size, the stars-are-far-away-suns theory was adopted.

What happened? Basically my son acquired a conceptual ecology which made my initial account become meaningful and plausible. Comparisons with balls and observations about the relation between distance and apparent size made some of the prerequisite concepts meaningful. An anomaly helped show the inappropriateness of one account and the plausibility of another. In short a conceptual change took place when an adequate conceptual ecology was present. *If, then, teaching basic concepts is a matter of facilitating conceptual change, the program of analysis requires identifying the components of a proper conceptual ecology.*

We need to deal with an objection. Consider the following argument to show that not all cases of learning basic concepts can be treated as instances of accommodation: 1. The view that all learning of basic concepts is accommodation seems to require that any current set of concepts, C, results from a change of some prior concepts, C_1. 2. But not all concepts can result from a change in prior concepts, for this would lead to an infinite regress of concepts. Therefore at least some concepts must be capable of acquisition without any predecessors.

This argument is simply a variant of what is a central paradox of epistemology. It was first stated by Plato in the *Meno* dialogue and is usually labelled the *Meno* paradox.[19] Plato's version goes: Inquiry is impossible. One cannot inquire into what is already known because it is already known. But one cannot inquire into something not known because one would then know neither the subject of the inquiry, nor what would count as an answer.

There are three traditional solutions to the Meno paradox. Pure empiricism maintains that knowledge can in fact be obtained from experience without the aid of prior knowledge. The laws of association show how it is possible to write knowledge on the blank tablet of the mind. The standard objection is Plato's. How could we learn anything from experience without some standards or criteria to tell us what we are looking for and when we have found it?

Plato maintains that there is no genuinely new knowledge. Instead knowledge is innate. What appears to be coming to know is in fact more like remembering something that we have forgotten. Inquiry enables us to state explicitly what in some sense we already know.

The third solution is suggested by Kant.[20] We do not possess innate knowledge of the facts we discover in an inquiry. But we do come into the world armed with knowledge of basic categories and forms of experience. Thus we possess some innate knowledge which enables us to identify particular features of experience. Inquiry is possible because we have an innate grasp of the basic structure of experience. We know the nature of the subject matter, and we know what counts as a solution. Perhaps the best way to distinguish Kant's view from Plato's is that it rests on distinguishing knowing the answer to an inquiry and knowing what counts as an answer. We do not, according to Kant, know the former, but we do know the latter.

Such a view has been developed for linguistics by Noam Chomsky.[21] Following the usual line against empiricism, Chomsky argues that the knowledge of language children acquire in a few brief years could never be explained on empiricist grounds. Children are not, of course, born with a knowledge of their own language. But they are, Chomsky holds, born with an innate knowledge of what Chomsky calls a universal grammar. The universal grammar specifies the basic structure of any possible language. It enables the children to sort through the chaos of linguistic phenomena and to identify those features of language which show the grammar of their own language.

An important variation on this theme is suggested by Jean Piaget, who has quite properly been called a developmental Kantian.[22] Piaget[23] ascribes adult conceptual abilities to schema which enable the individual to order and investigate experience. These schema are not present from birth. Instead they develop by processes of assimilation and accommodation from an initial substratum of perceptual and psychomotor habits through several stages until the adult stage of logical operations is reached. Piaget accordingly reaches a basically Kantian position, but without postulating innate ideas. For him schema develop from the interaction of biological factors and experience.

The account of accommodation I have given here is a variation on Kant. A conceptual ecology can be regarded as specifying the criteria of what counts as a plausible conceptual innovation. Moreover I believe that some variety of developmental Kantianism (not necessarily very similar to that of Piaget) is called for as the solution to the objection with which I began this discussion. A view that traces the early origins of concepts to basic behavioral patterns which are not themselves exactly concepts but which mature with interaction with experience into concepts is required. I will not develop such an account. My purposes will be best served by spelling out the difference between two different accounts of the learning of basic concepts.

Imagine that instead of the response just provided I had said: "Yes, while I still believe that most concepts are formulated and selected because of a conceptual ecology in which the overthrow of some prior conceptualization has a role and while I still believe that concepts play an important role in learning and inquiry, I must also grant that some concepts—the ones with which we begin inquiry—must be acquired as empiricists claim since it appears they could not be acquired in any other way." The consequences of this concession are immense.

Such a response is an admission that classical empiricism is fundamentally correct. It may have modestly erred in failing to notice how useful concepts are (once acquired) in further investigation, but concepts are acquired fundamentally as empiricists claim. They are constructed by associations linking the basic atoms of experience. Thus the consequence of the concession is to turn my entire account of the role of concepts in inquiry and learning into a set of new wrinkles on the old empiricist face. Traditional empiricism turns out to be right after all. It simply needs stating in a more sophisticated form.

The pedagogical consequences of the concession are to render unnecessary the notion that learning a new concept be treated as a process of accommodation. The establishment of a conceptual ecology may have some heuristic value in explaining a new concept, but in principle it can be ignored since there is another, and more fundamental, account of how basic concepts are acquired. We may, when it is helpful, treat the teaching of a basic concept as a problem of accommodation; but often it will be more efficient to introduce basic concepts directly without bothering to create a suitable conceptual ecology.

I do not claim here to have shown that any variety of developmental Kantianism is correct. I have barely suggested what it is. I believe however, the case against empiricism is persuasive. I find it simply inconceivable that a traditional empiricist view can succeed. The case I have presented here should have developed a conceptual ecology which gives an accommodation in the direction of developmental Kantianism initial plausibility. What needs to be done is to develop the conceptual machinery necessary to assimilate the phenomena of learning to such a view. Such an undertaking will be long and complex. Perhaps when we have had enough experience with it new anomalies will have emerged and we will need a new accommodation. Until then I believe an adequate case has been made for conceiving learning as a matter of accommodation and assimilation.

The Program of Instruction

How does a teacher present the material of accommodation and assimilation? Once we have the ingredients what do we do with them?

The epistemological views developed here are neutral to many issues of pedagogy. They do not suggest any grounds for choosing between (for example) lecturing, discussion, or discovery learning.

The claim may seem surprising. The position taken here may seem to require students to discover for themselves anything they can genuinely claim to know. I have in fact treated the student faced with a new idea like a scientist working on the fringes of knowledge. Do not such claims make a case for discovery learning? I believe they do not.

Consider what is meant by discovery learning. We may think of discovery learning as learning in a way that one would have to learn if there was no one to learn from.[24] This notion suggests that in promoting discovery learning the teacher must organize the student's experience so as to lead the student to find the desired concept without telling the student what the desired concept is. The teacher's task is to generate the proper conceptual ecology, but it is the student's job to find a concept that fits the niche.

But nothing in my argument requires the student to generate a concept which fits the niche. My claims that learning is thinking and that students are analogous to scientists on the forefront of knowledge require that the student *see* the connection between concepts and the ecology which selects them and the evidence which warrants them. But seeing the connections does not entail discovering them in any sense of discover which excludes being told. The phenomena of seeing the connections when told what they are is such a familiar part of experience that any view which denies it must be wrong. No view can coherently argue that it is impossible to do what is done.

We can identify some components of good pedagogy by focusing on a different problem. I have suggested that thinking or reasoning is a rule-following activity. When the student is engaged in looking for a concept to fit a given niche or is trying to use a concept to solve a puzzle, the student is applying intellectual standards and criteria to the making of rational judgments. The student is, in short, following rules.

Let us construct a simple account of how people learn to follow rules. There are two central conditions: the rule to be learned must be *exhibited* to the learner, and the learner must have *feedback* on his performance. These conditions, however, cannot be necessary for learning a rule. Obviously not all rules are learned as the result of some social transmission. Otherwise conceptual innovations would be impossible.

Consider first the idea of feedback. The central fact to grasp is that *rules are standards or criteria for doing things*. A basic criterion for distinguishing a rule from a natural law is that violations of a rule are considered mistakes whereas violations of a natural law refute the law. That an important feature of rules is the notion of a mistake indicates that *learning a rule is a matter of bringing one's actions into accord with a standard.* This suggests several things. It suggests that we need to resist passive notions of the transmission of concepts. Having a concept is not just a matter of being in a certain cognitive state, it is a matter of possessing certain skills. It is reasonable to suppose that *cognitive skills, like other skills, require practice.*

Practice should be distinguished from exercise. The key ingredient of exercise is repetition. In muscle development the crucial thing is not to do an exercise correctly but to do it often. Exercise is not a matter of bringing action into conformity with a standard. Practice, however, focuses on learning to do something correctly. Its point is to bring actual performance closer to desired performance.

The key element in practice is feedback. If one is expected to bring performance into conformity with a norm, one needs a source of information concerning the ways in which current performance departs from the norm. Accommodation and assimilation can both be considered in this way. Both having an ecology and possessing the concepts and strategies of assimilation are matters of possessing the criteria for making judgments and performing intellectual tasks. It is reasonable to assume, therefore, that part of acquiring the skills of accommodation and assimilation is practice and that one of the teacher's roles in the process is to be a source of feedback.

One cannot practice a skill until one has grasped some approximation of the rule which defines successful performance. The rule needs to be exhibited. This point should not be formulated as though learning a skill had two distinct phases—understanding the rule and bringing action into conformity with it. The point of practice is not only to teach the flesh to execute a skill the spirit has already grasped. Practice facilitates grasping the rule, but one cannot begin to practice a skill until one has at least a primitive grasp of what one is doing. Learning a simple concept may illustrate the point. Suppose we wish to teach a child the concept of a cat. We may begin by finding one, pointing and saying "cat." The child may then begin to apply 'cat' not only to cats, but all medium-sized mammals of the same shape. Feedback ("That's not a cat, it's a dog") will help the child to refine the rudimentary concept. Again, however, the child cannot do this until there is a concept to refine; and note that to grasp a rudimentary concept the child needs a conceptual ecology. The acts of pointing and naming must be understood.

The teacher must, then, exhibit the rule to be learned. Perhaps the best way to express the teacher's role is to say that *the teacher should be a model of competent performance. We may succinctly express the basic components of the act of instruction as modeling and feedback.*

These notions provide an antidote to views which provide excessive emphasis on learning from experience. *Experience is always socially mediated*. Teachers should conceive of their role as providing the concepts which make meaningful experiences possible rather than in terms of avoiding the sin of stepping between students and their experience with concepts and interpretations which are somehow inauthentic because they are not the student's.

This idea can be put in a different way. Any reasonable teaching must recognize what may be called *the two faces of learning*. On one hand *it is important to view learning as involving the student's rational reconstruction of experience*. The student must see the connections between ideas and how ideas are related to experience. Seeing these connections is something one must do for one's self. One person cannot understand for another. On the other hand *most learning is the initiation into public and shared concepts which have been developed or evolved because people have found them useful in dealing with experiences. A rational view of learning must keep the personal and the public aspects of learning in balance.* To lean too far toward the personal can cut the student off from concepts and human resources which are invaluable to learning. People cannot improve concepts they haven't learned. But to go too far toward the public can turn learning into indoctrination and can stifle thought.

We can also approach the processes of modeling and feedback by asking what sorts of social relations they assume between student and teacher. The relation here is essentially *a master-apprentice relationship*. The role of the master in such a relationship is providing a model of competent performance in the art to be learned and of responding to the student's performance. The student in turn acquires an art by practicing it under the guidance of an accomplished practitioner. *An effective master-apprentice relation has a number of social requirements. It requires a degree of intimacy. It requires the apprentice to trust the master's skill when he or she is not in a position to appreciate the point of all that the master does. The master's authority must be the authority of expertise, not of command. The submission of the student should be voluntary. Conversely the master must earn the trust of the student and treat the student with the respect due to one who has voluntarily placed himself under the master's care.*

D. CURRENT INSTANCES

In 1959 a group of eminent scholars and educators gathered at Woods Hole on Cape Cod to discuss the structure of knowledge. Part of the motivation for the conference was a sense that neither were the various curricula of the public schools rigorous enough nor did they present subject matter so that students could think in terms of its concepts. Should not students think like scientists? As Jerome Bruner has put it:

"Intellectual activity anywhere is the same, whether at the frontier of knowledge or in a third-grade classroom."[25]

The key to more rigorous curricula and to getting students to think as scientists do is to teach the structure of knowledge. This concept is best described by Bruner in *The Process of Education.*

The curriculum of a subject should be determined by the most fundamental understanding that can be achieved of the underlying principles that give structure to the subject. Teaching specific topics or skills without making clear their context in the broader fundamental structure of a field of knowledge is uneconomical in several deep senses. . . . Such teaching makes it exceedingly difficult for the student to generalize from what he has learned. . . . Learning that has fallen short of a grasp of general principles has little reward in terms of intellectual excitement. . . . Knowledge one has acquired without sufficient structure to tie it together is knowledge that is likely to be forgotten.[26]

What Bruner describes approximates what I have called the process of assimilation. One does not simply teach the specific facts or skills of a discipline; instead one teaches them in the context of the basic concepts of a discipline. Moreover the structure of the discipline is seen as prior to the detail of the discipline. The primacy of concepts in learning seems clearly recognized.

Resulting educational programs have been reasonably faithful instances of assimilation. The way arithmetic is taught in the new math is typical. Students are not just taught facts of addition. Instead they are taught the basic concepts of set theory and learn to see facts of addition as instances of these.

The structure of knowledge approach has an identifiable program of assimilation. Does it also have a program of accommodation? How are basic concepts taught? The answer to this question is unclear.

When asked how abstract concepts can be taught to children, Bruner responds: "The general hypothesis that has just been stated is premised on the considered judgment that any idea can be represented honestly and usefully in the thought forms of children of school age, and that these first representations can later be made more powerful and precise the more easily by virtue of this early learning."[27]

This idea is explicated in Piagetian terms. Children are seen as going through cognitive stages defined by the nature of the intellectual operations they are capable of performing. The stages of interest in schooling are the stages of concrete operations in which thought is characterized by the mental representation of concrete actions and the stage of formal operations in which the individual learns to manipulate hypothetical propositions rather than being confined to prior experience.

Bruner embodies these stages in the notion of a spiral curriculum in which basic concepts are taught first in a way comprehensible to a person at the stage of concrete operations and are later reformulated in terms suitable to formal operations. Concepts are taught initially in a highly experiential way and reformulated when the child has become more cognitively advanced.

Is this a program of accommodation? There are several relevant pieces of evidence. Bruner often describes the movement from the concrete to the formal representation of a concept in ways appropriate to accommodation. Moving through the stages of development can be facilitated by asking good questions—presumably questions which suggest anomalies or puzzles to be solved which, in turn, require a better formulation of the concept. But if Bruner envisages a process of accommodation, it is a different sort of accommodation than I have described. For Bruner the conceptual change envisaged lies between different formulations of the same concept, whereas the view of accommodation that I have suggested views change as occurring between substantively different concepts. In Bruner's view there is not a change of concepts, but a change in the ways children represent concepts. My account of accommodation does not preclude changes of this sort, but it assumes changes in the content as well as the manner of representation of basic concepts. Finally Bruner's account of how concepts are acquired at the level of concrete operations is an empiricist one. Concepts are described as gotten from experience by induction. The process envisaged seems to be one in which students see what is common in a number of examples. We can then conclude tentatively that Bruner has an inadequate account of accommodation and tends to lapse into empiricist descriptions of concept formation.

Kohlberg in his theory of moral development treats the acquisition of concepts as a matter of accommodation.[28] He regards moral development as moving through six invariant stages, each of which is characterized by a distinct moral conception. During the first stage, for example, morality is seen as a matter of punishment and obedience. When individuals have reached the fifth stage they see morality as fulfilling the conditions of agreements or contracts. At stage six morality is a matter of acting on principles which are universal and consistent. These stages are invariant in that the latter stages cannot be achieved without going through the former. People do not, however, always achieve the highest stages. Reaching stage six is rare.

Kohlberg views the achievement of a given stage as an accommodation to the inadequacies of its predecessors. Moral education thus proceeds by exposure to moral conflicts and to moral discussions. The point seems to be both to generate anomalies for the student's current moral viewpoint and to facilitate acceptance of a higher stage.

Kohlberg's views then seem a reasonably faithful example of my position on pedagogy. Each moral stage represents a way of assimilating moral phenomena. Acquiring new moral concepts is a matter of accommodation. Something of the flavor of this can be seen in an extrapolation of one of Kohlberg's examples.[29] He illustrates a stage-five response to a moral issue by quoting from Plato's *Crito*. Here Socrates refuses to flee Athens when sentenced to death for corrupting the youth. His argument is that he is bound to obey the laws because his having chosen to live under them implies a kind of contract to accept the judgment of the laws. How can a city continue to exist if the laws are destroyed by private persons? Kohlberg juxtaposes this response regarding the problem of civil disobedience to a stage-six example presented by Martin Luther King, where King distinguished between the duty to obey a just law and the duty to disobey an unjust law.

We might account for the move from stage five to stage six in the following way. Persons whose morality is governed by a contract model will have difficulty in assimilating certain sorts of moral phenomena. They will have difficulty with those cases where their agreements commit them to approving acts which seem morally abhorrent. Perhaps they have agreed to accept the results of a decision-making mechanism which then makes a noxious decision. The attempt to assimilate such an event generates an anomaly. Stage-five morality can lead to a commitment to immoral acts.

What would a solution to this anomaly entail? What a solution must do to succeed is account for our general duty to obey the law while also showing how there can be exception to it. What is required then are more general principles (such as equality or respect for persons) which are truly universal and which contain both the duty to obey and to disobey as instances. Such principles would consitute an accommodation to the deficiencies of stage five.

The structure-of-knowledge movement, as exhibited in the writing of Bruner and exemplified in curricular innovations such as the new math, provides cases of educational views and practices which can reasonably be regarded as instances of assimilation. Such programs seek to educate by focusing on the basic concepts of a discipline and assigning these concepts a central role in comprehending the detail of a discipline. The structure-of-knowledge movement lacks a program of accommodation. Indeed it lacks any clear idea of how basic concepts are to be presented or how they are learned. Kohlberg's program seems unique among available educational enterprises in that his views and practices exhibit a program of accommodation. Perhaps the most fruitful area for pedagogical research is the investigation of how to teach basic concepts as cases of accommodation.

CHAPTER 4

Even here one man can make a bureaucracy with his mouth.

—ERNEST HEMINGWAY

Empiricism and Liberal Values

No doctrine is as essential to liberal views as the idea that people are capable of rational self-directed action. In liberal societies people are held as responsible for governing their own lives. In the private sphere liberals object to government paternalism—not only because they believe that individuals have a right to self-determination—but because they believe that they have the capacity for it. No one is in a better position than individuals to come to rational decisions concerning what is in their best interest. Free people will make better decisions about their own lives than even the best-intentioned government.

Much the same can be said concerning the public sphere. Here liberals have advocated democratic decision-making. This reflects the belief that individuals have a right to influence those institutions which make determinations concerning them, but another aspect of the democratic argument springs from the belief that free people are capable of self-government. Collective self-determination invests a great deal of trust in the rational capacity of individuals.

Such views play an important part in liberal arguments concerning schooling. A liberal and democratic society must, above all, educate its citizens, for in doing so it is making people competent to determine their collective destiny and manage their private affairs.

Let me summarize these ideas by asserting that *liberals have perceived a strong connection between the values of freedom and reason.* A free democratic society relies on the competence of individuals to manage their private lives and to participate in public deliberations in rational ways. Moreover, liberals hold, only in a free society do people have the opportunity to develop their rational capacities, for only then do people need to rely on their own judgment and the opportunity to encounter the diversity of opinion and experience which facilitate the growth of reason.

It is therefore supremely ironic that empiricist epistemology has evolved in a way that modern behaviorists can hardly make sense of rationality. Moreover it behooves us to take a close look at the consequences of this failure, for it is possible that behaviorism not only will generate a false view of pedagogy but will undermine a view of human beings essential to liberal political ideals. If this is the case, a view of schooling constructed on behaviorist assumptions may be a Trojan horse in the liberal state.

Many behaviorists, chiefly B. F. Skinner, have held that the idea that men are free is incompatible with the possibility of a science of human behavior. Since, they claim, a science of behavior exists, people are not free. Human values and institutions rooted in ideas of freedom are based therefore on prescientific mythology. Moreover these values which once played an important role in freeing people from oppressive social institutions have become counterproductive in that the belief in human freedom has become an obstacle to employing available technologies of behavioral engineering. We accordingly need a new view of social organization, one in which human behavior is controlled by the proper deployment of positive reinforcement.

Against these views *I shall argue that there is no conflict between the possibility of a science of behavior and the idea that people are free. This supposed conflict stems from an erroneous view of what freedom is. I shall also hold that the real conflict between behaviorism and liberty stems from the inability of behaviorism to make sense of rationality and the centrality of rationality to freedom.* In short Skinner has mislocated the issue. When it is properly located, what is revealed is the poverty of behaviorism rather than the mythological assumptions of liberal democracy.

A. LIBERTY PRO AND CON: THE ISSUES

To begin we first need a clear statement of the issues. I shall begin by considering how liberals have linked freedom and reason; I do so by examining John Stuart Mill's "On Liberty." I then shall formulate the behaviorist objections to freedom as expressed by B. F. Skinner.

Mill develops his position concerning civil liberties by distinguishing between public and private acts. A society is entitled to extend its authority over an area of conduct only if that area involves actions which affect the well-being of others. Private actions are not proper objects of control. Mill defends two kinds of liberties, which he calls freedom of opinion and individuality. Freedom of opinion is the right to express one's beliefs. It includes freedom of speech and press, and it involves the free exercise of religion and freedom of association. Individuality is the right to act on one's preferences.

Mill here summarizes his arguments on the freedom of opinion.

First, if any opinion is compelled to silence, that opinion may, for aught we can certainly know, be true. To deny this is to assume our own infallibility.

Secondly, though the silenced opinion be an error, it may, and very commonly does, contain a portion of truth; and since the general or prevailing opinion on any subject is rarely or never the whole truth, it is only by the collision of adverse opinions that the remainder of the truth has any chance of being supplied.

Thirdly, even if the received opinion be not only true, but the whole truth; unless it is suffered to be, and actually is, vigorously and earnestly contested, it will, by most of those who receive it, be held in the manner of prejudice, with little comprehension or feeling of its rational grounds. And not only this, but, fourthly, the meaning of the doctrine itself being lost or enfeebled, and deprived of its vital effect on the character and conduct: the dogma becoming a mere formal profession, inefficacious for good, but cumbering the ground and preventing the growth of any real and heartfelt conviction from reason or personal experience.[1]

Mill develops a defense of free opinion by discussing the marketplace of ideas. Just as the competition of economic markets produces the best goods at the cheapest cost, so free intellectual markets produce the best intellectual wares. Competition among ideas, the process of criticism and debate, is held to be a basic condition of refining and improving our ideas. Only a society which permits free and open debate will be able to engage in rational decision-making. In a closed society ideas continue to be believed beyond the point where the evidence against them has become persuasive because those ideas are enforced by the power of the state. New and invigorating ideas are not adopted because the state excludes them.

Individuality is defended on similar grounds. Only a society which permits people to experiment with new ways of living will gain the experience which permits the rational evaluation of life plans. Individuality permits experiments in living and generates a useful repository of social experience.

Mill views liberty as a condition not only for the exercise of rationality but also for its development.

He who lets the world, or his own portion of it, choose his plan of life for him has no need of any other faculty than the ape-like one of imitation. He who chooses his plan for himself employs all his faculties. He must use observation to see, reasoning and judgment to foresee, activity to gather materials for decision, discrimination to decide, and when he has decided, firmness and self-control to hold to his deliberate decision. And these qualities he requires and exercises exactly in proportion as the part of his conduct which he determines according to his own judgment and feelings is a large one.[2]

The development of rationality requires incentives and practice. Rationality is unlikely to develop under conditions in which it is not needed. Mill's argument thus suggests an important social principle: *Open institutions produce competent people.* It has an equally important corollary: *Closed institutions produce incompetent people.*

To take these claims seriously is to desire a society in which individuals enjoy a wide range for personal decision-making and a substantial opportunity for participating in collective decision-making. *A liberal society seeks to achieve a wide and democratic distribution of rationality.*

Consider now Skinner's case against freedom. Skinner's arguments are directed against the idea that people can be autonomous or that they have free will. Mill begins his essay by distinguishing between the question of free will and liberty, holding that they are independent questions and that he is concerned only with the latter. Skinner's views on the relation are unclear. Often, however, he seems to believe that political issues are determined by his arguments against autonomy. Why? Consider this passage from *Science and Human Behavior*: "The hypothesis that man is not free is essential to the application of scientific method to the study of human behavior. The free inner man who is held responsible for the behavior of the external biological organism is only a prescientific substitute for the kinds of causes which are discovered in the course of a scientific analysis. All these alternative causes lie *outside* the individual."[3] The argument is simple. Science studies the causes of events, but a free act is one that has no cause. Therefore an attempt to study behavior scientifically assumes behavior is causal, not free.

What social implications follow from the fact that people are not free? Skinner claims our belief in human freedom is problematic because it prevents us from applying the available technology of behavior to the control of human beings. Consider this typical argument: "Our culture has produced the science and technology it needs to save itself. . . . But if it continues to take freedom or dignity, rather than its own survival, as its principal value, then it is possible that some other culture will make a greater contribution to the future."[4]

Skinner believes that we need more control, not less. But recommending an increase in control is not very useful when the precise nature of social institutions is concerned. Moreover precise recommendations as to who decides what and who shall be free to do what under certain conditions are hard to discover. We may begin, however, to reconstruct Skinner's point of view by noting his comments on values.

So far as the individual is concerned, the good is positive reinforcement. "The only good things are positive reinforcers, and the only bad things are negative reinforcers."[5] Skinner appears to extend this "physical-thing-language hedonism" into social ethics. The social good seems to be a maximization of positive reinforcement. "Presumably, there is an optimal state of equilibrium in which everyone is maximally reinforced. But to say this is to introduce another kind of value. Why should anyone be concerned with justice or fairness, even if these can be reduced to good husbandry in the use of reinforcers?"[6]

This passage marks a transition in which the criterion of an adequate culture is not its capacity to produce "the greatest positive reinforcement for the greatest number," but its capacity to survive. "The simple fact is that a culture which *for any reason* induces its members to work for its survival, or for the survival of some of its practices, is more likely to survive. Survival is the only value according to which a culture is eventually to be judged, and any practice that furthers survival has survival value by definition."[7]

Are these views consistent? Whether policies promoting the maximization of positive reinforcement simultaneously promote cultural survival is not clear. Even the concept of cultural survival is obscure. Has a culture founded on concepts of freedom and dignity survived when it adopts modifications of the kind that Skinner recommends? At the social level he has two values—the maximization of positive reinforcement and survival—and the relations between these values remain obscure.

How are these values to be achieved? Skinner answers that we need to design a culture. Designing a culture involves identifying survival-producing and/or reinforcement-maximizing behaviors and creating them through the suitable management of positive reinforcers. Since the designing of culture is a technological problem, presumably we shall need a technological elite.

> . . . the most effective control from the point of view of survival will probably be based upon the most reliable estimates of the survival value of cultural practices. Since a science of behavior is concerned with demonstrating the consequences of cultural practices, we have some reason for believing that such a science will be an essential mark of the culture or cultures which survive. The current culture which, on this score alone, is most likely to survive is, therefore, that in which the methods of science are most effectively applied to the problems of human behavior.[8]

Skinner is careful to add the caveat that "this does not mean, however, that scientists are becoming self-appointed governors."[9] He fails to illuminate further the question of how decisions are to be informed by scientific wisdom. We might summarize his views by suggesting that a society which survives will be governed by science, but not necessarily by scientists.

Skinner has inherited a great deal from the liberal philosophers who have done so much to propagate the noxious literature of freedom and dignity. His emphasis on positive reinforcement and his use of a maximization criterion are reminiscent of utilitarianism. Moreover his comments on the social role of science and his uneasiness about a simple affirmation of technocracy express his attempts to resolve a characteristic dilemma of modern liberalism. Liberals have been firm advocates of scientific patterns of thought and decision-making as well as of free and democratic institutions. They have reconciled these strains, in effect, by making every person his or her own scientist. Rationality is to be democratically distributed. Thus decision-making can both be scientific and democratic.[10] But the twentieth century has been hard on this point of view. Most sciences have advanced to the point where it is difficult for even the well-educated person to follow, let alone have a reasoned opinion about, developments in more than a few endeavors. The result is to pose a choice to liberals between decisions that are rational, but made by a technological elite, and decisions which are democratic. This dilemma is expressed in the passing of effective power from legislative branches of government to executive branches and their bureaucracies which have the resources to develop legislation on complex technical issues. The dilemma is also sharply focused on education. Skinner can be regarded as choosing one of the paths provided by this fork in liberal thought. In opting for a society where decisions express the judgment of a technological elite, he is following part of the logic of the philosophy of freedom and dignity.

We should not be trapped by Skinner's usual hostility to views containing freedom-oriented terminology and thereby overlook his ambivalence concerning liberal institutions. Consider:

A rather obvious solution [to the abuse of power] is to distribute the control of human behavior among many agencies which have so little in common that they are not likely to join together in a despotic unit. In general this is the argument for democracy against totalitarianism.[11]

Diversification permits a safer and more flexible experimentation in the design of a culture. The totalitarian state is weak because if it makes a mistake, the whole culture may be destroyed.[12]

In such passages Skinner expresses basic liberal commitments, and they cause us to wonder what the fuss is about. Perhaps Skinner does not object to liberal institutions so long as they permit suitable input for science. What does Skinner object to?

B. AUTONOMY AND LIBERAL INSTITUTIONS

Perhaps we should turn to the relation between Skinner's objection to autonomous man and his political views. Why do Skinner's views on autonomous man lead to a rejection of liberal political values?

Skinner believes that liberal institutions justify themselves by promoting autonomy. "The struggle for freedom and dignity has been formulated as a defense of autonomous man rather than as a revision of the contingencies of reinforcement.[13] Liberals thus seek to organize society to defend a myth.[11]

A review of Mill's arguments suggests that this is a misleading characterization, however. Mill argues that attaching penalties to the expression of ideas or the trying of new ways of living is counterproductive. Such penalties limit a society's capacity for self-renewal and for rational deliberation. Mill does not mention autonomy here. Furthermore, Mill's arguments consist of empirically investigable claims. He asserts a relation between a class of social actions (such as censorship) and their consequence on social deliberations and social policy. Perhaps these claims are false, but they are not unscientific in that they assume behavior to be uncaused. Quite the contrary. These claims therefore, cannot, be disposed of on a priori methodological grounds.

Liberals have, however, also valued autonomy, and have thought it to be a virtue of liberal institutions that they give room for the development of a capacity for autonomous decision-making. Mill's argument concerning the development of reason can also be constructed as a claim concerning the development of autonomous judgment. Let us see, then, if autonomy can be defended.

Skinner's crucial point is assuming that an autonomous act is an uncaused act. Thus no free act can be given a scientific explanation. But this claim is not self-evident.[14]

Consider what an unexplicable act would entail. It must be unrelated to any event which proceeds it. It must simply happen. But free acts are not like that. People make choices in light of events and of their desires. They can usually give reasons for their choices. They do not say "It just happened that I did this." Indeed an uncaused act could hardly be a free act. Such acts must happen independent of a person's wants or circumstances. As such they must happen to people who are, thus, victims, not free agents. The assumption that a free act is unexplained is suspicious. Consider a few examples.

Case A: Mr. Jones is an employee of an automobile company. This company requires employees to buy its own cars and has fired employees who buy cars from the competition. Mr. Jones is afraid of losing his job. Therefore he buys his new cars from his own company.

Case B: Mr. Smith has a suitable car. But Mr. Smith has been seeing a commercial in which a certain new car is associated with a strong masculine character. Since Mr. Smith has an unconscious need to think of himself in these terms, he buys one of these cars. Smith is not aware of the actual explanation of his act.

Case C: Mr. Black needs a new car. He discovers a consumer publication which shows him that he can meet his needs most effectively by purchasing a small foreign car. Therefore he buys a small foreign car.

Case C has the best claim to be an autonomous act. In Case A Jones is not autonomous. His act is coerced. In Case B Smith fails to be autonomous because he is victimized by unconscious needs and a manipulative advertisement. Black, however, can reasonably be viewed as autonomous. He makes a reasoned choice based on his needs and on plausible information concerning how they can be met.

Most noteworthy here is that each act is given an explanation. What distinguishes Black from Smith and Jones is not that Black's act has no explanation, but that Black's act involves a specific kind of explanation. It is a reason-explanation. Black acts on the basis of evidence concerning what it would be reasonable for him to do.

These examples suggest some properties of an autonomous act: 1. An autonomous act is not coerced. 2. An autonomous act is not caused by any psychological compulsion or unconscious state of which the person is unaware or over which he has no control. 3. An autonomous act is done for reasons. These criteria would require some refinement to become a fully adequate account. They suffice, however, for the point. There is no reason to assume that autonomous acts are inexplicable.

Skinner frequently argues that the advocates of autonomous man assume that if people are not controlled, they will be free. But people are never free: there are always causes for their behavior. The elimination of deliberate social control does not eliminate control. It only disguises control, and in so doing it substitutes haphazard and potentially harmful sources of control for rational planned control. The real choice is not between control and no control but between planned control and unplanned control.

To the extent that this analysis assumes that people who object to control are attempting to make the world safe for uncaused behavior, the preceding remarks will suffice for a response. But we should ask what can be said in favor of limiting social control.

Recall Mill's arguments. Mill attempts to limit social control, but he does not object to social control per se. Instead he objects to attaching penalties to expressions of opinion, and he argues that not engaging in this form of control has beneficial social consequences. Mill is for some forms of control and against others for reasons particular to the form and objects of control. To control or not to control isn't the question.

Few advocates of freedom and dignity have been so absurd to believe that when we have eliminated deliberate control over behavior, people instantly begin to exhibit uncaused acts. Even a modest look at literature in political theory should convince the reader that when people object to planned control they do so because they prefer self-regulating, informal, or more participatory mechanisms of social regulation. Some persons are so bold as to hope that people can learn to behave reasonably by persuasion and evidence. Perhaps they are wrong. Perhaps deliberate control is better. But if this is the case, it has to be shown on the basis of empirical evidence. Perhaps nothing is quite as anomalous about Skinner's arguments as the willingness of this empiricist's empiricist to reject perfectly plausible political options on the basis of a priori methodological considerations without benefiting from a study concerning their actual consequences.

We are again led to conclude that Skinner has not asked a sensible question. We are asked to be for planned control or chaos. We are supposed to be either for freedom or against it. But sensible questions cannot be formulated in such broad and gross categories. Issues concerning social authority need to be formulated through detailed questions about the consequences of particular uses of authority and the consequences of forebearance. No rational person can be simply for or against freedom.

Why does Skinner give us this sort of choice? He seems dominated by the mistaken notion that to advocate freedom of any kind is to advocate free will. Only such an assumption permits him to confront the whole tradition of liberal democracy via a discussion of the methodological commitments of science. But since this analysis is historically incorrect, how are we to account for Skinner's assumption beyond noting that he seems not to have read much of the literature of freedom and dignity to which he objects? A plausible response to this question is that Skinner's approach to a science of behavior blinds him to a basic value of liberal democracy—rationality. The concept of rationality cannot be formulated on behaviorist assumptions. Skinner therefore cannot make sense of the real values of liberty. Accordingly he generates an attack which is not to the point.

C. FREEDOM AND REASON

Skinner's "science of behavior" is incompatible with liberal concepts of freedom, but not for the reasons Skinner gives. *Behaviorism excludes freedom, not because it shows there are no uncaused acts, but because it shows that there are no rational acts. Liberal values make little sense apart from rationality.*

Consider indoctrination. Here the issue is students' freedom of choice with respect to belief. The relevant issues can be formulated through a distinction between persuading and indoctrinating. The distinction is typically employed to differentiate between cases when persons are free with respect to a change in beliefs from cases in which they are unfree. To say that persons have been indoctrinated is to say that something has been done to them. Their beliefs have been changed, but they have not changed them. To say that they have been persuaded is to suggest that they are active with respect to their beliefs. They have changed them.

The distinction between persuasion and indoctrination is tied to processes such as giving reasons or changing one's mind because of available evidence. To persuade people is to give them reasons for changing their minds. To indoctrinate them is to cause belief in some other fashion. The distinction between persuasion and indoctrination is thus dependent on a language in which the distinction between the giving of reasons and other kinds of influence can be stated. The distinction between persuasion and indoctrination is an application of the broader distinction between a reason-explanation and a mechanistic explanation. When a person has been persuaded, there should be a true reason-explanation for the change of belief. When someone has been indoctrinated, there is a true mechanistic explanation of the change of belief. Therefore, insofar as a behaviorist language is unable to employ those kinds of logical concepts necessary to formulate the concept of a reason-explanation, that language will also be unable to make sense of persuasion and will be unable to distinguish between persuasion and indoctrination.

Since Skinner seems as unhappy with the concept of dignity as with the concept of freedom, we should also look at the consequences of the inability to formulate a concept of rationality for the concept of human dignity.

Consider this passage from Immanuel Kant.

Rational beings . . . are called *persons* because their nature already marks them out as ends in themselves—that is, as something which ought not to be used merely as a means—and consequently imposes to that extent a limit on all arbitrary treatment of them (and is an object of reverence). Persons, therefore, are not merely subjective ends whose existence as an object of our actions has a value *for us*: they are *objective ends*—that is, things whose existence is in itself an end, and indeed an end such that in its place we can put no other end to which they should serve *simply* as means; for unless this is so, nothing at all of *absolute* value would be found anywhere.[15]

Kant concludes his discussion with this norm: "Act in such a way that you always treat humanity, whether in your own person or in the person of any other, never simply as a means, but always at the same time as an end."[16]

Kant's idea that persons are to be treated as ends rather than means provides a useful way to formulate a concept of human dignity. What is most significant is the suggestion that persons are appropriately treated as ends because they are rational agents. It follows from the behaviorist inability to formulate an adequate view of rationality that they will be unable to formulate the distinction between persons and nonpersons—that is between things which are rational agents and things which are not rational agents. Moreover, from a Kantian point of view, the inability to formulate an adequate view of human beings as rational agents results in relegating them to being nonpersons. If rationality is what separates persons from nonpersons, any view which is unable to formulate an adequate perspective of rationality will relegate human beings to the status of nonpersons. And once we are no longer able to distinguish between persons and nonpersons, we will be unable to apply Kant's principle. We will be unable to justify treating human beings as ends. We are then entitled to ask how the distinction between persons and nonpersons will be formulated from a behaviorist perspective. What will the behaviorist say is the relevant reason for treating people with respect?

Rationality is also a prerequisite concept to making sense of such rights as free speech or individuality. Our consideration of Mill should have shown that liberals see the importance of liberal institutions in developing and exercising rationality. A view like Skinner's which has difficulty with the concept of rationality will similarly have problems making sense of civil rights. The virtues of a marketplace of ideas will not be effectively stated in a language of reinforcement.

These arguments are important for understanding how behaviorists are going to view education. *Behaviorists looking at an educational system will see it as behaviors varying in desirability and as a system of reinforcements varying in effectiveness. They will ask themselves questions concerning how these reinforcements can be more effective in eliciting the behaviors desired. Certain questions will not occur. Behaviorists will not ask if some kinds of control are inappropriate to certain educational goals. They will not ask if they have a right to select what behaviors are to be learned, and they will not ask whether the effectiveness of education might be enhanced by lessening the degree of educational management, not by increasing it.* These questions won't be asked because they assume a view of the world which the behaviorist's concepts do not equip him to see. People who ask such questions will not be understood. Moreover we should not hastily assume that only full-blooded Skinnerians will approach education with these sorts of conceptual barriers to comprehending liberal values. Aspects of a behaviorist world view are often accepted by people who would not normally be considered behaviorists. Perhaps the most virulent form of the behaviorist disease is well contained, but public education currently suffers from an epidemic of a milder strain.

D. ACCOUNTABILITY

One place to examine the symptoms of a less virulent strain of behaviorism is the current demand for accountability in schooling. Since accountability often generates a need for behaviorist technology, it can easily become a vehicle for the introduction of behaviorist mentality into public education. Perhaps, we can get a grasp on how behaviorist categories generate attitudes toward education by looking at a case. I have chosen Leon Lessinger's *Every Kid a Winner: Accountability in Education*, a popular book. It nicely displays the mentality of accountability.

Lessinger's commitment to a behaviorist program of analysis is exhibited in this remark about the importance of "specific performance criteria":

The key to this process is the framing of objectives in terms of performance. Let us see why. If I live in Detroit and have as my objective a visit by road to Los Angeles, it is not sufficient merely to be told that the direction is southwest. I need more specific instructions. Similarly in education, the general direction of faculty to teach students "to understand and appreciate science" is not sufficient. To be useful, the general direction must be supplemented with a set of operational steps. Thus we might supplement the science objective mentioned above by listing such projects as the dissection of a frog in a science laboratory, or we might ask the student to demonstrate an application of Ohm's Law in an experiment with electricity.[17]

Consider now the view of the student implicit here:

This right to know is not satisfied by providing a school desk for the child, putting books in front of him, and having a teacher go through the steps of a specified curriculum. It is satisfied only by objective proof that, after going to school, he can exercise the necessary skills and apply his knowledge. We are talking about demonstrable results, not merely ten or twelve years' exposure to a program that may offer a measure of success to some of the children (or even to most of them). In a sophisticated technological society, each child has a right to be taught a mastery of the essentials, *by whatever means are necessary.*

Stated in this way, the point seems indisputable. Who would argue that, as a matter of policy, we ought to allow a significant fraction of our children to go into the adult world without the means for earning a decent living or being responsible citizens? Yet that is what we do. In other spheres we do much better. In building rockets we engage in "zero-defect" programs of quality assurance, for we know that if a single part fails, the rocket fails. Can we not find ways to do as well for our children?[18]

Lessinger later asserts: "Under the new mandate, schools are asked to give each student the competence he needs, regardless of the difficulties; and that means *regardless of his initial or apparent interest, his cultural background, his home life, or his ability* as measured by culture-bound tests. In effect, this act asks the schools to *guarantee the acquisition of necessary skills.*"[19]

What I find interesting about these ideas is the assumption that the student is completely passive. Education is conceptualized on a production model. Learning is the product, teaching is the production process, the child is the raw material. Learning is something done to the child whose own values are not important and whose cooperation is not required. Accountability is illustrated by quality-control examples. On such a model, to limit the schools' obligation to providing the child with adequate resources for learning is objectionable. If the child is treated as a thing that undergoes learning, it makes about as much sense to say to the child "Here is the opportunity to learn; avail yourself of it" as it does to say to a sheet of metal "Here is the assembly line; make yourself into a car." According to Lessinger we can guarantee that children learn. Indeed we can guarantee that they learn *whether they want to or not.* Our obligation to "learn" the child extends to cases in which the child is uninterested in learning. Therefore children are not expected to avail themselves of the opportunity to learn, nor are they assumed to be responsible for learning. The responsibility appears to be the school's alone. A child's resistance to being taught is understood as a defect in raw materials. It is something to be remedied. It receives none of the consideration that the wants or interests of free agents ought to receive even if they ought to be ultimately overruled. Educational rights involve the right to be educated whether one likes it or not.

The ease with which it is assumed that children are entirely passive and that they have no legitimate rights in directing their own education gives one pause. That many would find Lessinger's comment to apply to almost any educational situation at any level raises concern. If we extrapolate the trend there is reason to wonder whether educators and students soon will find accountability oppressive, undermining the student's and the teacher's freedom of choice in education, eliminating students' responsibility for their own education, and loading excessive responsibility on the school. Lessinger seems to have difficulty viewing children as persons instead of materials.

The assumption that the student is passive, an assumption required if the educator must guarantee results, is not obvious. Why does it seem obvious to Lessinger; why is it becoming increasingly obvious to others in education? Perhaps a major influence has been that ideals of freedom have been eroded by the conceptual system of behaviorism. If I am right concerning the intellectual background of the passive language in which Lessinger's view of accountability is couched and if I am right that the clash between behaviorism and values of freedom results from a mistaken view about freedom, the trend it suggests is ominous and apparently threatens not only freedom in education but civil liberties. *A variety of civil rights and liberties depends on thinking of persons as free, active, responsible agents, and will not long survive the intellectual habit of conceptualizing human behavior in a passive language.* Indeed I will argue in the final section of this book that the very idea of people having equal rights is linked to what it means to be a person. If this is correct, the capacity for evil in a view that erodes that concept is great. We accordingly can believe that educators are moving toward the adoption of a behaviorist-like conceptual framework which will erode not only freedom in education but human rights.

It is not clear that this passive language which is increasingly being employed in the professional jargon of educators reflects an explicit commitment. This is not surprising, but it does suggest some interesting properties concerning the way in which a conceptual change often takes place. Such a change can result from one's unreflectively adopting new verbal habits. Students often enter an educational program talking about what children do and about how to teach them and leave talking about their behavior and how to change it. They tend to adopt the language largely used in the education community. In doing so they change from an active language which facilitates thinking of persons as free and responsible into a passive language which makes it difficult to think of persons as agents and easy to think of them as objects of manipulation. It is doubtful that in many cases such a change reflects any intellectual commitment, but it may lead to some because it is a passive language. Such language makes it difficult to express ideas which assume that persons are free active agents. The language had hidden commitments. Thus students who have undergone such a language change may discover that their values about education have also changed—not because they have changed them but because their verbal habits have altered what it seems possible to say or think.

I doubt that American educators can be argued out of their historical commitment to thinking that education is an instrument to liberate individuals. Reading *Beyond Freedom and Dignity* is unlikely to affect wholesale ideological changes in the profession. Yet I believe there is a danger that American educators will undergo a transformation in educational values caused partly by the hidden conceptual commitments of prevailing jargon. Educators need to take seriously how they talk and to be careful that they mean what they say.

We now face the serious possibility that we will back into a behaviorist view by our affection for enterprises such as accountability and our consequent employment of behaviorist technologies and behavorist language. Having done so, we may find that our liberal democratic values have become unintelligible to us. Empiricism's heir, behaviorism, may indeed be a Trojan horse in the liberal state.

II

Public Education and Private Values

Liberals often conceive liberty by distinguishing between public and private areas of life. The state has a right to legislate values or actions only when they are in the public sphere. The individual should be autonomous in the private sphere. This conception raises significant difficulties for public schools. As public institutions how can they deal with values without encroaching on the private sphere? How can they not deal with values and still fully educate their pupils? Public schools cannot solve this dilemma. In a liberal state publicly controlled schools cannot educate their students. It will take several chapters to state exactly what I mean by this. So that the threads of the argument do not become entangled, however, I shall begin with a brief summary of what this claim entails.

I do not mean that schools cannot succeed in teaching basic skills such as reading, writing, and arithmetic. Instead, I hold that liberal public schools cannot coherently transmit private values, and I hold that the transmission of private values is necessary for genuine education to occur.

I will not argue the second thesis in detail. I shall treat it as self-evident that an educated person should have attained reasonably developed tastes and acquired sensible opinions as to what things are good. My intent is to show how liberal ideas function to order the curriculum of public schools and the social relations under which this curriculum is transmitted. I believe that liberal public schools work best in attaching instrumental values to the knowledge they deal with and that as a consequence schooling reflects the triumph of means over ends. I shall leave it to the reader to confirm that a schooling system which provides instruction in the instrumental skills of living, but which fails to permit individuals to develop any rational notion of what to live for, is defective. The dilemma of public schools is teaching only the means of living, not what to live for.

Why should liberal public schools have difficulty with private values? The answer is that private values are private and that as such the school as an arm of the state cannot take a stand on them. Religious values may serve as paradigmatic here. A religion, if it is anything, is a comprehensive viewpoint from which perspective on other areas of life is gained. I once met a gentleman who was fond of saying that no fact was ever adequately understood until it was seen as a God-created fact. Anyone with a religious point of view must believe something like this. Other domains are not adequately grasped until they are assimilated into the religious outlook.

Yet our society has felt so strongly that religion is a private affair that it has adopted a constitutional provision which excludes the state from giving support to one religion over another and from preventing individuals from exercising their religious convictions. This is all well and good, but when applied to schooling it becomes problematic, for the religious person must find religious categories fundamental to genuine education, and public schools, as agents of the state, cannot deal with religious concepts.

Public schools need not exclude all private values. Teachers are not precluded from exhorting students to love Shakespeare or to love astronomy as they are precluded from exhorting students to love God. But liberal public schools may preclude teachers from *insisting* that their students love Shakespeare or astronomy. We may feel that schools are entitled to compel students to learn to read and write. If students fail in these areas they will become a social liability. But if they do not love Shakespeare, they harm no one, perhaps not even themselves. What right do we have to insist on this? The answer is that in a liberal society public schools have no right to insist that students adopt any particular set of educational values. When private values such as a love of Shakespeare are such that no one in the community is likely to find them offensive, the school may display them smorgasbordlike for students to sample. But schools will also be obliged to keep such things to the periphery of school life. Thus music, art, literature, even pure science or math—the enterprises which add meaning, reason, and value to experience—are relegated to the status of extracurricular activities. In creating such a classification schools teach that such values are acceptable—but unnecessary to life.

This state of affairs is not clearly objectionable. It is reasonable for a society to satisfy public educational concerns in public institutions and to allow private educational concerns to be privately pursued. Additional facts, however, suggest that there is a problem. Public schooling has become so dominant a part of the education of American youth as to weaken the effectiveness of education in the private sphere. Public schools also tend to create age-horizontal rather than age-vertical social relations. They thus inhibit the development of social relations which make possible the transmission of private values.

On the one hand public schools occupy too large a piece of educational space. Public education has grown from a state in which most students went only for a few years' instruction in basic skills to a point where children are institutionalized for a major part of their lives from five to eighteen. The expansion of public schooling has occurred at the expense of the educational capacity of family, community, and church, many of whose functions have either been transferred to public schools or neglected.

The expansion of schooling is not the sole cause of the weakening influence of other socializing influences. To a large extent it is an effect of this weakening. The influence of the church has declined as a function of loss of faith. Economic and demographic changes have weakened the educational potential of community and family. Nevertheless numerous educational tasks once performed informally outside of school have now been transferred to schools so that in the public mind education and schooling are synonymous.

Schools, however, are ineffective places for transmitting private values. They do not place students in intimate contact with adults whose shared values set the tone and determine the concerns of the school. Instead, students are set in formal and distant relations with adults whose lack of shared values is unlikely to generate any community of educational concerns. The student's intimate associates are instead peers in age. Public schools thus invite students to establish age-segregated communities of mutual ignorance whose culture is characterized by its lack of insight, its shallowness of experience, and its rejection of adult sources of insight and experience. Public schools seem ideal institutions for a society that wishes to commit cultural suicide. They are likely to be dominated by those instrumental concerns on which adults can agree. They will be ineffective devices for transmitting other values. Therefore liberal public schools cannot educate and will represent a triumph of means over ends.

This compact set of claims presents the agenda for section II of this book. We will have to look in detail at how a liberal point of view influences what public schools can and cannot be about. In chapter 5 we will examine the aspects of liberal theory which point public schools toward some things and away from others. In chapter 6 we will look at recent attempts to deal with values as represented in schemes of moral and values education. In chapter 7 we will consider how public schools transmit liberal values by examining recent controversy on student rights. In chapter 8 we will look at how public schools deal with the values of work. This should give us a reasonable picture of the dilemma of public schooling in a liberal society.

I know of only one way of preventing men from degrading themselves, namely, not to give anybody that omnipotence which carries with it sovereign power to debase them.

—ALEXIS DE TOCQUEVILLE

What's Public about Public Schools?

A. A LIBERAL THEORY OF SCHOOLING

Why would a liberal state have public schools? I take it for granted that education is a good and necessary thing and that in technological societies education has to involve formal instruction in schools. But why *public* schools?

Public schools require infringements on individual liberty. Attendance is required. This may appear to violate the liberty of children, but in fact the point of coercion is parents. Parents must, on penalty of fine or imprisonment, send their children to school. A second kind of coercion is financial. To pay for schools individuals who own property or who earn an income must pay a percentage of the value of their property and income.

Before we conclude that these forms of coercion are reasonable, note that much in the way the liberal state is conceived suggests that the practices are objectionable. The essence of the liberal state is that the state exists to regulate competition among individuals for private goods. From this notion it follows that the government must not seek to establish a public conception of good. It must not act so as to impose one person's conception of a worthwhile life on another. The government's legitimate sphere of action is limited to regulating competition between individuals for their individual goods. Thus a government must justify its acts by showing that they are necessary to enforce fairness in the competition for private goods or that they are designed to promote some legitimate public objective.

The question of why a liberal society should have public schools can also be stated as an economic question: Why not allow education to be provided by the private sector of the economy? If people want education, they will be willing to purchase it. When enough people are willing to pay for education, other individuals will emerge to provide the service. Is there anything objectionable about this view of how education should occur in a liberal society?

For the liberal this question is an issue of liberty and of efficiency. If values may legitimately differ, individuals should be free to choose the goods and services they wish to pay for, and the economy should be free to respond to such expressions of free choice. Any attempt by a government to regulate what people can purchase or what people can sell must be justified by the same criteria as any other infringement on personal choice. Why then do we not allow consumer choices to determine what sort of education we will have? What reasons are there which might justify the violation of free choice involved in a liberal state providing compulsory public education? Must not public schools inevitably lead to public regulation of private values?

Consider John Stuart Mill's remarks: "All that has been said of the importance of individuality of character, and diversity in opinions and modes of conduct, involves . . . diversity of education. A general State education is a mere contrivance for molding people to be exactly like one another: and as the mold in which it casts them is that which pleases the predominant power in the government . . . it establishes a despotism over the mind, leading by natural tendency to one over the body."[1] A problem exists: how public schools can deal with private values in a liberal state.

These remarks do not enforce the conclusion that public schooling is illegitimate, given liberal assumptions. They do suggest, however, that public schools in a liberal society should have justification. *If there are to be public schools in a liberal state, these schools should be dominated by concerns which are clearly public. Moreover such schools must avoid encroaching on individuals' private concerns.* We should expect therefore that the public/private distinction will be important in determining what public schools do and do not involve. Moreover this distinction should be a key to understanding the problems public schools have in dealing with values.

The public/private distinction is not clear. Indeed it has been highly problematic. If we are going to understand its role in public education, we will have to achieve a clearer view.

The central idea of a private value or action is that it ought to concern only the individual. Private matters are not the legitimate business of social or governmental authority. Public values or actions, by contrast, legitimately involve collective decisions and legitimately may be advanced or prohibited by social or governmental authority.

The distinction is intended to separate human affairs into one group which can and one group which cannot be the business of collective choice. But it does not inform us of the basis on which this distinction is to be made. That is the problem to be solved.

We would be mistaken to proceed as though there must be some single criterion which is sufficient to separate human affairs into a public and a private domain. Instead there are various grounds which lead to the conclusion that some endeavors should be considered private and that other endeavors should be public. The trick to understanding the public/private distinction is having a reasonable sense of what these grounds are and how they can be applied to education.

Consider first some grounds for treating some value, belief, or action to be a private matter.

1) *Extensiveness of consequences:* One of the standard ways liberals have attempted to mark the private sphere is by distinguishing between those actions which affect the well-being of others and those which do not. This is a difficult distinction to make sharply. We may agree, however, that actions which have few or unimportant consequences for the well-being of others should belong to the private sphere.

2) *Desirability of consequences:* Some liberties are justified because the consequences of not regulating a certain range of activity are socially desirable. Liberals have often defended such liberties as free speech, free press, or academic freedom on the grounds that free and open debate has desirable social consequences.

3) *Personalness:* Some values, beliefs, or activities are so close to the center of a person's concept of life or of self that they ought not to be made objects of public decision. Religious beliefs or practices are paradigmatic. People often hold their religious or moral convictions in a way such that they cannot willingly consent to have them made objects of public regulation. Any such attempt will be experienced as an attack on the self—a violation of the sanctity of the individual. Likewise public scrutiny of personal or family intimacies can be experienced as an attack on the self. Liberals have tended, therefore, to see highly personal matters such as religion or family relations as part of the private sphere.

4) *Lack of objectivity:* One reason for considering a value to be private which is often given in educational contexts is that there are no rational criteria for its assessment. It thus becomes a matter of personal preference or taste. Arguably it is inappropriate for educational institutions to exercise any authority over such matters. Matters of taste should be treated as part of the private sphere.

5) *Controversial Matters:* A final reason for treating something as private is that opinion about that matter is sufficiently divided and sufficiently intense that any attempt at collective decision is likely to have undesirable consequences. Public schools therefore may avoid a topic on grounds that it is simply too controversial to handle fairly in a public context.

Liberals primarily have applied the public/private distinction to actions. The reader will have perceived that frequently I have applied it to values or beliefs as well. This is important if the distinction is to prove useful in talking about schools, for in an educational context we are often more concerned with what people believe and with what they value than with what they do. In many social situations it is appropriate to regulate only actions. It would surely be out of bounds in a liberal society to attach criminal penalties to what people valued and believed as well as to what they did. But in education the issues are not what people will do but what they will be. We are not concerned primarily to prohibit undesirable actions. Instead educational debates concern what values and beliefs the state may or may not propagate. In educational contexts the public/private distinction must be applied to the propagation of values and beliefs.

In determining what is private one must distinguish tastes from beliefs. Tastes or preferences are those things which one desires. Beliefs are those propositions which an individual holds to be true. The reason for stressing this distinction is that preferences tend not to raise issues of truth while beliefs do. This suggests that the grounds to tolerate a diversity of tastes are different than the grounds to tolerate a diversity of beliefs.

When people differ in tastes, it does not necessarily follow that they have disagreed about anything or that one person must be right and the other wrong. There are no logical reasons for someone who likes olives to be challenged in this preference by someone who prefers pickles. Here a part of the grounds for tolerance is that nothing is at stake in people's preferences beyond their likes and dislikes.

Beliefs do raise issues of truth. When people disagree about their beliefs, at least one of them must be wrong. Reasons can be given for or against holding a belief. Consequently tolerance of diversity in belief cannot be argued for simply on the grounds that there is no rational way to challenge a person's choice. One's beliefs can be false. Tolerance of diverse beliefs thus requires an argument which shows that tolerance serves some public good or an argument which shows that a person's convictions ought not to be violated by society.

Within the domain of beliefs, to distinguish individuals' fundamental convictions from their other beliefs is useful. Fundamental convictions lie at the core of their understanding of life and its duties and obligations. Religious beliefs and basic moral convictions fall into this category. To compel a person to violate fundamental convictions constitutes a strong attack on the person.

Most beliefs—let's call them *common beliefs*—do not fall in this category. Most of us believe that there are nine planets in the solar system. None of us is likely to find the meaning of our existence challenged if someone discovers a tenth.

The point of tolerance may also differ between common and fundamental beliefs. Arguments concerning the importance of free and open debate usually concern common beliefs. With fundamental convictions it becomes equally important that society leave individuals in peace to affirm and practice their values as that the process of criticism and debate be promoted. Most people will attach more importance to the right to practice their religion than their right to debate it.

I do not pretend that this classification of private values is perfect. Obviously the distinction between fundamental and common beliefs involves a matter of degree as well as kind. Clearly all preferences are not simply matters of personal taste. It is difficult to imagine what a rational debate concerning whether pickles taste better than olives would entail. But it is not hard to imagine a rational debate concerning whether Beethoven is better than the Beatles. Here there is room for reason to get at least a foothold. Taste is not just a matter of taste. Finally beliefs and taste can interact. Beliefs may legitimate preferences, or people may form associations around beliefs, and these associations may be expressed in a culture incorporating a set of preferences.

These distinctions do have some utility in our discussion. They help explain some of the strategies public schools have employed in dealing with private values. The general rule has been that schools are supposed to be neutral about values.[2] But there are different ways to be neutral, ways which correspond (roughly) to the classes of private values noted.

The rule has been that schools may not deal with fundamental convictions. Public schools have typically sought to avoid dealing with religious issues. Parents and educators do not seem to think that schools can discuss religious beliefs while not supporting or undermining any of them. Schools thus have been expected to avoid the topic altogether. This has resulted in eliminating prayer and Bible reading from the once omnipresent morning exercises, and it has been pressed to the point that even the voluntary singing of secular music associated with religious holidays has been rejected. One can decorate the room, but not "Deck the Halls."

Where convictions differ, but are not fundamental, schools may adopt a different attitude. Neutrality is likely to be understood as promoting an open discussion in where the school's duty lies promoting a fair presentation of issues. Political issues are paradigmatic. Students will be encouraged to debate issues and candidates (within the normal range), and teachers will be encouraged to keep their opinions to themselves.

Tastes receive still a different treatment. Schools typically provide opportunity for students to acquire and express a variety of tastes. Participation is voluntary, however. The most obvious examples are sport, music, and art, which are usually available to students as extracurricular activities. Even the intrinsic values of the regular curriculum are treated as extracurricular. Students may be required to take English, math, and science; but no one is likely to insist that they love Shakespeare, appreciate an elegant equation, or admire a powerful explanation. Teachers will often feel it is important that students be exposed to such values, but their acceptance is treated as a matter of taste. Schools display a smorgasbord of private values for students but enforce acquaintance with only a few and acceptance of none.

This is not a complete inventory of how schools can respond to values in a public context. There are a number of particular difficulties which require special responses. Consider, for example, some problems which flow from the schools' attempts to promote democratic values.

Promoting democratic political beliefs and attitudes is an important part of the public function of schooling. Surely a society that wishes to govern itself by liberal democratic principles must teach these principles and seek to develop loyalties to them. Nevertheless, this endeavor can bring the school into conflict with an individual's fundamental convictions.

One recent issue has concerned saluting the flag. This exercise has been intended to promote patriotism and love of country. Certain religious groups have declined to salute the flag on the grounds that their allegiance to God precludes their expressing allegiance to a state or its flag. The exercise in patriotism offends their fundamental conviction. The chief response to this sort of issue is to grant to the state its right to use the schools to promote patriotism, but at the same time to grant to the individual citizens the right to opt out when their fundamental convictions are offended. Thus, courts have maintained the rights of parents to send their children to private schools[3] and have upheld the right of religious dissenters not to participate in saluting the flag.[4] Opting out is a basic strategy for reducing the conflict between public education and private values.

A more perplexing difficulty is the contradiction between the school's duty to promote democratic values and its inability to enforce an ideology on its staff. If schools are expected to promote democratic values, it seems reasonable that they have a right, indeed a duty, to expect a commitment to these values from teachers. How can an institution promote values its members do not accept? At the same time to insist that teachers subscribe to a political creed is to stifle free and open discussion and to attach state-imposed penalties to expressions of opinion. Thus basic liberal values are violated. Can an institution promote a set of values by violating them?

Perhaps the sensible attitude for schools to adopt is benign partisanship, the key to which is a reliance on reason and persuasion. The school must assume that liberal democratic values will commend themselves to most teachers sufficiently that they will be willing to participate in their promotion voluntarily. Those who dissent, however, cannot be subject to sanctions on that account. It is hard to see what other viewpoint permits schools to promote liberal democratic values without simultaneously violating them.

This inventory should give us some idea of the kinds of private values schools have to contend with and the strategies schools adopt to avoid treading on them. The general rule is that where values are intensely felt and where sharp differences exist, schools will be expected to avoid them altogether. In areas where people are likely to recognize the legitimacy of a range of options or where values are seen as a matter of taste, schools will be permitted to promote impartial discussion or present values for voluntary selection.

Public schools ought to promote enterprises which are legitimately public. The primary sense of a public value is that such values are legitimate objects of public choice, public action, and public coercion. I shall list five aspects of the public which connect to this central definition. It is not clear that each of these is public in quite the same sense. There seems to be a family resemblance between these different kinds of public goods rather than a single unchanging meaning. Moreover considerable overlap exists between several of these categories. Nevertheless, if public schools are to be legitimate social institutions, they must be justified by serving some public need. Consider five different ways of conceiving the public function of public schools.

1. *Schools should promote the conditions for fair competition.* In the concept of a liberal state one of the functions assigned to the state is the promotion of fair competition for private goods. The final section of this book explores equality of educational opportunity as an institution for creating fair competition. Suffice it now to note that providing an equal chance to acquire the means to compete is a fundamental public task of schooling.

2. *Schools should promote goods with significant neighborhood effects.* Certain goods produce benefits for persons other than those who pay for them. If I buy and eat an ice-cream cone I receive the entire benefit of the cone. If, however, I invest in an education, the resulting improvement in my capacities or character may produce benefits for other people. These benefits are neighborhood effects. In determining how much of a good to purchase I will consider its benefits to me, but not its neighborhood effects. The result is that for goods with substantial

neighborhood effects, the aggregate investment in the good may be less than what actual demand would justify. Individual investments will produce less of a good than people collectively wish to have. Thus, for goods with significant neighborhood effects, free markets do not reflect consumer sovereignty. Such goods therefore are legitimate objects of public decision because public choice is necessary to reflect private demand adequately. Since education produces such neighborhood effects, education (or those parts of it which produce neighborhood effects) is a public good.

3. *Schooling should prevent harm to others.* Schools may function to protect the public against the incompetence of its members. The usual kinds of incompetence are political and economic. Schools protect people against the harm that ignorance can do to democratic institutions.

4. *Schools should promote universal instrumentalities.* Suppose a thing is a means to almost any end. Such a commodity would be something all rational people want regardless of other desires. It would be a means to most private goods, whatever they happen to be. Such goods can be considered to be public both in that reasonable people would agree about their desirability and in that their fair distribution would be essential to promoting social justice. The Harvard philosopher John Rawls lists these "primary goods" as rights and liberties, opportunities and powers, income and wealth, and self-respect.[5] Schooling can play a role in creating the conditions for the effective employment of rights and liberties. Education is itself a basic opportunity and is thought to be important in society's providing for acquiring the talents on which income and wealth depend. Schooling also has a role in enhancing self-respect or detracting from it. Clearly how teachers and peers regard a student affects his or her self-regard. Equally important may be the student's success in school and the lessons learned about what's relevant to judging people. The school is often the child's first contact with a highly competitive and evaluative social institution. It would be surprising if it did not affect the student's self-regard. These universal instrumentalities can thus be treated as appropriate areas for public schools.

5. *Schools should promote transcultural rational enterprises.* Such enterprises as mathematics and science are public in the sense that their claims are subject to public rational standards and are not matters of personal taste. While this sense of public is remote from the central conception we have been dealing with, it nevertheless contributes to legitimizing the pursuit of such enterprises in public schools.

This point may be best seen by emphasizing the transcultural character of such rational enterprises. Let us define a culture as an organized set of preferences shared by the members of a group. In this sense to speak of French, Japanese, or African culture is to speak of tastes in food, dress, poetry, art, architecture, and music. These aspects of culture are private because attachment to them is justified by preference or history, not reason. There may, of course, be standards of excellence in, for example, French cooking; but these pertain to the refinement of tastes, not to the truth or falsity of claims about the world. That culture in this sense is a matter of taste is confirmed by the fact that we do not feel any need when confronted by a person who likes French cooking or French poetry and another who prefers Japanese cooking or poetry to decide who is right. Nor is there any inconsistency in liking both. Rational enterprises, however, are not just organized preferences. Their claims exhibit an objectivity that transcends culture. Thus, while science or math, like all human enterprises, originate in a culture and may begin as an expression of that culture's values, their claims exceed its bounds. There is no French science in the sense that there is French cooking.

Rational enterprises do not present the same difficulties for public schools as do divergent cultures. Cultures may be dealt with by schools like private preferences. They may be presented by the school so long as participation is voluntary. What the school cannot do is exhibit a preference for one culture over another. Rational enterprises are not, however, subject to these limits. Their objective transcultural aspects mean that they are more than a matter of preference. This public character justifies the school in making rational enterprises central to the school's task. They need not be treated as extracurricular, and the school may put them at the center of its idea of education without great concern that private values are being treaded upon.

We now have to consider what sorts of educational enterprises are public. Consider first an argument which suggests that *each of the senses of public is best fulfilled by an education which emphasizes the development of rationality.* We must again remember the link between political liberalism, the emerging natural sciences, and the empiricist epistemology by means of which they were interpreted. Liberals have been confident that once people are liberated from the bonds of ignorance and tradition and are educated in the arts of reason and science, they will become masters of their own fate—competent to manage their own affairs and to participate in the collective management of public affairs. If we wish to create such people the emphasis must be on creating individuals who know how to collect information and to deal with it in rational ways.

The curriculum which such a viewpoint generates will emphasize basic literacy, mathematics, and science. Literacy is a condition of assessing information in our society. Mathematics and science are those enterprises most suitable for training the mind to rigorous and clear thinking and in enabling the student to cope in a rational fashion with day-to-day problems. Other disciplines such as history may also have such virtues and may teach the "laws" of history and politics.

Liberals have often viewed the chief functions of education as political and economic. They have, however, not assumed that achieving these goals requires political indoctrination or specific vocational training. Instead it is assumed that the rational individual will be both politically and economically competent. A rational person will quickly learn the specific ideas and skills needed to meet specific political and economic demands and will be better able to adapt as political and economic realities change. An emphasis on political and economic values need not, therefore, lead to an emphasis on political indoctrination or vocational training.

An emphasis on basic skills and basic disciplines is public in each of the five senses noted above. This obtains because rationality—the key value of the liberal's curriculum—is basic to each sense of public.

In this discussion I have suggested the connection between rationality and political and economic competence. An approach to basic skills and basic disciplines can serve the public function of protecting society from political and economic incompetence. It is also arguable that rationality is either a primary good itself or is implicit in the list. Rationality seems quintessentially a universal instrumentality. It is something all rational persons want. It is by definition assumed in the development of a rational set of private values or a life plan. Moreover rationality is important in exercising political rights and exploiting economic opportunity. It thus seems a requirement implicit in having rights and liberties, opportunities and powers, and income and wealth. Its connection with self-respect is less clear, but it is not implausible to suggest that rationality is important to self-respect as well. Rationality is therefore a public good in the sense that primary goods are public.

Similar arguments show that rationality is of public concern insofar as promoting fair competition is concerned. If rationality is important to political competence or to economic opportunity, then its equitable distribution is a key part of the state's duty to ensure equal opportunity.

Rationality can also be held to have significant neighborhood effects. Insofar as education develops individuals into competent and productive citizens, everyone shares in the growth of each individual's capacity. Rationality is a public good in this sense as well.

Finally rationality is public in the sense that it is transcultural. This (at least on conventional epistemological assumptions) is simply a matter of definition.

Note that some mention of political and economic competence occurred in the discussion of each of the senses of public except the last. This isn't surprising, given the significant degree of overlap between the various senses. It entitles us to another conclusion—that liberals tend to see the public function of education largely in its capacity to promote political and economic competence. We may thus summarize a liberal view of public schooling by saying: *The central public functions of schools is the fair distribution of political and economic competency by developing the individual's rational capacities through an emphasis on basic skills and basic disciplines.*

B. RELIGION AND PUBLIC SCHOOLS

The preceding discussion has provided an abstract commentary on how liberal notions of the private and the public function to determine a conception of education in a liberal state. We can grasp these issues more firmly by examining them in some concrete cases.

The distinction between the public and private spheres is embedded in the First Amendment to the Constitution, which guarantees such liberties as freedom of religion and freedom of speech, press, and assembly. Here I wish to deal with the Supreme Court's handling of problems concerning how religion is to be dealt with in public schools.

Consider first *Pierce* v. *Society of Sisters.* The case concerns a 1922 Oregon statute which required all children between the ages of eight and sixteen to attend a public school. One of the plaintiffs was the Society of Sisters who operated a Catholic parochial school. The Court held that while Oregon might compel children to attend some school and could regulate all schools in ways consistent with the state's legitimate interests, it could not prohibit parents from sending their children to private schools. The grounds for this decision were that the Oregon statute arbitrarily destroyed the value of the property of those who operated private schools and that it interfered with the liberty of parents to direct the education of their children. The case is therefore not clearly a First Amendment case, although it is commonly read as one.[6]

The Court justified the right to a private education in the following words:

We think it entirely plain that the act of 1922 unreasonably interferes with the liberty of parents and guardians to direct the upbringing and education of children under their control. . . . The fundamental theory of liberty upon which all governments in this Union repose excludes any general power of the state to standardize its children by forcing them to accept instruction from public teachers only. The child is not the mere creature of the state; those who nurture him and direct his destiny have the right, coupled with the high duty, to recognize and prepare him for additional obligations.[7]

The state's interest in public education is also maintained.

No question is raised concerning the power of the state reasonably to regulate all schools, to inspect, supervise and examine them, their teachers and pupils; to require that all children of proper age attend some school, that teachers shall be of good moral character and patriotic disposition, that certain studies plainly essential to good citizenship must be taught, and that nothing be taught which is manifestly inimical to the public welfare.[8]

The Court seems to have a public/private distinction in mind; however, the concept is not clearly expressed. The private sphere, the sphere of parental discretion, is represented in the remarks that the state may not standardize students and that parents have the right and duty to prepare them for additional obligations. The state's legitimate (public) interests are represented in the suggestion that the state may promote citizenship and prohibit subjects "inimical to the public welfare." The solution *Pierce* offers to the conflict between public schools and religious values is essentially to permit those who feel that the public schools either fail to promote or conflict with their values to establish private schools. The right extended is a variety of the right to opt out.

A second case in which the right to opt out for religious reasons is maintained and which expresses a clearer concept of the public function of schooling is *Wisconsin* v. *Yoder*. This case concerns the attempt by the State of Wisconsin to enforce its compulsory education statutes against a group of Amish parents who on religious grounds wished their children not to attend public schools after the eighth grade.

The Court expresses the conflict between the schools and the religious values of the Amish in these words:

Amish objection to formal education beyond the eighth grade is firmly grounded in these central religious concepts. They object to the high school and higher education generally because the values they teach are in marked variance with Amish values. . . . The high school tends to emphasize intellectual and scientific accomplishments, self-distinction, competitiveness, worldly success, and social life with other students. Amish society emphasizes informal learning through doing, a life of "goodness," rather than a life of intellect, wisdom rather than technical knowledge, community welfare rather than competition, and separation, rather than integration with contemporary worldly society.[9]

Having recognized the conflict between Amish religious values and the values of the public school, the Court proceeds to address the issue of whether the public's interest in compulsory education is sufficient to override the Amish's religious liberty. Justice Berger expresses the Court's agreement with the State of Wisconsin concerning the nature of the public's interest in education:

The state advances two primary arguments in support of its system of compulsory education. It notes, as Thomas Jefferson pointed out early in our history, that some degree of education is necessary to prepare citizens to participate effectively and intelligently in our open political system if we are to preserve freedom and independence. Further, education prepares individuals to be self-reliant and self-sufficient participants in society. We accept these propositions.[10]

Here the Court identifies the public interest in education—the interest which justifies compulsion—as the achievement of political and economic competence. From this point the Court's argument is a factual one showing that Amish children become good citizens and self-reliant individuals without the need of a high-school education. It thus exempted them from Wisconsin's compulsory education statutes.

Here we have a clear affirmation by the Court that the central public concerns in education are political and economic competence. It is the public's interest in those which justifies state compulsion. It is also worth noting that in *Yoder* the Supreme Court does not pretend that public schooling is value-neutral. Instead the Court contrasts the values of the Amish with the values promoted by public schools. Moreover the Court seems to hold that individuals are protected from the school's encroachment against their private values only when these values have religious roots. "A way of life, however virtuous and admirable, may not be interposed as a barrier to reasonable state regulation of education if it is based on purely secular considerations; to have the protection of the Religion Clauses, the claims must be rooted in religious belief." [11]

We should thus not seek to read *Yoder* as limiting schools to promoting economic and political competence or insisting on strict value-neutrality. The point is rather that only the fundamental public needs of promoting political and economic competence are viewed as suffcient to override religious scruples. When, however, these fundamental public interests are not threatened, *Yoder* extends a more extreme form of opting out to those whose scruples are offended by public schools. They need not attend school at all.

The Court has insisted that schools be neutral with respect to religious notions in a different sense. Part of the First Amendment prohibits the state from effecting "an establishment of religion." In a recent case, *Abington School District* v. *Schempp,*[12] the Court held that the establishment clause prohibits religious exercises such as prayer and Bible-reading in public schools. Here the Court struck down a Pennsylvania statute which required "at least ten verses from the Holy Bible shall be read, without comment, at the opening of each public school on each school day. Any child shall be excused from such Bible reading, or attending such Bible reading, upon the written request of his parent or guardian."[13]

The following comments express the essence of the Court's grounds for striking down the statute.

Almost twenty years ago . . . the Court said that "neither a state nor the federal government can set up a church. Neither can pass laws which aid one religion, aid all religions, or prefer one religion over another. . . ."[14]

Public schools are organized "on the premise that secular education can be isolated from all religious teaching so that the school can inculcate all needed temporal knowledge and also maintain a strict and lofty neutrality as to religion."[15]

Here the Court seems to limit the opting-out strategy to the free exercise of religion clause. When the secular curriculum of the schools is seen by someone as conflicting with religious scruples, the Court offers the individual the opportunity to withdraw, providing that doing so does not threaten some vital public interest. The Court does not, however, permit this strategy to justify a school's promoting any explicitly religious point of view. Schools may not avoid the charge that they have violated the establishment of religion clause by holding that those who wish need not participate. Here the school must maintain its neutrality by excluding any semblance of support for religion.

The Court also identifies religious neutrality with a secular education. This notion of neutrality must be stated correctly if it is to make sense. The Court has not erected an assumption that schools must be strictly neutral to all values, only religious values. Neither is the Court claiming that a secular curriculum avoids conflict with religious values. If that were the claim *Yoder* would be nonsense. Rather the Court's claim makes sense if we hold that the point is that by limiting itself to a secular curriculum, the school avoids taking a stand for or against any religion. That neutrality does not exclude possible unintended conflict with religious interests. Finally the Court apparently rejects the notion that neutrality could be understood as providing equal access for all religions to the public schools while preferring none of them. It does countenance a study of comparative religion or religion as history, but it seems to reject a "marketplace of ideas" conception of neutrality which permits a diversity of religious practice and advocacy in schools. Religion is excluded.

It is tempting to see the Supreme Court as affirming the public character and thus the legitimacy of the transcultural (or in this case the transreligious) values of a secular curriculum. In a concurring opinion Justice Brennan expresses this public character of the secular curriculum, expanding the point beyond religious issues. "It is implicit in the history and character of American public education that the *public* schools serve a uniquely public function: the training of American citizens in an atmosphere free of parochial, divisive, or separatist influences of any sort—an atmosphere in which children may assimilate a heritage common to all American groups and religions."[16] In short, Justice Brennan sees the secular curriculum as public in that its concerns transcend cultural and religious differences. It is thus the fifth sense of public which identifies the public with transcultural rational enterprises which is at the root of the identification of neutral with secular.

The foregoing is hardly an adequate summary of the complex issues of religion and public education. It will do for our purposes, however, and it does support some conclusions concerning the Supreme Court's conception of the public and private distinction and concerning the Court's strategies for solving conflict.

In regard to the public/private distinction the court has given explicit protection only to those values which are clearly rooted in religious views. *Pierce,* however, implicitly recognizes a wider range of private values and offers the protection of private schools to those who feel offended by public schools for whatever reasons. The Court's concept of the public character of education picks out the creation of political and economic competence as the fundamental public interests in education. It is these interests which justify coercion. The Court also can be viewed as regarding these objectives as served by a secular curriculum which is also public in that it involves transcultural rational enterprises.

The basic policies the Court has adopted for resolving conflict between the public and private spheres in education are that the Court excludes religion from the public schools except as it might be encountered in the secular parts of the curriculum. When religious or other private values conflict with the secular curriculum and secular values of the school, the court will permit the offended parties to opt out either to a private school or even (as in the case of the Amish) to no school. The Court also suggests that when the public's interests in political and economic competence are threatened, it will permit compulsion even when that might lead to conflict with private and even religious values.

We can understand these views more fully by exploring two objections expressed in a dissenting opinion by Justice Stewart in *Schempp.* Initially Stewart holds that for those who wish to withdraw from public schools to pursue or protect better their fundamental convictions in a private education, the court's policies have the consequences of making the availability of a basic right dependent on the ability to pay.

It has become accepted that the decision in *Pierce v. Society of Sisters . . .* was ultimately based upon the recognition of the validity of the free exercise claim involved in that situation. It might be argued here that parents who wanted their children to be exposed to religious influences in school could, under *Pierce,* send their children to private or parochial schools. But the consideration which renders this contention too facile to be determinative has already been recognized by the Court: "Freedom of speech, freedom of the press, freedom of religion are available to all, not merely to those who can pay their own way."[17]

   This argument has its context in a larger discussion concerning whether excluding prayer and Bible-reading from public schools might not raise the issue of "a substantial free exercise claim on the part of those who affirmatively desire to have their children's school day open with the reading of passages from the Bible."[18] Stewart argues:

For a compulsory state educational system so structures a child's life that if religious exercises are held to be an impermissible activity in schools, religion is placed at an artificial and state-created disadvantage. Viewed in this light, permission of such exercises for those who want them is necessary if the schools are truly to be neutral in the matter of religion. And a refusal to permit religious exercises thus is seen, not as the realization of state neutrality, but rather as the establishment of a religion of secularism.[19]

   This argument deserves some analysis. We should distinguish the claims that exclusion of religion from the schools involves "the establishment of religion of secularism" from the claim that "religion is placed at an artificial and state-created disadvantage." The first claim ascribes to the state the advocacy of a particular point of view, secularism, which is both religious in character and hostile to the claims of traditional religion. The second claim merely implies that the state has acted in a way which has unintended but harmful consequences for religion. The first claim is therefore the stronger one.
   J. Robertson McQuilkin, president of Columbia Bible College, states a version of the first claim. "The religion of secularism must be disestablished. Judeo-Christian religion and, along with it, religious values and Christian morality have been barred from many public schools, while at the same time the frankly secularistic position has been established. And yet secularism is religious in nature. Man-centered and limited to the realm of the material, it has all the basic elements of religion: absolutes based on faith, values based on these absolutes, ultimate allegiance, evangelistic fervor, and an emerging 'priesthood.'"[20]
   Such a claim is difficult to confront because it is not clear what factual evidence would be required to substantiate it. If on one hand the truth of the passage requires commitment by professional educators to a positive, yet secular, interpretation of life and a recognized and successful intent among educators to use schools to promote this point of view, then the claim is false. If there is such a positive yet secular philosophy guiding the actions of those who run the schools, they have been remarkably successful in hiding the ideology and their own activities. The religious and philosophical commitments of professional educators reflect the diversity of views exhibited in the general population.
   On the other hand there are enterprises in public schools which are motivated by secular ideologies, and there are individuals in public schools who use their positions to promote secular ideologies and to at-

tack religion. (Much the same could be said of those with religious views.) Perhaps some biology professors exceed their duty to teach the scientific theory of evolution and advocate evolution as a fundamental way of interpreting existence, or perhaps some popular views of moral education are seen by their advocates as secular alternatives to a religious point of view. It is questionable, however, that such incidents add up to any official commitment by the schools to a religion of secular humanism.

What is operating in McQuilkin's remarks is a mixture of "He that is not for me is against me" logic with a bit of paranoia. It is easy for one with an intense commitment to a religious viewpoint to see a certain unanimity in the views of those persons outside the community of faith. They are united in rejecting some fundamental truth. Is that not sufficient to regard them as representing a single point of view? In this way the chaos of viewpoints which actually characterizes public-school personnel is easily reified into a unified secular ideology. As easy as this step is, however, it is a mistake. This variant of the claim that schools have established a secular religion is unsubstantiated.

The weaker claim that the exclusion of religion from schools puts religion at a disadvantage is quite plausible. Public schooling may dominate education to a degree which interferes with the capacity of parents to provide a religious education for their children. This will particularly be the case if by a religious education one has in mind the generation of a religious interpretation of life and learning, rather than mere instruction in a creed.

There may be an equally serious difficulty. I have insisted in the first section of this book that what people learn is a function of their current beliefs as well as of what they are taught. We therefore need to ask not just what schools teach concerning religious issues but what children learn.

Consider the example of sex education. Religious leaders frequently claim that sex education ought to be conducted in a religious context and that secular sex education inculcates views and practices inconsistent with religious conviction. School officials in turn claim to present factual information and to advocate or reject no moral point of view. Parents are free to provide whatever religious interpretation of sex they desire. The schools are properly neutral.

We must, however, consider the matter from the adolescent's point of view. Psychologists claim that youth are constantly testing the limits of adult authority. In this fashion they not only discover themselves and their capacities but also find the real values of their society. We are also told that Americans tend to be highly other-directed and to gain much of their sense of right and wrong from what they see as commonly done.

Let us express these observations as principles of inference. The first point becomes "Anything adults do not object to is permissible." The second is "Anything that is commonly practiced is permissible." Consider now the conclusions which an adolescent armed with these principles of inference will draw from a value-neutral description of sexual facts and practices. The inferences is that no sexual practices are morally noxious (although one may have to take care to avoid undesirable consequences). The reader may agree with these conclusions, but the point is that they are incompatible with traditional religious views of sex. There are, then, reasons to suspect that, even when instruction about sex is neutral, what students learn will not be. Public schools may communicate significant lessons about religious values despite the fact that they don't teach them. I therefore find the conclusion that the exclusion of religion from public education puts religion at a disadvantage highly plausible.

I do not conclude, however, on the basis of this argument that the majority opinion in *Schempp* is incorrect. Mandatory prayer and Bible-reading do not count as state neutrality. Instead *the proper conclusion to draw is that the conflict between private values and public schools cannot be resolved to the degree that public schools dominate the educational process. To the degree that education equals public schooling parents will desire public schools to express their fundamental values, for failure to do so is the failure to communicate these values at all. Yet public institutions cannot legitimately promote private values.* Indeed it is unlikely that they can avoid having negative consequences for many of these values.

Private values therefore should be promoted by private means. The current need for American education is to strengthen such private means. The heart of the conflict between religion and schooling is not that public schools are inevitably antireligious. It is that in implicitly equating education with public schooling, Americans have created a need to bring their private values into public schools. Yet this is a need public schools cannot legitimately meet.

One final remark: I have thus far presented the conflict between public and private values as a conflict between the secular curriculum and religious values. Religious values, however, are only a class of private values. That values are not religious does not mean that they are not private or that they cannot conflict with the values of the school. We therefore must examine the problem as it arises in a nonreligious context.

CHAPTER 6

Moral and Value Education

Programs in values education or moral education have been increasing in recent years. Parents and public officials have been progressively concerned that schools transmit more than skills and disciplines. Schools must also develop the child's character. How to keep Johnny moral after school has become a matter of deep concern.

This concern may be related to recent events. Adolescent violence and vandalism often are cited as reasons for the interest in moral education. Of greater significance is that people should find it obvious that moral or values education is a task for public schools.

From a liberal point of view, moral education is problematic when conducted in a public school. How can schools deal with issues of value and morality without infringing on the private sphere?

The answer has considerable bearing on my contention that public schools in a liberal state cannot educate students because these schools cannot adequately transmit values. If one can discover some technique for transmitting values which is both successful and legitimate, my claim will have been substantially refuted. On the other hand, if attempts to solve this difficulty fail, another piece of evidence will have been found to confirm my contention.

Consider some strategies which might be employed to teach values in a way that does not infringe on the private sphere. Values might be dealt with in some value-neutral way. This can mean a number of things. Educators might make the school a forum for discussing values without taking a position in any debate. Or they might describe values without advocating any. These approaches, however, do not immediately commend themselves, for what is wanted is not that children should learn about values, but that they should acquire a suitable set of values. We wish children to be moral—not to make them philosophers or anthropologists. Values educators have thus not wished to be confined to teaching about values.

The trick to teaching values while still remaining neutral may reside in teaching how to reason about values. If we can teach moral reasoning, then we can help students to select sensible moral principles without taking a stand on moral issues and without interfering with the free choice of students in selecting their own values. This strategy should commend itself to any liberal. It recognizes the centrality of rationality to liberty. It proposes to deal with values by teaching people how to think about them rather than by indoctrinating people in some particular set. It assumes, however, the suspicious notion that there are ways of reasoning about questions of value which do not themselves involve value-assumptions.

Another way of legitimating values in a public institution is to restrict oneself to public values. If some value—say honesty—is vital to human beings doing business with one another with maximum effectiveness and minimal injury, such a value may be treated as public, and even a liberal public school can seek to advance it. The most obvious public values in a liberal state will be those of liberalism itself. Thus the school may legitimately promote values such as tolerance and a respect for others' rights.

The investigation of values and of moral education will be concerned to see if these strategies are successful. Is it possible for public schools to teach anything important about values without encroaching on the rights of individuals?

I have thus far been using the words *value* and *moral* interchangeably. I will not elaborately analyze these terms. There is little in the argument which will not be adequately served by our intuitive concepts. I do wish to suggest two ways of distinguishing value issues and moral issues.

The concept of value often seems the broader of the two. One may hold that all moral issues are issues of value, but that not all value issues are moral. Whether or not a painting is a good painting is, for example, a value issue, but not a moral issue. Here, however, it will be convenient to use a narrower notion of value. I discuss values when what is at stake is a person's desires, tastes, or preferences. I talk about morality when what is at issue is the rightness of conduct.

This usage reflects a standard philosophical distinction between the right and the good. Right concerns conduct. Moral theory is the theory of right action. Good concerns the evaluation of objects or the worth of events. The theory of the good or value theory is thus concerned with determining what sorts of things are worthwhile. Both right and good can be applied to actions. They reflect the difference between "It would be right to do X" and "X-ing is enjoyable."

The distinction between value theory and moral theory requires us to divide our question. The broad question "Can public schools legitimately deal with values?" now must be separated into: (1) Can public schools legitimately deal with values (individual preferences or goods)? and (2) Can public schools legitimately deal with moral questions?

We need to conduct independent investigations of values education and moral education. As they are now construed, these are different topics. I first examine a popular view of values education called value clarification. Then I look at the views of Lawrence Kohlberg on moral education.

A. VALUE CLARIFICATION: HEDONISM WITH A SHRINK

Value clarification proposes to help us *think* about preferences. Consider, for example, this remark from *Values and Teaching* by Raths, Harmin, and Simon, the basic text on the subject: Value clarification "is based on a conception of democracy that says persons can learn to make their own decisions. It is also based on a conception of humanity that says human beings hold the possibility of being thoughtful and wise and that the most appropriate values will come when persons use their intelligence freely and reflectively."[1]

It is not clear that preferences can be weighed rationally. Isn't a preference simply something one likes? What is there to think about? Isn't the idea that we can discover our likes equally absurd? A liking is a state of consciousness. By definition it is something of which we are immediately aware. How could we not know what we like? Thus, if liking is all there is to a preference, how can there be any thinking about it?

Perhaps we should begin with two sets of questions: 1. Is it possible to be rational about preferences—that is, is it possible to give reasons which show that one preference is better than another or which show that one ought to like one thing more than another? Can a preference be an object or rational choice? How? 2. Is it possible to discover one's preferences? How is it possible not to know what one's preferences are?

Let us start by making the hedonist assumption that liking or desiring something is what is meant by calling something a preference and that gaining our preferences is a major part of a worthwhile life. But let us also admit that our preferences do not just happen to us. They are often, if not always, objects of choice. We can decide what we want. This does not show that questions about rational preferences have answers, but it does show that they have a point. If our preferences merely happened to us, it would make little difference if they were rational. In fact, however, we can decide what we will like or choose to cultivate a taste. Even when we can't, we can avoid pursuing some desire when there is a reason. We are not mere victims of our passions.

But how can we be rational about preferences? The most obvious need for reasoned choice among preferences arises because preferences may conflict. They can be inconsistent with one another or with the means available for their realization. Hence we need to order our preferences and to reconcile them. Achieving a set of organized preferences requires much thought. We must know in detail the consequences of acting on our preferences and the contingencies on which realizing them depends.

We should not simplistically understand the conflicts and interactions between preferences. There is a degree of transfer between preferences so that to acquire a preference for one sort of thing generates additional preferences for similar things and can blossom into a full-blown life-style whose preferences are linked or reflect a common core of value. Thus, when one learns to enjoy art or poetry, one may also come to desire tranquility or an attractive work setting. Or the temperament acquired through developing one's taste in art may be reflected in one's tastes in music. These considerations need to be weighed when one works toward an organized and rational set of preferences.

It is also likely that reasons can be given for preferring some things to other things even if one is not so inclined. Consider, for example, Mill's remark in *Utilitarianism* when he argues that true happiness resides in the life of the mind. "It is better to be a human being dissatisfied than a pig satisfied, better to be Socrates dissatisfied than a fool satisfied. And if the fool, or the pig, are of a different opinion, it is because they only know their own side of the question. The other party to the comparison knows both sides."[2]

Mill suggests that despite what we currently like there may be other things which are genuinely more likable. Some tastes appeal at the outset but quickly bore or reveal their shallowness. Others may not please at the outset, but once one learns to see what they offer, they exhibit countless variety and depth and provide for longer and deeper enjoyment. Such considerations enable us to tell someone who prefers the Beatles to Beethoven that Beethoven is nevertheless better. Such remarks mean that a person who acquires a taste for Beethoven by learning his music will ultimately find that Beethoven has more to offer.

Thus reasons can be advanced to show that some preferences are better than others. Mill's claim that the life of the mind is ultimately the most satisfying strikes close to the truth, but is too narrow. John Rawls formulates the idea well in what he calls the Aristotelian principle. "Other things equal, human beings enjoy the exercise of their realized capacities (their innate or trained abilities), and this enjoyment increases the more the capacity is realized, or the greater its complexity. The intuitive idea here is that human beings take more pleasure in doing something as they become more proficient at it, and of two activities they do equally well, they prefer the one calling on a larger repertoire of more intricate and subtle discriminations.''³ Some such claim seems necessary to render a hedonist ethic consistent with the fact that it is possible to give reasons which show that one object or act is genuinely better than another. In the arts such arguments commonly appeal to the capacity of the objects to elicit a sophisticated response or subtle discrimination. Rawls's Aristotelian principle thus states the psychological presupposition of the objectivity of aesthetic modes of reasoning.

Another way of giving reasons for preferences stems from the connection between preferences and beliefs. In many cultures art and music express, and are justified by, the culture's fundamental beliefs. Medieval art and socialist realism both illustrate this point. Fundamental beliefs typically exclude some preferences and certify or legitimate others. Art, music, architecture, entertainment, and sport often take their themes and their tonality from their society's religious or moral convictions. It is thus possible to be rational about preferences when we explore the relations between preferences and fundamental beliefs.

A final way to be rational about preferences stems from the fact that notions of justice will influence one's concept of permissible or desirable preferences. Justice excludes certain sorts of preferences. A concept of justice which includes liberty and equality will reject preferences which involve taking pleasure in the oppression or humiliation of other human beings. Moreover a society which wishes to function according to justice will be committed to just institutions and just acts, and these will reflect the preferences of its members. It is possible to imagine a society in which the demands of justice are accepted by the population simply as a duty. It seems better, however, for people to act justly because they genuinely wish to do so.

These considerations indicate that preferences are more than one's initial likings. What people initially like is at the root of their preferences. But a preference can and ought to be a product of reflection and choice concerning one's likings. Values can be rational in a variety of ways.

Liberals have tended to see thought about preferences as a matter of ordering desires and relating them to available means that are constrained by the demands of justice. They have not generally subscribed to anything like the Aristotelian principle (Mill is an exception) for psychological reasons. Bentham's notion that pushpin is as good as poetry has been the basic sentiment. They have also tended to ignore the relations between preferences and fundamental beliefs because their emphasis on scientific thought and its hostility to tradition and received authority has made them suspect many claims about fundamental convictions.

Owing to these emphases, liberals have seen the choice of preferences as a matter of individual choice having little to do with initiation into a culture characterized by values shared by its members. That there is a degree of transfer between preferences, that sophisticated preferences are developed by people modifying and improving a cultural tradition, and that preferences express basic convictions are the kinds of considerations which suggest that preferences are not random. But liberals rarely have seen the choice of preferences as having to do with initiation into a culture. They have thus tended to see the right of free choice among preferences to be more nearly a defense of individualism than of pluralism.

This individualist focus concerning preferences is reinforced by empiricist epistemology. Empiricists have emphasized learning from immediate experience. This is not simply a view of science but a view of how we learn what we like. We come to associate feelings of pleasure and pain with certain objects or events. But an epistemology which sees learning as a matter of modifying a set of concepts in light of experience is also likely to see the selection of a rational set of preferences as the initiation into and modification of a cultural tradition. It will recognize that individuals who fail to rely on a cultural tradition are no more likely to achieve a rational and sophisticated set of preferences than individuals who ignore the received views and problems of a science are likely to develop a rational view of nature. Rationality about preferences, like rationality about nature, is more profoundly a group enterprise than liberals have been willing to admit.

This point suggests that a view of values education which envisages setting out values smorgasbordlike and helping students choose among them will not contribute markedly to the development of genuinely rational and sophisticated tastes.

We now turn to our second set of questions. Is it possible to discover one's preferences? How is it possible not to know what one's preferences are? If preferences are rational likings, it is possible not to know one's preferences. One will not know one's preferences if one does not know what it is rational to want. Finding out is a matter of reasoning.

There are two ways in which one might be said to discover one's preferences. One can discover them in action. The question How do you know if you'll like it if you haven't tried it? reflects the point. Introspective data on whether one likes something may be unreliable without experience concerning the object or act in question.

Another possibility for discovering one's preferences involves the unconscious mind. If there are mental states which one cannot call to consciousness at will and if preferences exist among these states, then it is possible to have an unconscious preference and not to know what one's preferences are. Discovering one's preferences might then be a matter of making them conscious and might involve rejecting superficial or phoney preferences for real preferences.

These remarks suggest some things that values education might involve. It should involve some experience with the objects of possible preferences and might even involve a little therapy.

Consider what sort of program these ideas might lead to. A curriculum which focuses on mathematics and science and supplements these with literature, art, history, philosophy, and music is required. These enterprises are important to developing rational and sophisticated preferences. They provide some of the intellectual resources people have developed to think about values. Science and math provide tools through which people come to understand the consequences of their actions. Literature and the arts likewise are repositories of ways people develop taste and discrimination. They allow people to experience their world more fully. We should add sports and crafts to the list, recognizing that there is an excellence of the body as well as of the mind.

This view of values education tends to see values education as inherent in the normal curriculum. But it does not give full play to the link between values and particular ethnic and religious traditions. Moreover, it is short on experience and "therapy." It may, however, be the best a public school can do. Schools cannot become intimately involved with particular ethnic or religious traditions. Formal educational institutions also are limited in their ability to provide some kinds of experience, although real contact with the arts and sport and vicarious contact with other aspects of life through literature and history are important. Schools are not appropriate places for therapy. The connection between the standard curriculum and values ought to raise our suspicion about views which provide techniques of values education unrelated to what people have found to be rational about their world.

Let us return to a consideration of values clarification. The view presented by Raths, Harmin, and Simon has a starting point which seems compatible with liberalism. They do not propose a particular set of values. Instead they wish to teach students how to think or to clarify their own values. And they regard this view of value education as an extension of democratic attitudes. Raths and the others do not, however, distinguish between values and morals. Thus, while the view they develop seems at first a theory about preferences, they extend it into the moral arena, but I shall treat their views as though they were exclusively concerned with preferences. Later we shall look at the consequences of not distinguishing between preferences and moral claims.

Raths thinks that the problem of values results from being unclear about them. Persons knowing their values are described as positive, purposeful, enthusiastic, and proud. People who are unclear about their values are seen as apathetic, confused, or irrational. Their existence lacks direction. The basic goal of value clarification is that people gain a clear idea of their values.

But it turns out that Raths and his coauthors desire values fundamentally to have authenticity, not clarity. Values should be personal. Raths claims that "if children—or adults, for that matter—are to develop values, they must develop them out of personal choices. We are also saying that these choices, if they are possibly to lead to values, must involve alternatives which (1) include ones that are prized by the chooser; (2) have meaning to the chooser, as when the consequences of each are clearly understood, and (3) are freely available for selection."[4]

Raths believes that respecting the personal character of values is a moral and legal obligation of teachers.

In a society like ours, governed by our Constitution, teachers might well see themselves as obliged to support the idea that every individual is entitled to the views he has and to the values that he holds, especially where these have been examined and affirmed. Is this not the cornerstone of what we mean by a free society? As teachers, then, we need to be clear that we cannot dictate to children what their values should be since we cannot also dictate what their environments should be and what experiences they will have. We may be authoritative in those areas that deal with truth and falsity. In areas involving aspirations, purposes, attitudes, interests, beliefs, etc., we may raise questions, but we cannot "lay down the law" about what a child's values should be. By definition and by social right, then, values are personal things.[5]

Raths sees values as emerging from experience. Experience is not a clear term. Little in this passage or elsewhere suggests that Raths sees much connection between values and any cultural, intellectual, or religious tradition. Generally traditions are things to be liberated from. Raths also sees the right to personal values as rooted in their nonrational character. There is no right or wrong about values; no truth or falsity. Therefore we cannot be authoritative about them. In these notions Raths seems well within the empiricist tradition. Experience is set against tradition. There is no truth about preferences. Preferences are what one likes. Taste, not reason, is central.

The basic strategy of values clarification is to ask questions which focus the student's attention on some issue about values. Often such questions are one-liners in response to something the student has said. Questions are often variants of "Have you thought about this?" or "How do you feel about that?" In other cases something called a value sheet is used. A value sheet is a short provocative passage on some issue involving values together with a short list of questions designed to focus the student's thoughts. Good questions focus the student's attention on values without moralizing or condemning and without revealing any preferred point of view. They are designed to help students decide what they really think or feel. Raths lists seven features about what value clarification should do. The first three are illustrative: "1. Encourage children to make choices, and to make them freely. 2. Help them discover and examine available alternatives when faced with choices. 3. Help children weigh alternatives thoughtfully, reflecting on the consequences of each."[6]

I note an apparent inconsistency. Raths claims that value clarification should promote critical thinking about values. He also claims that values are matters of opinion about which there can be no right or wrong. What, then, is there to think about?

Raths is not inconsistent on this point, however. The earlier discussion on reason and preferences should suggest that it is possible to reflect on preferences and to select some and not others without necessarily assuming that statements of the form "X is good" have truth value in the same way that "Grass is green" has truth value. That reasons can be given for preferring some things to others does not mean that individuals or groups may not legitimately differ in their preferences or that when they differ, someone must be wrong. Nevertheless the apparent paradox in Raths's views should lead us to inquire what role thought plays in the evaluation of preferences.

Raths characterizes the role of thinking in value clarification: "Thinking may help us to see the alternatives which are relevant, and valuing helps us in the process of choosing from among these alternatives. Thinking may help us to anticipate a variety of consequences associated with the alternatives, but valuing leads us to make a choice from among the weighted consequences."[7]

Here Raths sees thought as a tool for achieving a set of ordered preferences. In choosing we must weigh alternatives. To do that we must know the consequences of our acts. Once we know the consequences of our acts, choosing may still seem a matter of what we like. Reason can only help to make clear what will result from our actions, but it seems not to have a further role in evaluating or comparing the outcomes of different choices. Raths considers the question of whether it is possible to be rational about preferences by noting that insofar as achieving a set of preferences is a matter of knowing the consequences of choices and actions it can be a rational activity.

Much of what is suggested concerning how to clarify values is based on the assumption that the task is not to evaluate one's preferences but to discover what they are. For example, a list of typical clarifying questions includes: "Is this something that you prize?" "Are you glad about that?" "How did you feel when that happened?" "Have you felt that way for a long time?" "Would you really do that or are you just talking?" "Is that a personal preference or do you think most people should believe that?" "Would you do the same thing over again?"[8] Some questions assume that values are discovered through action or experience and by reflecting on how we feel about them. Others suggest that our real values may be hidden from us by the ways we have learned to talk or behave in responding to the expectations of others. There is always the task of distinguishing real feelings from those adopted because they are socially approved. It is this suggestion that we may have to discover how we really feel which accounts for the droll title of this section of the chapter. The strategies of value clarification are not those which we normally associate with therapeutic or clinical contexts, but some do assume that we may have to discover our true feelings.

Rationality in Raths's system thus functions to help discover true feelings and to ensure that in ascertaining true feelings we weigh the consequences of our choices.

Raths does not foresee any broader role for rationality. We do not find a sense that despite one's current feelings, clear or otherwise, other preferences might be better. Value clarification does not envisage anything like the Aristotelian principle. Nor is there any sense that values might have a connection with fundamental beliefs or convictions which have truth value. Values are not seen as objects of refinement or as expressions of a more comprehensive view of life. They are expressions of current feelings illuminated by a grasp of the consequences of choices, but unilluminated by any sense of what people have discovered to be good and unilluminated by any sense of a connection with fundamental beliefs about life.

This view of what reason can and cannot do explains why Raths sees little connection between value clarification and the normal curriculum of the school. The standard curriculum can provide access into values clarification, but Raths does not see the arts and sciences as resources for sophisticated thought about values. There is no sense that preferences are enhanced by art and literature. In fact there is no sense that math and science might be relevant to understanding the consequences of our acts. Indeed Raths seems to regard students as sufficient unto themselves to think about values. That thinking might be assisted by appropriating the intellectual resources people have developed for thought seems alien. In this respect value clarification reflects the psychology and epistemology of classical empiricism. Preferences emerge from unmediated experience and are a function of what we discover ourselves to like. Intellectual or cultural traditions are a source of bias, not a source of wisdom. Value clarification thus has an impoverished view of the potential of reasoning in developing preferences. It is impoverished in the same way and for the same reasons that traditional empiricism is impoverished.

The most noteworthy omission in Raths's perspective is any sense that preferences can be constrained by moral principles or by the demands of justice. Here Raths's view becomes puzzling and inconsistent. Consider two examples. Raths records a discussion between a teacher and a student named John concerning immigration in which John says: "Well, they [immigrants] work so much cheaper that a decent American can't get a job."[9] The teacher responds not by attacking John's claim, but by asking for an example. Raths commends the teacher: "What about the prejudicial statement about immigrants which John made and which started off this dialogue? Can a teacher, in good conscience, ignore such poor critical thinking? One answer is that a frontal attack is not always the most effective."[10]

What grounds does Raths have for assuming that John's opinion *is* a matter of poor critical thinking? After all, the respect due to students' personal values was supposed to be rooted in the idea that there is not a matter of right and wrong in values. But Raths assumes John is wrong. He does not even suggest that John is entitled to his stupid opinion. The only issue raised is the most effective way to change John's values.

Possibly John is uncertain about his feelings about immigrants and after a bit of clarification he would feel differently. It is also possible that John's comments reflect his true feelings. In this case Raths's view suggests no grounds for questioning John or for doing anything other than respecting his preference regarding immigrants.

Consider next part of a conversation concerning honesty reported by Raths:

Ginger: Does that mean that we can decide for ourselves whether we should be honest on tests here?

Teacher: No, that means that you can decide on the value. I personally value honesty; and although you may choose to be dishonest, I shall insist that we be honest on our tests here. . . .

Ginger: But then how can we decide for ourselves? Aren't you telling us what to value? . . .

Teacher: Not exactly. I didn't mean to tell you what you should value. That's up to you. . . . All of you who choose dishonesty as a value may not practice it here, that's all I'm saying.[11]

The teacher here is in an absurd position. (Raths, who commends the teacher's handling of the discussion does not see this.) The teacher is in this dilemma because he subcribes to Raths's view that values are simply opinion. He therefore cannot be authoritative about them. He cannot claim that one ought to be honest; he can only say that he personally values honesty. Any attempt to enforce a policy of honesty is therefore unjustified. (The students understand this.) But the teacher wishes to enforce such a policy. He tries to solve the problem by expressing the view that it is all right to compel others to act in accordance with one's personal values so long as one does not seek to compel them to agree with one's values.) We are left altogether in the dark as to why we should agree with this unusual concept of tolerance. Such a position might make sense if the teacher thought that honesty was genuinely better than dishonesty. Liberal societies often insist that people act in certain ways regardless of whether they agree that they should. But the condition of justifiably doing so is that the society believes that the law or policy in question is reasonable and in the public interest. Nothing that is merely a personal value can be legitimately enforced.

One way of putting the difficulty is that Raths has not seen that *preferences can be evaluated in terms of their consistency with basic standards of justice.* A preference for Americans and a dislike for immigrants is not on a par with a taste for pickles and dislike of olives. The former is objectionable because it conflicts with norms of justice. The latter is a matter of taste. A second way to make this point is that Raths takes a theory which makes sense as a theory of preferences and treats it also as a theory of morals. He thus extends principles which govern likes and tastes to cases which concern the regulation of public conduct. He uncritically allows a theory of good to become a theory of right. Questions of honesty, justice, and respect for persons are treated as though they involves pickles and olives.

I have not provided any argument to disprove this move. Respected philosophers have argued that moral claims are matters of personal preference.[12] Here I only note that the view is counterintuitive and that Raths seems to stumble into it uncritically. I take it as intuitively obvious that *issues of justice are not just matters of taste and that the contrary opinion requires justification.*

We have yet to inquire as to whether or not value clarification employed in a public school represents an illicit encroachment by a public institution on private values. Does value clarification succeed in remaining neutral? I believe that value clarification fails to be neutral.

Value clarification involves a set of values. The authors of *Values and Teaching* attach a high value to personal choice. Accordingly the value of authenticity is a commitment of value clarification. Moreover value clarification assumes aspects of hedonism. It assumes that values are fundamentally a matter of how one feels or what one likes, and it limits thought to ordering preferences by the consequences of acting on them. Hedonism is an ethical theory that is incompatible with other ethical theories. It is a matter of noting that people differ in the sources for happiness. *The hedonists's "different strokes for different folks" involves a kind of value neutrality but a kind of value neutrality which presupposes a substantive moral theory.*

Value clarification is thus neutral in one sense but not another. It makes no assumption about what people should like. But it is not value neutral because it involves commitments to authenticity and a form of hedonism. These commitments are values. They are taught by the process of value clarification. And they are incompatible with values and moral convictions of both a religious and secular character. The claim to neutrality, then, is spurious.

Perhaps, however, these values about which value clarification is not neutral are public values and legitimately are encouraged by a public school. Might not one hold it to be a public good to teach children to exercise independent judgment? A liberal society needs people who are not easily manipulated and who make up their own minds. Perhaps the schools need not be neutral here.

Hedonism is harder to defend in this way, but it might be argued that in teaching a "different strokes for different folks" ethic, value clarification promotes tolerance and a respect for different values. Tolerance and respect are public values legitimately encouraged by schools.

These claims have some force. They are, however, weakened by the fact that authenticity is not exactly autonomy and "different strokes for different folks" is not quite tolerance.

I have attached the label *authenticity* to Raths's notion that values should be personal in order to distinguish it from autonomy. Autonomy signifies a capacity for rational and independent judgment. The core of the concept is the ability to make decisions on the basis of evidence. Autonomy thus requires reasoning and judgment and the psychological capacity to resist manipulation and to act in accordance with one's judgment. Authenticity differs from autonomy in that it involves an increased emphasis on choices that are personal, choices that reflect one's real feelings; and it entails a decreased emphasis on the notion that choices should be rational or strongly rooted in evidence.

The central value of value clarification is authenticity not autonomy. Value clarification does assign a role to thinking, but its point seems to be that values should reflect one's true feelings. Thought is a handmaiden to the feelings. This is not to object to authenticity. Authenticity forms a part of a reasonable theory of preferences. But authenticity does not have the same claim to be a public value as does autonomy. A liberal democratic society requires individuals to be capable of independent rational judgment. It is hard to see, however, that a capacity for authentic choice has an important public function. It may be a good, but it seems a private good.

The problem with treating "different strokes for different folks" as a view of tolerance is its narrowness. It does involve one kind of tolerance —the kind appropriate to differences in taste. But this is at best only a small part of the kinds of tolerance required by a liberal society. Differences in fundamental convictions and political ideals are not just matters of taste. Yet they are the cases in which tolerance is most important and hardest to come by. The "different strokes for different folks" standard does not provide grounds for religious tolerance or for free speech and free press. Thus, if we wish to teach the sort of tolerance appropriate in liberal societies, we will need something more potent than value clarification.

What results is that the defense of value clarification which turns on the claim that authenticity and tolerance are public values legitimately promoted by the schools is marginal. Authenticity and the limited tolerance involved in value clarification do overlap with autonomy and the broader tolerance involved in liberal theory. But they are identifiably distinct. They are not clearly public values and are thus not clearly legitimate values for promotion by the school. Moreover the fact that value clarification potentially involves sharp conflict with other religious and secular points of view and the fact that it divorces the process of value education from involvement with public rational enterprises suggests that it is not value-neutral. The fundamental difficulty with value clarification, however, is its corruption of public values. Its failure to limit value clarification to preferences is a catastrophe. *Value clarification makes public values such as liberty and equality into matters of taste and feeling. In doing so it undermines their claim to be morally obligatory.* We should value justice regardless of how we feel about it. We may compel individuals to behave justly. The basis of such obligations is the objectivity of the claims of justice. We need not maintain that the demands of justice are always clear or that the arguments for a particular conception of justice always convincing. Reasonable opinions about justice are difficult to obtain. But to treat liberal and democratic values as though they were on a par with pickles and olives undermines their obligatory character and the legitimacy of any attempt to enforce them. Public schools have an obligation to promote liberal democratic norms in rational and noncoercive ways. This obligation will probably not be fulfilled if teachers deal with liberal values in the way in which Raths deals with honesty. In this regard, then, value clarification is highly objectionable. In the form outlined by Raths, Harmin, and Simon, it ought not to be employed by public schools.

B. KOHLBERG ON MORAL EDUCATION

We have already examined the views of Lawrence Kohlberg in chapter 3. I consider the general features of learning assumed by Kohlberg to be sensible.

Now we ask about the legitimacy of Kohlberg's theory of moral education, its suitability to public schools. Can the schools practice moral education as envisaged by Kohlberg without encroaching on the individual's right to autonomy in the private sphere? To answer this question we will have to look at the substantive features of Kohlberg's moral theory. Here I will assume that the "essential Kohlberg" is captured in stage six since this is the stage which Kohlberg regards as fully adequate and since the others are preliminary to it.

Before describing the particular features of stage six we need to note some of the more general features of Kohlberg's views on ethical theory. Kohlberg's theory concerns right, not good. He is concerned to develop principles which regulate conduct. Further Kohlberg claims that the argument for his moral theory is not dependent on any theory of value. The rightness of an action does not depend on its maximizing some good.

Kohlberg also claims that his moral theory is objective. He insists that the moral principles asserted in his theory are rationally defensible and universally binding.

Consider now Kohlberg's description of stage six.

The universal ethical principle orientation. Right is defined by the decision of conscience in accord with self-chosen ethical principles appealing to logical comprehensiveness, universality, and consistency. These principles are abstract and ethical (the Golden Rule, the categorical imperative); they are not concrete moral rules like the Ten Commandments. At heart, these are universal principles of justice, of the reciprocity and equality of human rights, and of respect for the dignity of human beings as individual persons.[13]

Kohlberg suggests criteria for the adequacy of any moral principle. Such principles should be comprehensive, universal, and consistent. The moral principles involved in stages one through five are inadequate because they fail to meet these standards. Maxims such as "Do unto others as you would have others do unto you" express the demand for comprehensiveness, universality, and consistency. Kohlberg also indicates the nature of some of the substantive ethical concepts which fulfill these standards. They include equal rights and the obligation to respect persons by treating them as ends rather than means.

This sketch does not do justice to the complexity of Kohlberg's theory, but it is sufficient to ask whether the use of his program for moral education in a school violates the student's right to autonomy in the private sphere.

Kohlberg views his stages as descriptions of the principles of moral reasoning employed by individuals. He might wish to defend the appropriateness of his approach for public schools by affirming that he is teaching moral reasoning, not specific moral claims. Moral education attempts to improve the quality of moral reasoning by seeking to help the student move in the direction of a more adequate set of moral principles. These moral principles do not involve the school in taking a stand on current controversial issues. The school therefore can engage in moral education without getting involved in substantive moral debates. For example one might aspire to generate a commitment to equal rights on the part of the student without taking a stand on the ERA.

Kohlberg's views may be neutral concerning the burning issues of the day, but there is an obvious sense in which they are not neutral. For Kohlberg's views involve a substantive moral theory. There are alternatives to it. It is perhaps commendable that schools can employ Kohlberg's theory without getting entangled in sensitive topics. But why should schools support a view in which morality is seen as a matter of engaging in actions which are in accord with abstract ethical principles? Some Americans are ethical relativists, and others see morality as a matter of behaving in ways prescribed by some moral code such as the Ten Commandments or as doing the will of God.

Kohlberg's views are less likely than those of value clarification to clash with ideas people hold dear. Kohlberg's views are easily reconciled with some interpretations of a Judeo-Christian point of view. Perhaps God is a stage six. Kohlberg claims that Jesus was.

If one is not going to be neutral it is better to not be neutral in ways which are unlikely to offend principles which real people are inclined to hold. On the other hand the fact that one's views are unlikely to be offensive to very many people is not the same as being neutral. Kohlberg's theory does involve a controversial ethical theory which can and is denied by rational people. Therefore it is not neutral.

The claim that the commitments of Kohlberg's theory have a public character and thus can be promoted legitimately by public schools has considerable plausibility. Consider that the substantive moral commitments of Kohlberg's view are the principles of justice, equality, and respect of persons. These are the kinds of moral commitments for which liberal democratic institutions have normally argued. Thus Kohlberg's commitments can correctly be described as a variant of those commitments required for a justification of liberal democracy.

This defense of Kohlberg's legitimacy in public schools seems to me to be a qualified success. It is a success because Kohlberg's moral commitments are a variant of the basic principles of liberal democracy. They can claim to be public values, whose promotion can reasonably be held to be the duty of public schools. The defense is a qualified success because Kohlberg's views are one version or one formulation among others of these values. It is still not obvious why schools should support one formulation of democratic values over others. For reasons already suggested, however, this bit of partisanship seems benign. Moreover, if schools are to promote liberal democratic values, they must do so by promoting some formulation of them. Kohlberg's variant is better than most. Kohlberg's enterprise thus seems to me to have a legitimate place in public schools. In fact it is a form of citizenship education and thus is part of one of the central public functions of public schools.

C. SUMMARY

We need to take stock of where the discussion of the last two chapters has left us. I began these chapters with the claim that public schools in a liberal state cannot educate because they cannot transmit values. What can now be said for this contention? We have found reasons to divide this question so as to reflect a distinction between preferences and morals. Presumably both concepts are important to a reasonable view of an educated person. An educated person will have achieved a rational, sophisticated, and well-ordered set of preferences. And a well-educated person will have achieved a rational sense of justice and a rational view concerning proper conduct toward other persons. Schools, however, may differ in their capacity to deal with preferences and morals. Let us begin, then, with preferences.

The discussion in the last two chapters has suggested at least three reasons to believe that liberal public schools will have difficulty in assisting students in developing this rational set of preferences.

1. *The failure of value clarification:* Value clarification is the leading contender among views concerning how to facilitate the development of preferences. It has been found to be inadequately neutral and to have an insufficient appreciation of the role of rationality in generating desirable preferences. Moreover it illegitimately treats issues of justice as questions of preference. It is thus problematic on both moral and pedagogical grounds. That one view concerning value education is inadequate does not entail the view that liberal public schools cannot teach values. That value clarification faithfully captures some of the central attitudes of liberalism does, however, make its failure a consideration.

2. *The inability of schools to deal with fundamental convictions and culture:* The insistence that schools be neutral has been understood to exclude religious considerations and other fundamental convictions from

schools. Neither can public schools enthusiastically pursue values rooted in various ethnic cultural traditions. But preferences are often rooted in religious or moral convictions. Moreover cultures can be considered as organized sets of preferences. The inability of public schools effectively to transmit preferences with these sources limits their capacity to transmit values.

3. *Liberal schools fragment values:* I have suggested some epistemological considerations which suggest that sophistication in preferences requires the student to become an initiate into a cultural or intellectual tradition and to function as a junior member of a community led by adults united by a serious commitment to shared values. Liberal public schools, however, present a smorgasbord of preferences before students who lack the sophistication to explore or choose reasonably among them, and they deprive the student of the aid of a community of adults with shared values. Students are therefore unlikely to be able to avail themselves fully of the intellectual and cultural resources needed to realize the Aristotelian principle.

These difficulties, all of which stem from the inability of a public institution to commit itself to the full development of a set of preferences, are mitigated by the notion that the standard curriculum can be an important resource for developing sophisticated preferences. Moreover enterprises such as science and mathematics and to a lesser extent literature, art, and music have a claim to be public and therefore to be legitimately promoted by schools. Here arise factors which I will explore fully in the next chapters which suggest that the potential for developing sophisticated preferences which the standard curriculum has will not be fully exploited by public schools. These factors involve the tendency of schools to adopt a take-it-or-leave-it attitude toward the values inherent in subject matter, the inability of schools to develop communities in which the values of subject matter are shared, and the tendency of schools to give subjects like math and science a largely vocational cast.

We therefore continue to have considerable reason to be cynical about the capacity of public schools to assist students in developing rational preferences.

Moral education has, however, fared better. The reason is that Kohlberg's moral views include a set of concepts such as fairness, justice, equality, and respect for persons which form the basis of a liberal democratic view of society. These concepts are thus public values that are legitimately promoted by public schools. They are a part of the duty of the schools to promote citizenship. Thus, in the writings of Lawrence Kohlberg, we have discovered a theory of moral education which is plausible from both a moral and a pedagogical point of view.

There is, however, a small cloud or two on the horizon. In the next chapter I will suggest that the inability of schools to deal with preferences limits its capacity to perform its citizenship role as well. In chapter 8, I will argue that the school's duty to promote citizenship has been largely undermined by its preoccupation with and conception of promoting economic competence.

CHAPTER 7

A wise man heareth his father's instruction.
                                                    —SOLOMON

Student Rights

On February 24, 1969, the U.S. Supreme Court handed down the decision concerning students' rights, *Tinker* v. *Des Moines.* [1] This case concerned several students who wore black armbands to school as a protest to the Vietnam war and violated a school regulation. The case has generated a revolution in judicial attitudes toward adolescents in schools. The decision has been extended into areas such as student discipline and the right of due process.[2]

In upholding the right of John and Mary Beth Tinker to wear black armbands to school against the wishes of the Des Moines School District the Court held the following:

1. The wearing of an armband for the purposes of expressing a point of view is "the type of symbolic act that is within the Free Speech Clause of the First Amendment."[3]

2. People have rights in schools. In Justice Fortas' words: "It can hardly be held that either students or teachers shed their constitutional rights . . . at the schoolhouse gate."[4]

3. Students are legal persons for constitutional purposes. Fortas writes: "In our system, state-operated schools may not be enclaves of totalitarianism. School officials do not possess absolute authority over their students. Students in schools as well as out of school are 'persons' under our Constitution. They are possessed of fundamental rights which the state must respect."[5]

4. Free exchange of ideas is an important part of the students' educational process. Fortas quotes Justice Jackson in *West Virginia Board of Education* v. *Barnette*: "That they are educating the young for citizenship is reason for scrupulous protection of Constitutional freedoms of the individual, if we are not to strangle the free mind at its source and teach youth

to discount important principles of our government as mere plattitudes.''[6] I quote Justice Brennan: "The classroom is peculiarly the 'marketplace of ideas.' The Nation's future depends upon leaders trained through wide exposure to that robust exchange of ideas which discovers truth 'out of a multitude of tongues, [rather] than through any kind of authoritative selection.' ''[7]

5. Free speech is permitted so long as it does not lead to the material and substantial disruption of the school's program.[8]

The third and fourth points express what is philosophically important in *Tinker*. The statement that students are legal persons, for constitutional purposes, results in eliminating the distinction between minors and adults. As far as the Constitution is concerned, persons are persons regardless of age. In a concurring opinion Justice Stewart expresses doubt on this point. "I cannot share the Court's uncritical assumption that . . . the First Amendment rights of children are co-extensive with those of adults. . . . [A] State may permissibly determine that, at least in some precisely delineated areas, a child . . . is not possessed of that full capacity for individual choice which is the presupposition of First Amendment guarantees.''[9]

The other point of philosophic interest lies in the Court's remarks concerning the importance of a "marketplace of ideas." The Court believes that a marketplace of ideas provides the most fruitful context for learning and especially for training children for their role as citizens in our "disputatious society."

I wish to build a case against both of these notions. I do not intend to argue against student rights, however. I believe that withholding rights to students is worse than extending them. But my purpose is to show that liberal societies generate educational dilemmas to which solutions in public institutions are unlikely.

A. CHILDREN AS PERSONS

Of course children are persons. Children can be presumed to have, or have the potential for, those capacities which distinguish persons from things. They are moral rational agents. Therefore it is immoral to treat children as though they were conceptually indistinguishable from tables, cats, and rocks. As persons children have rights. They must be treated as ends, not means. Their wants and needs must be taken as having prima facie validity.

Do children have the same rights as adults? The primary fact is that children do not fully possess many of those characteristics which define being a person. Children are rational agents in the same sense that an acorn is an oak tree. Children, unlike chairs and kittens, have the potential to become moral rational agents—but they are not yet. But liberals discern an intimate connection between rights and rationality. Various rights and liberties are justified because they promote the growth or exercise of rational capacities or because they permit the individual to develop and effectively pursue a rational life plan.

What rights do persons have because they are *potentially* moral and rational agents? Do some rights have a competence requirement? More particularly, do the rights at stake in *Tinker* v. *Des Moines* have a competence requirement? The issue is the justification of paternalism. When is a person (or a society) entitled to substitute his judgment concerning the good of another for the second person's judgment?

Consider Mill's "On Liberty." This passage follows Mill's basic statement of his principle of liberty: "this doctrine is meant to apply only to human beings in the maturity of their faculties. We are not speaking of children or of young persons below the age which the law may fix as that of manhood or womanhood. Those who are still in a state to require being taken care of by others must be protected against their own actions as well as against external injury."[10] Mill specifies two groups who are "not in the maturity of their faculties"—children and barbarians. Concerning the latter he says: "Despotism is a legitimate mode of government in dealing with barbarians, provided the end be their improvement and the means justified by actually effecting that end. Liberty, as a principle, has no application to any state of things anterior to the time when mankind have become capable of being improved by free and equal discussion."[11]

Liberty is appropriate only to those in the maturity of their faculties. The reasons for this restriction of liberty are that those not in the maturity of their faculties need protection against their own actions, and that they are not capable of improvement by free and equal discussion. And Mill suggests the rights and duties of those in paternalistic relationships: the obligation of those persons in authority is the improvement of those under their control.

The restriction of liberty to those in the maturity of their faculties indicates Mill's willingness to attach a competence requirement to the liberties that he advocates. Actual, rather than potential, rationality is required. But Mill sheds little light on how we are to decide whether a person has achieved such a condition other than to identify it with that age "which the law may fix as that of manhood or womanhood." The concept of maturity, however, involves a number of difficulties.

It is not clear what maturity is or that it does not vary according to different purposes. Maturity is not intelligence alone: it also involves the emotional stability and predisposition to act wisely. And a person may be sufficiently mature to act responsibly in one area without being sufficiently mature to act responsibly in another. Maturity and rationality are not the kinds of qualities that one either has or does not have. They come in degrees. Presumably children acquire them gradually over a number of years. Finally there is little reason to assume that the rate of maturation is very constant. Thus at any given age it can be expected that we will find individuals at substantially different levels of maturity.

These complexities indicate that to draw a legal distinction between those who are sufficiently mature to participate in some class of rights and those who are not will be arbitrary. It will exclude from participation many who are capable and extend rights to some who are not.

The attempt to distinguish a broad class of those who are too immature to exercise basic liberties by legislating adulthood involves a significantly different approach to restricting the rights of children than the one taken to restricting the rights of adults. Our society does permit the liberties of adults to be restricted when adults lack the rational capacity to care for themselves. We restrict those who are mentally retarded or who become insane or senile. In such cases we respond to the particular circumstances of particular individuals. Moreover society has erected legal institutions which presume the competence of adults and which require it to be proven otherwise before rights are restricted. When, however, we fix an age of maturity and make reaching that age a condition of exercising some class of rights, we erect a legal presumption of the incompetence of a large class of persons, and we preclude them from so much as the opportunity to present evidence challenging this presumption.

These comments do not show that the rights of children may not be limited on grounds of their immaturity. Nor do they show that establishing a legal age for adulthood is an objectionable way of doing so. My remarks ought to suggest, however, that the procedure is not self-evidently right and that it should be undertaken for good cause.[12]

What reasons exist for restricting rights on the basis of maturity? Mill suggests that immature persons need to be protected from the consequences of their own acts and that the normal benefits of liberty may not accrue to the immature who are incapable of being improved by free and equal discussion. The force of these problems can be illustrated by voting. The point of voting is to express the right of persons to an equal influence on those institutions which make decisions affecting the capacity to pursue one's interests. Extending the voting franchise to the immature does not enable them to pursue or protect their legitimate interests, for immature people have an inadequate grasp of what their real interests are and on what their realization depends. Moreover the extension of the franchise to the immature prevents mature persons from using the vote as effectively to protect their interests, for it introduces an irrational element into the voting process. Voting thus ceases to reflect accurately either where the real interests of a majority lie or accurately to reflect any aggregation of true preferences. When the immature vote, they do not realize the benefits of voting and they harm the process.

Can such an argument be constructed concerning the liberties discussed in "On Liberty" and at issue in *Tinker* v. *Des Moines*? Let's remind ourselves of the liberties involved and the arguments for them. Mill distinguishes two basic classes of liberty—liberty of opinion and liberty of action. Among the arguments given for these liberties these are most relevant:

1. *The marketplace of ideas argument:* The improvement of ideas and the decisions and policies which flow from them is a result of free and open discussion.

2. *The experiment in living argument:* Liberty permits the testing of new patterns of life and new ways of doing things.

3. *The individual knows best argument:* Individuals are the best judges of what is in their own interest.

4. *The personal competence argument:* Liberty promotes the growth of personal judgment and competence.

Is extending liberty of thought and action to children likely to generate any of the benefits suggested by Mill's arguments? Whether we are talking about freedom of thought or freedom of action makes a difference. Children, particularly small children, need to be protected from the consequences of their own actions. Children under the age of seven or eight need close supervision to prevent them from getting into situations which can easily lead to significant physical injury. Even children through junior-high age and into high school require a significant degree of adult supervision. Such supervision requires a limit on their freedom of action which would be intolerable if applied to adults. It is less obvious that harm can result from freedom of expression.

A certain degree of maturity is required if any of the benefits suggested by the first three arguments are to be realized. Each of these arguments obtains only when the individuals involved have developed their rational capacities sufficiently so as to be able to profit from criticism and debate, to learn from their experience, or to be the best judge of their own welfare. Are such assumptions reasonable for children?

To answer that question we must ask what is to count as benefiting from criticism and debate or from one's own experience. Children of any age are capable of learning from discussion and from their own experience. Teachers are frequently told that good pedagogy involves creating active rather than passive roles for children in the classroom. Classroom discussion is surely part of such an active role. Moreover parents are often exhorted against overprotecting their children, the argument being that children learn from their mistakes. Don't these claims show that the desirable outcomes of liberty can result for children as well as for adults?

Several points can be advanced against this position. If we allow the individual's growth to count as one of the benefits of liberty envisaged by the first three arguments, that has the consequence of eroding the distinction between them and the fourth. That argument concerns the capacity of liberty to promote the individual's growth. Mill envisages that freedom of expression and action will lead to new additions to human knowledge and new discoveries concerning how people may best live. When we want to know whether we reap the benefits of liberty envisaged in the first three arguments when liberty is extended to children, we are not asking whether the individual learns something from participating in criticism and debate, but whether participation leads to the over-all improvement of the ideas being debated. When benefiting is understood in this way, it is unclear that extending liberty to the immature is productive. Children are rarely capable of fully grasping what is at stake in adult debates on matters of serious concern, let alone making a positive contribution to the debate.

Finally, when adults decide to extend various liberties to children, what they are extending to children is not liberty as Mill envisaged it. Liberties are extended by adults to children in a paternalistic fashion. Such liberties are a gift from the adult to the child. They are extended when the adult believes the child will profit, but the adult continues to be the judge of the child's interests and to hold the power to withdraw liberty for the child's benefit. Consider the examples of classroom discussion and of children learning from their mistakes.

Most teachers believe that discussion is useful pedagogically. But many teachers see discussion primarily as a motivational device. Students are more likely to be attentive and interested when they are participants in classroom activities rather than spectators. The teacher rarely approaches a classroom discussion assuming that students will contribute to human knowledge. The teacher hopes that students will refine their own ideas and see something they have not seen earlier. Teachers will assume a directive and paternalistic role in the process. They will introduce new data or ideas when they seem needed and will want to steer the discussion in a profitable direction, and they will retain the right to terminate the discussion when it takes an unprofitable turn. In short the teacher manages the process. The student may have the freedom to express an opinion concerning the topic at hand, but this freedom is delegated and tentative and may be withdrawn at the teacher's direction if the educational situation demands it.

Similar comments apply to the child's learning from experience. Good parents allow their children enough freedom for them to learn and explore. But sensible parents also recognize that good results depend on extending a suitable degree of freedom to the child. It makes little sense to permit free choices where children are not sufficiently mature to learn from the consequences of their acts. When children act in situations too complex for them to grasp how their actions produce consequences, the consequences of their acts appear magical. There is also reason to believe that children who are given a range of choices beyond their ken cope by developing rigid and irrational patterns of action. Excessive freedom is pedagogically counterproductive. And, particularly in the case of younger children, too much liberty can have immediate and harmful consequences. Children and adolescents often only dimly recognize the potential consequences of some of their acts and therefore need protection from their own poor judgment. A range of freedom may be good for children, but it needs to be the sort of freedom which is controlled by adults.

Therefore it is far less likely that the benefits of liberty will result when liberty is extended to minors, and it is far more likely that harm will result. Maturity does, therefore, seem a reasonable prerequisite to granting the liberties discussed by Mill, and there do seem to be good reasons for distinguishing the rights of adults from the rights of minors. The usual arguments for liberty make little sense when applied to those not in the maturity of their faculties.

But consider an objection. I have omitted one of Mill's arguments. One of the benefits of liberty was supposed to be that it facilitated the development of personal growth and maturity. Is there not a paradox here? Liberty appears to be a condition of the development of personal maturity. Yet people are not entitled to liberty until they have achieved a degree of maturity.

To deal with this objection we need a sense of what rights persons have in paternalistic situations.

Consider first John Rawls: "The principles of paternalism are those that the parties would acknowledge in the original position to protect themselves against the weakness and infirmities of their reason and will in society. . . . Paternalistic intervention must be justified by the evident failure or absence of reason and will; and it must be guided by the principles of justice and what is known about the subject's more permanent aims and preferences, or by the account of primary goods."[13] In Rawls's view paternalism is justified because rational agents who choose under impartial conditions would agree to it to protect themselves against the possibility of their own incompetence. In particular cases paternalism must be justified by the evident failure of reason or will.

The most important feature of Rawls's remarks concerns the duties toward those subjected to paternalistic institutions. Here Rawls suggests two standards. When deciding for others we should decide either according to our understanding of their settled and rational preferences or, failing here, according to the theory of primary goods.

The basic sentiment here is unobjectionable. The duty toward individuals subjected to a paternalistic situation is to decide in ways reflecting their best interest. How do we do this? We cannot, of course, do what they want. Such individuals' expressions of wants can be assumed to be irrational. We can, however, act according to our judgment of what such persons would want if they were rational. Thus we can decide according to our understanding of their rational preferences. Of course we may not know these. And there is a special problem in the case of children, for children may not have developed many enduring or rational preferences. Here we can fall back on the notion of a primary good.

Recall that for Rawls a primary good has the character of a universal instrumentality. Rawls defines a primary good as something rational people want whatever else they want. He lists the primary goods as rights and liberties, opportunities and powers, income and wealth, and self-respect. This list of primary goods provides general criteria according to which we can judge the interest of persons under paternalism.

Rationality bears an intimate connection to these primary goods. Rationality is assumed when rights and liberties are granted to individuals. Moreover the importance of rationality in exercising opportunities and developing capacities is obvious. Rationality seems quintessentially a universal instrumentality. The implication is that the primary obligation toward someone subjected to paternalism is to act so as to eliminate the need for it, and the fundamental aspect of this obligation is the creation or restoration of the individual's rationality.

The next issue is that if liberty is a part of the environment which leads to the development of the individual's personal competence, is not paternalism self-defeating? Doesn't paternalism perpetuate the need for paternalism by restricting the conditions for growth? The solution to this paradox consists in distinguishing between actual liberty (as argued for by Mill) and freedom of choice extended to an immature person by someone in authority over him. Let us label these *liberty* and *paternalistic freedom*.

Liberty is a right, but paternalistic freedom is not. Liberty is not something a society benevolently extends to a person provided it is used wisely. It is something persons are entitled to however they use it. It may not be withdrawn by authorities on the grounds that individuals are using it in ways judged incompatible with their own interests. Paternalistic freedom, by contrast, is something extended by one person to another because the hope is that it will produce desirable consequences. Moreover it may be withdrawn at the discretion of the person in authority if it has negative consequences. Paternalistic freedom is dispensed.

The extent of liberty and paternalistic freedom may therefore differ. Mill argues the range of liberty is the private sphere of action. The range of paternalistic freedom, however, is determined by what is judged to promote the growth of the individual. Usually the range of paternalistic freedom will be less than that of liberty, but that is not necessarily true. If children learn from their mistakes, it may be profitable on occasion to allow them to experience the results of an excess of liberty.

The paradox of paternalism can be resolved. Those not in the maturity of their faculties are not entitled to full liberty. But freedom of choice can be dispensed paternalistically when its availability has desirable educational consequences.

Thus far my argument suggests that the majority opinion in *Tinker v. Des Moines* is philosophically incorrect. Students may be persons, but there are good reasons to distinguish the rights of adults from the rights of minors. Students will be profitably served by a degree of freedom, but that does not mean that they have a right to adult liberties.

There is one additional line of argument to be considered. I have argued this chapter in terms of Mill's defense of liberty. Mill's argument defends liberty because it leads to rational decision-making which in turn promotes the common good. These are reasonable arguments, but there are other more central ones. I will later argue that rights are ultimately rooted in what it means to be a person, not in what are useful means to the common good. Does this make a difference in considering the rights of the immature?

It does make this difference. *Part of what it means to be a person is that a person's wants and beliefs must be treated as objects of respect.* Children are persons, and they do have wants and beliefs. These wants and beliefs thus have an a priori legitimacy. To say that they have such legitimacy does not imply that they may not be overridden for good reasons. Because children are immature we may often have to prevent them from acting on their wants or attempt to dissuade them from their beliefs. None of this, however, eliminates the obligation to treat the wants and beliefs of children as objects of respect. Even if we override them we cannot do so gratuitously or for reasons which are unrelated to the well-being of the child. To do so is to treat the child as a means, not an end—to fail to treat the child as a person.

It follows that the immaturity of children does provide grounds for the view that the rights of the immature should differ from those of adults. Children do require freedom to grow. But this freedom is different than adult liberty. It can be legitimately dispensed by those in authority and can be weighed in terms of educational criteria. But it also follows that *the arguments for distinguishing the rights of minors from those of adults do not diminish the fact that children are persons and that as such their wants and beliefs are objects of respect and should not be gratuitously overruled.*

Consider how these notions could be turned into legal policy concerning student rights. We might on one hand erect an assumption that children are legal persons possessed of basic constitutional rights. At the same time we would recognize that reasons exist for restricting liberty beyond what is permissible for adults. Schools, then, would be permitted to exercise such restrictions on showing that they serve some reasonable educational objective. Alternatively we might hold that minors do not have constitutional rights but that school authorities have the right to extend freedom to students when doing so encourages their growth. If we may assume that school officials and courts are possessed of unlimited benevolence and wisdom, these courses of action could and should lead to the same consequences. The rules governing student conduct would permit and prohibit the same acts.

There are, however, reasons to prefer the first plan, which gives better expression to the claim that the wants and beliefs of children are legitimate. The second plan relies excessively on the judgment and benevolence of school officials concerning the freedom of their students. Public-school officials do not have an exemplary record on this matter. Therefore it seems preferable to operate on an assumption in favor of students having the range of constitutional rights permitting exceptions as educational needs justify. In short we need to affirm the concurring opinion of Justice Potter Stewart. Students have rights, but not always those of adults.

B. RIGHTS AND SCHOOLS

These conclusions must be examined in more detail in the context of public schools. Recalling that the Supreme Court believed that extending First Amendment rights to students served important educational objectives, let me repeat the two earlier passages:

That they are educating the young for citizenship is reason for scrupulous protection of constitutional freedoms of the individual, if we are not to strangle the free mind at its source and teach youth to discount important principles of our government as mere platitudes.[14]

The classroom is peculiarly the "marketplace of ideas." The Nation's future depends upon leaders trained through wide exposure to that robust exchange of ideas which discovers truth "out of a multitude of tongues," [rather] than through any kind of authoritarian selection.[15]

Two different arguments are expressed. One argument rests on a concept of citizenship, primarily on the tacit assumption that what the student will learn about citizenship will depend more on what the school does than on what it says. Implicit is the view that the school functions as a model of social relations to the student. If we wish students to function well in a liberal democratic society, we must teach them in a liberal democratic school. Let us term this the *modeling argument.*

The second passage expresses a view of classroom learning. The marketplace of ideas is supposed to be an important feature of a desirable learning situation. This approach can be termed the *marketplace argument.*

Part of this argument is that free and open debate is a useful way to learn. But the Court seems to have more than this in mind. The point is also to teach students to function in an intellectually free situation and to learn to discover truth out of a multitude of tongues. The Court quite sensibly views this as something one needs to learn to do.

But if the school is to be a marketplace of ideas, it cannot be the same marketplace of ideas that Mill has in mind, for the right to participate in the marketplace of ideas has a competence requirement. Mill's argument for the marketplace of ideas is to subject opinion to the light of reason by permitting criticism and the posing of alternatives. This assumes that we are rarely certain of our ideas, but it also assumes that one opinion is not as good as another. Ideas can be improved by being examined. If this is the case, then there must be standards and criteria for the evaluation of ideas.

If there are standards and criteria for the evaluation of ideas, a marketplace of ideas is going to be productive only if the participants understand these standards and criteria. Ideas cannot be subjected to rational evaluation when the participants do not know what counts as a reason. It is the ability of the participants to weigh ideas according to rational standards which makes the difference between a marketplace of ideas and a tower of Babel.

In many classroom situations this aspect of rationality is missing. Students cannot participate in a marketplace of ideas because they do not have a firm grasp on what counts as a reason. A marketplace of ideas becomes possible only to the extent that students have internalized the standards of reason which apply to given situations. The marketplace of ideas is a game for the initiated. Conducting free and open debates is simply not a sensible way to teach physics, although it may make more sense in areas where standards of judgment are likely to be available to students prior to formal instruction.

The difficulty can be approached in a different way. A marketplace of ideas tends to assume a reasonable equality of expertise. For a marketplace of ideas to function each person must have something to contribute to the education of all. When the level of expertise differs substantially among the participants, the marketplace ceases to function. Those at higher levels of expertise will not find it worthwhile to attend to the opinions of the uninitiated. When fruitful exchange takes place, the role of the expert is to instruct, not to learn. Again this point is most appropriate in difficult subjects such as mathematics and science, in which the level of development and sophistication of the discipline permits the expert to be very much advanced over the novice. But the point applies in any area which has rational standards.

The deficiency of an unqualified marketplace of ideas as a model of classroom learning is that it does not attach adequate importance to the role of expertise in learning. It implicitly regards the student as an equal rather than as an apprentice to the teacher. An excessive emphasis on this sort of marketplace of ideas can be educationally counterproductive. Little truth is likely to result from pooling the resources of the ignorant. Students taught in such a way may, however, come to have an inappropriately high regard for their own views and fail to comprehend the role of reason in evaluating ideas. Premature participation in a marketplace of ideas can undermine the student's capacity to profit later from a free exchange of ideas by undermining respect for reasons and frustrating the teacher's ability to function as a model of competent performance.

Advocating a superior role for the competent in educating the intellectually uninitiated is not the same as advocating an appeal to authority to settle disputes or as advocating that the student be presented with only the perspective regarded as true by the schools' governors. The role of the expert in teaching is to function as a model of reason, not a model of totalitarian authority. In suggesting that we must choose between a marketplace of ideas and authoritarian selection the Court has committed the fallacy of allowing too few options. There is also the authority of reason and expertise. Moreover listening to student opinions and explaining what counts for and against them is a mark of respect for the student as well as good common sense about teaching. The teacher's role is not simply to forge appropriate intellectual standards, but to create and shape rational attitudes. Open discussion provides the teacher a chance to show what it means to be a reasonable person.

These comments suggest that some features resembling a marketplace of ideas are appropriate in the classroom. The classroom happenings described are, however, much closer to what I earlier characterized as a master/apprentice relationship than a marketplace of ideas, and they extend to students paternalistic freedom, not liberty.

We can now turn to the modeling argument. Must the school function like a liberal democracy if the student is to learn the role of a citizen in a liberal democracy? I assent to the Supreme Court's concept of citizenship. Citizenship has often been identified with an uncritical obedience of authority. In a 1929 case, *Pugsley* v. *Sellrmeyer,*[16] an Arkansas court upheld the expulsion of a girl for wearing talcum powder. The court reasoned that such an infringement of personal choice would be objectionable in any public institution except a school. The school is different than other institutions since it has among its legitimate tasks instruction in citizenship. Moreover, since obedience to authority is part of citizenship, and since enforcement of rules per se may teach obedience to authority, the enforcement of rules, regardless of their content, can be viewed as serving the legitimate educational goals of the school. In the school, it seems, no rule can be arbitrary.

In *Tinker* the Supreme Court, however, recognizes that citizens have the right to question and oppose as well as the duty to obey authority. It wishes to train students to be good citizens, but it has a suitable liberal and democratic view of what the citizen's role is. And, the Court reasons, if students are to learn to exercise their rights in a liberal state, they must be granted them in school. Students will learn to function in our society's marketplace of ideas, when the school is a marketplace of ideas. This is an appealing view of how the school should prepare students to be citizens in a democratic society. Let the school practice what it preaches. But I want to argue that it is unlikely that public schools will teach democratic or liberal values by modeling them.

Part of my case is taken from *Youth: Transition to Adulthood,*[17] a report of the Panel on Youth of the President's Science Advisory Committee. The book's thesis is that public schools have become dysfunctional by denying to students the opportunity to participate in adult roles and by segregating youth into institutions where they come into contact primarily with others of their own age.

The authors contrast the current pattern of socialization to that which prevailed as little as a century ago. Until recently formal schooling played only a small part in a child's education. The child was an important part of the economy of the family. Much of the child's education resulted from executing an economic role and from general participation in the life of the community. But as children have ceased to be economic assets and as the labor market has required more formal education of workers, the education of children has increasingly taken place in special institutions. And as formal schooling has taken over the task of education, children have been excluded from the adult world.

There are a number of undesirable consequences. Children now have only one way to grow up; they are denied the educational resources of the workplace, the community, and of older, more experienced persons; and they are denied the opportunity to be responsible for themselves or others. Moreover many students develop the psychology of outsiders. Since they are excluded from adult values and adult roles, they create their own values and their own roles. In short, schools which segregate youth from adults and place them into intimate contact with their own peers create the conditions for the development of a youth culture. They make it difficult for adults to transmit adult values successfully to the next generation.

The panel comments on the implications of age segregation for the development of political values:

The political repercussions to society of keeping a large and able fraction of its members as outsiders, with no history or experience of responsibility, until well after they are politically active, are certainly great. It creates a special political bias, in which many of the most able members of future elites become politically active while still in an outsider's status, still able to view the world only from the position of an outsider. It creates a warmhearted, sympathetic, and open political stance, one which focuses on certain principles like equal opportunity and civil rights but ignores others, such as honesty, reward for merit, and the rule of law.[18]

This passage leads us to expect that public schools will generate a positive set of attitudes toward First Amendment rights in schools. The schools will not, however, develop those attitudes toward rights because the school functions as an effective model of proper attitudes toward rights. Nor will they develop attitudes toward such rights which are altogether what one might desire.

Consider first the difference between a participant's and an outsider's view of rights. For people who feel themselves to be *in*—to be full participants in society—freedom of opinion is likely to be perceived as something which gains its import because of its role in collective decision-making. Free expression will be something that allows *us* to conduct *our* affairs sensibly. To the outsider, however, freedom of opinion gains its importance from the fact that it protects the individual from encroachment by the in-group. Liberty is worth having because it is what protects *us* and *our* views from encroachment by *them*.

If the panel's views on how schooling effects political attitudes are correct, students should develop favorable attitudes toward free expression. But they would not do so because the school has been a model of liberty, but because feeling themselves to be outsiders, they will feel the need of protection from encroachment by the adults in the school. One would expect that students would have an outsider's rather than a participant's view of their rights.

I am not objecting to the legitimacy of either set of attitudes toward free expression. Liberty should permit participation in social decision-making and should protect those with divergent views against the excesses of the majority. But an outsider's view of rights is a tragedy in a school, for it signifies the breakdown of workable relations between teacher and learner. Schools exist to teach students. When students feel the need to be protected from adult influence, the conditions for successfully transmitting adult ideas and values to children have been destroyed.

Do students tend to have an outsider's view of rights? Much anecdotal evidence suggests this. I spent several years at a midwestern university where I was involved with individuals working with local "free" schools and where I supervised an experimental course designed to give students an opportunity to achieve a high degree of participation in running a small piece of their own education. These opportunities were used primarily by students who saw them as an opportunity to have an education without adults. One incident illustrates nicely.

The event was a short discourse by a high-school girl attending a local free school. We were in a meeting designed to inform the public of what was happening. She expressed the view that free schools were good because they allowed her to escape the oppressive public schools. They were oppressive (she held in response to a question) because they made her come at 8 A.M., would not allow her to leave until 2, and they made her learn things that were irrelevant. At the free school she usually appeared at 10 or 11. She sat in the lunch room until noon while some students played guitars or read poetry. In the afternoon they became involved in their own interests. Now, she avowed, she was learning a lot of relevant stuff. (No one asked what.)

The example is no doubt extreme, but it is clear that the freedom that students have often demanded is freedom from the education that adults have wanted to provide. Students should feel oppressed by adults who treat them capriciously or harshly. Many students in recent years have felt oppressed by adults who wanted nothing more than to teach them something which the adults valued but which students did not. Such a sense of oppression suggests a strong out-group psychology.

Some harder evidence for this thesis exists in a survey a colleague and I took of the attitudes of some seven hundred upstate New York high-school students toward their own rights.[19] Our intent was to ascertain how supportive students were of the rights extended to them in *Tinker* v. *Des Moines* and also to perceive why students hold certain views.

Several of the items suggest that students support their own rights.

			Percentile
1.	The rights of freedom of speech and freedom of press should protect the right to criticize persons in positions of responsibility such as senators or mayors.	Agree	94
		Disagree	2
		Undecided	4
2.	The free speech of a student should give him the right to be critical of school authorities.	Agree	66
		Disagree	17
		Undecided	17
3.	A school should be able to limit a student's expression of opinion if what he says is in favor of communism or some other radical doctrine.	Agree	17
		Disagree	60
		Undecided	23

These results are a civil libertarian's delight. They exhibit a strong preference for free speech. But consider the following:

4. The faculty advisor for a student paper permitted students to print remarks critical of others only when these remarks were backed up with facts. Do you agree with this policy?

Agree 59
Disagree 27
Undecided 14

5. A student's expression of opinion may be limited when what is said might hurt someone's feelings.

Agree 66
Disagree 22
Undecided 17

The discontinuity between the tolerant responses (1–3) and the intolerant responses (4–5) requires comment. The fourth response may be connected to the phrase *backed up with facts.* But I believe the significant feature of both 4 and 5 is that students envisage them as referring to incidents among students whereas the first three are perceived as referring to incidents between students and adults. (Other items, interviews, and a factor analysis tend to confirm the point.)[20]

The general pattern of responses suggests that students respond specifically to issues. The principle of free expression does not determine the response but the issue and the circumstances of the item. The issue of communism or pornography is not disturbing to many students. They generated consistently tolerant responses on our "commie-porn" items. These issues are perceived as adult "hang-ups." Moreover students expect adults to permit themselves to be criticized by students. Students are least likely to be tolerant of free expression when that tolerance leads to stress within or challenges some value of the peer group.

These results make most sense when they are seen as indicating an outsider's view of free expression. Students tend to see freedom of opinion as something that allows them to criticize adults and liberates them from adult issues and ideas. They are less inclined to see freedom of expression as governing relations between peers. In short our results support the contention that youth tend to have an outsider's view of rights.

These results tend to undercut the Supreme Court's modeling argument. The age-segregated character of public schools promotes the independent enculturation of youth and resistance to adult values, even liberal political values. Indeed it is possible that the recognition of student rights increases the effects of age-segregation by justifying to students their resistance to adult values. The results also suggest that whatever tendency the schools have to promote positive attitudes toward civil liberties occur for reasons other than the school's capacity to function as a model of liberality. Indeed they may owe their efficacy in producing supportive attitudes toward civil liberties to alienating students from adults and creating in students a sense of being a minority group.

This pessimistic assessment, however, does not make a conclusive case against student rights. We must consider that children are persons and that their wants and beliefs should be respected and not gratuitously overruled. These factors constitute a strong case for extending rights to students, although these rights may be distinguished from those of adults in ways consistent with the principles of paternalism. At the same time we have found little reason to believe that extending First Amendment rights to students will generate the educational benefits hoped for by the Tinker court. The best conclusion still seems that of Justice Stewart. Students are entitled to First Amendment rights, but because they are immature and because schools are a unique sort of environment with purposes requiring adults to transmit ideas and values to students, these rights may be distinguished from those of adults.

C. TRANSMITTING VALUES

The previous arguments leave us in a quandary. We still have reasons to extend students the basic liberties of freedom of opinion and expression. These liberties are perhaps extended in a paternalistic fashion so as to reconcile them with educational goals, but nevertheless if we are to show students proper respect, we must treat their views and their values reasonably. On the other hand we have little reason to believe that the hopes envisaged by the Supreme Court will result from extending First Amendment rights to students. Indeed we can reasonably believe that extending these rights to students will tend to legitimate their sense that they are victims of adult imperialism against their own private values. When linked with age-segregation, student rights may do more to sanction youth culture than to educate students in the arts of democratic participation.

This sad state of affairs can be linked to the difficulties of transmitting values in public institutions. That link is not obvious. The villain in the latter part of my discussion is age-segregation. But what has age-segregation got to do with the public character of American education?

The key to the connection between the public character of American education and age-segregation is that the concept of age-segregation is not value-neutral. A certain conception of what is important, central, or serious about adult life is assumed. The assumption is that work is serious and what is learned in school isn't. I shall put the argument in five claims, amplifying each briefly.

1. Values are most effectively transmitted in communities in which students see themselves as junior members of a community united by shared values taken seriously by the adult members of the community.

2. The conception of age-segregation suggests that our culture treats work as serious, but not the intrinsic values implicit in many educational activities.

3. The public character of American education prevents adults in schools from appearing to be serious about those educational values which turn out to be private.

4. Students are more inclined to have their values formed by their associations with their peers than by their associations with their teachers.

5. Schools thus become poor places for transmitting values from adults to students, even when these values, like citizenship, are legitimately public.

Several of these themes will be given more detailed treatment in the next chapter. Here I want to simply sketch their meaning. The claim that values are best transmitted by communities in which students perceive themselves as junior members of a community united by shared values states a group version of the views expressed in chapter 3 concerning desirable social relations for effective instruction. There I described the teacher/student relationship as a master/apprentice relationship. Such a relationship should be voluntary, should generate a degree of intimacy between student and teacher, and should be based on trust and mutual respect. The teacher functions as a model to the student—not just of competent performance but of the values of the intellectual activity. My experience is that the teachers who have had the most enduring effects on students have not necessarily known their subjects best but have loved their subjects most. They were the ones who taught their students that what was being learned was worth learning.

The student's commitment to learning a subject—especially when that subject is valuable for its own sake rather than instrumentally valuable—cannot be fully rational. The value of many forms of intellectual activity is internal to the activity. One does not fully understand what is intrinsically valuable about science or mathematics or art until one has achieved some proficiency in these enterprises.

The student's commitment to learning some subjects therefore must be based on confidence in those who have recommended the enterprise as well as on a sense of the value of the activity. Children beginning to honk on a horn or struggling to learn basic arithmetic cannot experience the satisfaction of a good performance or the beauty of a complex yet simple equation. They must accept the testimony of someone they trust.

To gain a student's trust, the teacher must exhibit respect for the student. Modern schools unhappily have often sacrificed the intimacy required to bureaucracy and efficiency. The student must also see the teacher as serious about the values of the subject. Teachers who love their subjects are a testimonial to students that there is something in the subject to love.

This last aspect of trust concerns me. While individual teachers may often be serious about their subjects and may convey this to their students, it is very difficult for the school—the group of adults which collectively represent learning to students—to be collectively serious about the private values implicit in many subjects. Students sense this lack of seriousness on the part of adults. It thus becomes difficult for students to become committed to the values adults attach to learning, and it is easy for them to gain their values from their peers.

The public character of education prevents schools from exhibiting intense devotion to the private values implicit in subject matter. A public school will regard its central tasks as the production of students who are competent politically and economically. These goals can be pursued even to the point of coercion. But when the values of a subject matter pertain more to private taste than to political and economic competence, they become extracurricular. The school may present them smorgasbordlike for tasting and sampling, but it is unlikely to insist that either the students or the staff exhibit any commitment to any one set of those values. One may value music, literature, or science as one wishes, but the liberal school cannot exhibit strong attachment to them.

The student therefore does not see these values as included among the shared values which define the community of the school. The school, then, will not appear to be serious about such values. Students cannot be expected to be any more serious about such values than are their teachers and administrators. When the attitude exhibited by schools to the values of its subject matter is a take-it-or-leave-it attitude, students will be indifferent to negative.

A further reason for the lack of seriousness about the private values of subject matter is that schools are fundamentally serious about something else—preparing students for entering the world of work. Indeed the fundamental commitment of the schools is to the work ethic—the notion that meaning in life is achieved through work.

This commitment is implicit in age-segregation. That putting children in schools constitutes segregating them from the adult world assumes that what goes on in schools is not serious adult activity, but that work is serious adult activity. In a society that believes that adults gained meaning in life by participating in art or science—that the good life was the life of the mind—it would be impossible to regard placing children in institutions which provided access to these activities as segregating them from the adult world. Likewise a society which views work largely as of instrumental value—as a way to procure the means to pursue other things of intrinsic worth—could not view the exclusion of children from work as a fundamental loss for them.

Schools have a great deal of difficulty being serious about private values. The fact that schools are public prevents such private values from being shared by the community and from being treated by adults as matters of serious concern. Moreover the prevailing system of public values applied to the schools contains the implicit message that work is real, learning isn't. In these circumstances public schools cannot become communities in which private values are effectively transmitted. Students accordingly begin to look to themselves as the sources of their values. They tend to generate an independent culture and perceive themselves as outsiders to the adult world. This tendency is aggravated by the prevalence of the work ethic in which work is the fundamental value.

This independent enculturation limits the school's capacity to fulfill its role in teaching citizenship. Students' political views are formed more by their perceived status as outsiders than by their modeling of adults. Thus the school's failure to be a community of shared values can undermine its capacity to transmit even those liberal democratic values which are legitimately shared in public schools. Indeed, given a degree of alienation of youth from adult values, the attempt to introduce liberal ideas concerning rights into schools may serve more to legitimate a youth culture than to create a participatory democratic community.

The understandings of the greater part of men are necessarily formed by their ordinary employments.

—ADAM SMITH

Schooling and the Values of Work

Liberals have emphasized the vocational and instrumental components of schooling. The psychology of classical empiricism makes knowledge a servant of the passions and makes it difficult to express the notion that knowledge has intrinsic value. Knowledge like work is basically a means to get what you want. Liberals also wish to limit the role of public schools to distinctly public functions. The vocational aspects of knowledge are part of this public function. Public schools are supposed to promote the economic self-reliance of students. But whatever intrinsic values knowledge may have are a matter of individual preference. Thus the instrumental and economic aspects of knowledge lie closer to the central function of schooling than do the noninstrumental aspects of knowledge. Finally liberal attitudes have become linked with what is often referred to as the Protestant ethic or the work ethic. Here too the values attached to knowledge and to work are largely instrumental.

These factors give the public school a distinctively instrumental and vocational role in liberal ideology. Yet liberal ideology is ambivalent about what is meant by vocational education. At the heart of liberal attitudes is the idea that intelligence is a substantial economic asset. Producing people who are economically competent therefore need not entail training them for a specific occupation. Education is more likely to be seen as a matter of creating intelligent adaptive people who can learn and succeed at a variety of economic endeavors. Thus the fact that liberals have attached a vocational role to schooling is not the same as saying that liberals have supported a curriculum which emphasizes occupational training. In this view vocational education is not identified with training for a specific job. Moreover the entire curriculum has a vocational role—making people competent enough to fend for themselves in the economic domain.

Liberals are probably hostile to narrow occupational training. Liberals have assigned a variety of responsibilities to schools. These include citizenship training and the development of a set of rational preferences. Essential to these notions is the creation of rational independent people. The public schools also should promote equal opportunity. These values may be linked if the liberal school focuses on the democratic distribution of intelligence.

But some people have argued for vocational education as suited to those students presumed incapable of intelligent thought. They have thus looked at vocational training as a matter of teaching individuals to execute particular job skills by rote. Moreover, since vocational education so conceived is intended for the mentally inferior, it is to be assigned by means of intelligence testing. A low intelligence quotient is viewed as the primary requirement for admission to a vocational curriculum and the working class.

Such a view denies the entire package of liberal values concerning schooling. Schooling in this view has little to do with the democratic distribution of intelligence. Other views of vocational education are, however, possible even when vocational education is understood as job preparation. One need not have a view of work which sees work as unintelligent activity and makes low I.Q. the primary prerequisite for a vocational education. It is possible to see work as purposeful, creative, and intelligent and to devise a concept of vocational education to fit that concept.

Many persons are inclined to see current vocational education as reflecting illiberal views. This, they claim, results from the fact that the organization of the curriculum of the schools reflects the nature of the work which is generated by current economic and productive processes. Attitudes toward production have been much influenced by liberal views.

Here is liberalism at odds with itself about work and about the vocational role of schooling. On one hand liberalism emphasizes the value of intelligence and applies this emphasis to its conception of vocational education. Here there is little conflict between the economic role of schooling and its other functions. *On the other hand the organization of work generated by the economic views associated with liberalism produces a concept of vocational education clashing with other liberal values.* I believe those values concerned with the democratic distribution of intelligence are central to a liberal society. These values are often undercut by the ways in which we produce and distribute goods and services. Liberal attitudes towards work and towards the vocational role of schooling are therefore complex and inconsistent.

A. THE VALUES OF WORK

It will help in considering work and schooling to have a point of comparison. I begin by sketching a reasonable view about the values of work. The problem concerns the extent to which work can be intrinsically worthwhile. Clearly the primary value of work is instrumental. Work has a point beyond itself. People do not work primarily because they enjoy work, but because they need to work to provide for themselves the necessities of life and the goods on which the enjoyment of life depends.

We are not compelled, however, to suppose that activities which have an instrumental point cannot also be experienced as worthwhile in their own right. This being the case, it seems good sense to attempt to organize instrumental activities so that in addition to performing their instrumental function, they are inherently worthwhile. Of course when we think this way about work some potentially difficult choices are posed. When we look at an activity as simply an instrumental activity, we evaluate it only in terms of its efficiency. How successful is it in achieving its end? But when we also look at the act as an intrinsic good, we introduce other criteria for its evaluation which potentially can conflict with those of efficiency. Let us put this point by saying that tension between the quality and efficiency of work can exist.

Consider some features which enhance any activity.

1. *An activity should satisfy the requirements of the Aristotelian principle.* The Aristotelian principle claims that individuals enjoy the exercise of their realized capacities, and this enjoyment increases the more the capacity is realized, or the greater its complexity. Intrinsically valuable acts thus promote creativity, judgments, and skill. They are educative and growth-promoting.

2. *The quality of an activity is enhanced when it is purposeful—that is, when it has a rational and visible connection to some legitimate and worthwhile end.* Human beings should feel that they are contributing to some worthy end. It is perhaps easier to enjoy wrapping boxes of pencils than boxes of cigarettes. Moreover people need to understand what they are doing. The enjoyment of an act is enhanced when its connection with its end and its larger social context is understood.

3. *The quality of an activity is enhanced when it generates convivial human relations.* People are social beings. They enjoy activities which generate good conversation, cooperative effort, mutual support, and enduring friendships. Enjoyable activities bring people into such relationships.

4. *The quality of an activity is enhanced when it promotes personal independence.* People should exercise choice in their activities and have

some control over the direction of their lives. Activities which provide for choice and self-management are enjoyable.

5. *The quality of an activity is enhanced when it contributes to an individual's sense of self-worth.* This feature of an enjoyable activity is perhaps a composite of the preceding ones. Self-worth is linked to one's sense of competence, usefulness, and the esteem of others. Nevertheless it is perhaps the bottom line in the enjoyment of what we do.

When these criteria are applied to work, they may easily suggest a contrast between assembly-line jobs and, say, a craft. Assembly-line jobs can be viewed negatively on all of these criteria. They generate routine tasks which require little thought or talent and which can be performed without any sense of their connection with their end however worthwhile that end may be. Moreover they provide little need or room for convivial human relations.

Assembly-line jobs also fail to provide autonomy. The job requires little skill. Thus the worker is easily replaced. Nor do workers own their own tools. Thus they have little choice but to submit to the authority and direction of those who run the factory. They become wage slaves—replaceable cogs in the capitalist machine.

Craftsmen, however, own their own tools and create the things they make from beginning to end. They normally possess a high degree of autonomy in their work, and they can put all of the creativity and talent of which they are possessed into their tasks. A craft is therefore more likely to fulfill the Aristotelian principle. And a craft is more likely to be purposeful than an assembly-line job. Craftsmen are required to understand the connection between the various tasks in producing an object and the finished product; and if they are involved in marketing the product, craftsmen will have ample opportunity to understand the larger social and economic context of their work. Since craftsmen can perceive themselves as competent and self-reliant, they are also likely to possess considerable self-respect.

That a craft is more likely than an assembly-line job to generate convivial relations is less clear. That factor may depend on whether the craftsman works alone or with other craftsmen—or on the particular ways that work brings the individual into contact with others. But a craft does at least seem to generate a sense of membership in a group of craftsmen united by some shared values, and it seems less likely to generate antagonistic relations with other workers or with management.

These comments illustrate how the concepts apply to jobs, but I am not recommending a return to an economy dominated by small individually operated manufactures. Large-scale manufacturing industries are with us to stay. But one can ask how large-scale manufacturing can be organized to make work more craftlike. It is not self-evident that an efficient and productive economy must have as its price the generation of large numbers of routine, tedious, and alienating jobs. Cannot work even in large industrial facilities be ordered to promote more of those factors which make them intrinsically valuable rather than merely efficient?

The curious thing about this last question is that in the United States it has hardly been asked outside of academic circles. This fact itself needs consideration. When obvious questions are not raised, it is likely that they are not as obvious as is supposed. Such cases suggest the working of the hidden hand of some ideology. Is there some set of ideas in the public mind which prevents people from attending to an issue which should be addressed? To be more specific, is there something about a liberal point of view which inhibits questions about the quality of work? What is there in liberalism which underlies the concepts of intrinsic and instrumental value?

B. LIBERALISM AND THE WORK ETHIC

Several factors have prevented attention being paid to the intrinsic quality of instrumental tasks. One is a problem peculiar to schools or at least public institutions. Instrumental features of activities attach to public goods such as economic competence, while the intrinsic quality of activities is private. This theme need not be expounded here. Two other ideas need exploring, however: I want to look at the psychology of empiricism and at liberalism's association with the Protestant ethic.

Recall that classical empiricists tended to view the mind as furnished with sensations linked together by association. Most of these sensations are products of the external senses, but there are also inner sensations, including pleasure and pain. These sensations are the sole motives for action. According to the empiricist tradition people act to pursue pleasure and to avoid pain. The human being is a pleasure-maximizer.

These sensations of pleasure and pain are distinct events which are always in principle separable from the other sensations that are associated with them or with the actions or events which produce them. If, let's say, we get pleasure from the eating of an ice-cream cone, the pleasure is one thing, the taste of the ice cream a second, and the act of eating it a third. And there is nothing logical or inevitable about the association between these events. We eat the ice cream because we associate the act with the taste and the taste with pleasure, but there is no logical reason why these associations must obtain.

This picture informs us of the purpose of action and of knowledge. Actions are intended to maximize pleasure. Knowledge exists to inform us concerning which actions result in pleasure. Knowledge in a classical empiricist view will involve associations linking the mental residue of various sensations. Some of these sensations will be those of pleasure and pain. Others will be those characteristically produced by certain actions. When we have acquired a chain of associations linking an action of some sort with sensations of pleasure and pain, we know how to act so as to produce pleasure and avoid pain. For the empiricist knowledge involves the power to regulate actions so as to produce pleasure and avoid pain. That is its sole point.

We should stress that *pleasure and pain are distinct sensations which are contingently connected with other sensations and with actions, but which have independent existence and character.* This claim has two corollaries important to our account. They are (1) *that sensations of pleasure are the only things that are intrinsically valuable* and (2) *that actions and knowledge can only be of instrumental value.*

This is a startling result which is counterintuitive. One armed with a traditional empiricist psychology will not ask how to distinguish between instrumentally and intrinsically valuable acts. Nor is there an issue concerning whether knowledge or learning can be or should be intrinsically valuable. The instrumental character of knowledge and action is a commitment built into the empiricist viewpoint. Given the typical set of empiricist commitments, only sensations of pleasure are intrinsically good. All other values are instrumental. It may be that some events are more intimately connected with pleasure than others, as the taste of the ice cream is more intimately connected with its pleasure than the work which earned the money to purchase the ice cream. But the taste of the ice cream is still merely an instrument for producing the pleasure. The taste is one thing and the pleasure another, and the taste is valued only for its connection with the resulting pleasure.

Here is another case in which the concepts of traditional empiricism manipulate thought so that some issues are difficult to raise. I began this discussion with a question. Why is it that liberal theorists have tended to be attuned to the efficiency of work, but have been inclined to ignore issues concerning its quality? Part of the answer is that empiricist psychology has made it hard to formulate this question. Empiricism generates a set of concepts concerning the value of an act which mean that the act must be evaluated solely by its efficiency in producing an extrinsic end—pleasure. It is easy to treat profit or income as a surrogate for pleasure. But for someone who sees the world through empiricist glasses, it is conceptually difficult to attend to issues concerning the quality of work or of any activity. The concepts for making sense of the question are excluded by empiricist theory.

The problem has its analogue in behaviorism. The concept of an intrinsically valuable act cannot be coherently formulated within a behaviorist viewpoint. Behaviorism recapitulates the logic of its empiricist sire, requiring that the reinforcement be one thing and the act rein-

forced be another. Since positive reinforcement is the good and since reinforcement is always a distinct event from the act reinforced, there is no
such thing as an intrinsically worthwhile action. Actions can only be
means to positive reinforcement. Behaviorists are not conceptually
equipped to evaluate the intrinsic quality of actions. Actions will only be
evaluatable or not as positive or negative reinforcements are contingent
on them.

Thus a behaviorist looking at a classroom will assume that children
will learn only when induced to learn by some external reward. That
children may wish to learn to satisfy natural curiosity or that they will find
learning inherently rewarding is excluded on methodological grounds.
Such claims do not distinguish the behavior from its reinforcement. Likewise a behaviorist viewing the workplace will assume that the worker
is motivated purely by some contingency external to the activity. Money is
the obvious leading candidate. "Money," as Skinner informs us, "reinforces work behavior." Here we should not uncritically assume that some
of the features that add to the intrinsic worth of an activity cannot be expressed as reinforcements and thus be viewed as external contingencies of
the activity. But the point is that *an empiricist viewpoint makes it difficult
to focus on the quality of an activity. To do so the intrinsic qualities of an
action must be separated from it and viewed as extrinsic rewards which
are simply contingent on the act. An empiricist view, however, makes it
easy to focus on the externalities of an activity.* It is not, then, surprising
that people with an empiricist viewpoint will find it hard to perceive the
intrinsic values of learning or of work.

Empiricism also will have difficulty with notions such as the Aristotelian principle. Bentham once declared that "pushpin is as good as
poetry." His point was that the only relevant grounds for comparing one
pleasure with another (excluding their consequences) is to compare their
intensity. Thus, if people happen to find the pleasure resulting from the
simple game of pushpin equal to or superior to the pleasure resulting from
poetry, there are no relevant grounds for claiming that they are wrong.

Compare Bentham's remark to Rawls's discussion of some examples
of the Aristotelian principle. "Chess is a more complicated and subtle
game than checkers, and algebra is more intricate then elementary
arithmetic. Thus the principle says that someone who can do both
generally prefers playing chess to playing checkers, and that he would
rather study algebra than arithmetic."[1]

The difference lies in the psychology. Empiricism tends to undermine
notions such as the Aristotelian principle. Traditional empiricism regards
experience as occurring unmediated by concepts. Notions such as the
Aristotelian principle, however, seem more at home in a psychology
which regards experience as ordered by concepts.

Consider that the complexity of chess or algebra is not sufficient to make them more enjoyable than checkers or arithmetic. One must be able to *do* both. Rawls might better have said that one must be able to experience the complexity or subtlety of chess or algebra to enjoy it. The experience of any object, event, or activity is enjoyable when it is complex or subtle *and* when the individual has the concepts and the skill to experience that complexity and subtlety. The complexity and subtlety of the world requires concepts to perceive. One who does not possess them will not be able to see what is there and will not be able to enjoy the experience. If Beethoven is really better than the Beatles, it is because Beethoven is more complex and subtle than the Beatles. If most people do not enjoy Beethoven more than the Beatles it is because they have not learned to see Beethoven properly.

Experience is mediated by concepts. The concepts people have determine what they will see in an experience and thus the nature of the enjoyment they will derive from it. A view of experience which has little regard for the role of concepts in organizing experience will have difficulty attending to the point. Empiricism is thus at the root of "pushpin is as good as poetry." The hedonism of empiricism comes to emphasize pleasure, because it lacks a concept of mediation. And thus it has difficulty making sense out of another aspect of the intrinsic value of activity.

The final influence on liberal attitudes towards the values of work is the Protestant (or work) ethic. Here we find a viewpoint which attaches the intensity of religious commitment to a set of attitudes toward work and which, like empiricist psychology, tends to value efficiency over the quality of the activity.

Protestantism is not liberalism. Nevertheless the affinity between Protestant theology and liberal attitudes is clear. One of the central doctrines of the Reformation is the priesthood of the individual believer. Individual Christians, according to this view, do not need the clergy to mediate between them and God. God dispenses His grace and forgiveness directly to the individual. Likewise individuals are responsible for their conduct directly to God. People are not in need of an ecclesiastic hierarchy to commune with God. In such beliefs we see in theological form doctrines which became of central import to liberal political thought. Protestantism tends to make people equal before God; it undermines the privileged position and authority of the clergy; and it makes each person morally autonomous. It places on persons the burden of interpreting the will of God for themselves. Just as empiricism makes each person his own scientist, Protestantism makes each person his own theologian.

It is widely claimed that Protestant attitudes toward work have been crucial to the development of capitalist economic institutions (or that the development of capitalist institutions has generated Protestant attitudes toward work). The connection has been worked out in books such as Max Weber's *The Protestant Ethic and the Spirit of Capitalism*[2] and R. H. Tawney's *Religion and the Rise of Capitalism*.[3] My discussion owes a considerable debt to these works.

The crucial doctrine of the Protestant ethic is the notion of a calling. Traditional Christian attitudes toward economic activity treated work as a necessary evil. One's duties in life were otherworldly. The individual was to worship God and to prepare the soul for the next life. Work was to provide the means to pursue these ends. But to seek to acquire more than the necessities of life was evil. The economic watchword was "take no thought for the morrow." The church sought to keep economic activity in bounds with such moral notions as fair price and restraints on usury (interest). The notions that markets should set prices or that one might profit from what should be an act of charity were morally noxious. There was no religious duty to increase productivity, and capitalist notions of exchange were inhibited by religious ethics.

The major Protestant reformers, Luther and Calvin, accepted much of this point of view. But they added to it the notion that one's worldly occupation had the status of a calling. One was chosen by God not just to be a priest or a monk, but to be a farmer or a carpenter.

To make a person's job into a calling is to make the performance of the job into a religious duty. Farming thus ceases to be just a means of providing necessary food and is transformed into a religious observation. The performance of one's job is an act of worship. In doing one's job well, a person is giving glory to God. Such ideas transformed the otherworldly attitude of devout Christians. Involvement in the affairs of the world was changed from a necessary evil to be dispensed with in a perfunctory manner, into a religious observance to be pursued with all the dedication that the pious can muster.

Such views ultimately helped to undermine the suspicion of Protestants toward capitalist economic institutions and helped to liberate economic activity from the bonds of Christian ideals of fairness and charity. Now the attitude toward wealth is reshaped. The Christian is not supposed to covet wealth. The gain of riches is not the point of work. The Christian's duties toward riches are to be a mixture of thrift and charity, not avarice and luxury. But it cannot be denied that God rewards those who discharge their duties faithfully. Therefore riches, when they come to the person who faithfully discharges duties to God through work, should not be rejected.

The notion that God rewards the faithful transforms attitudes toward capitalist institutions. Wealth and poverty represent God's judgment on virtue and vice. The rich are rich not because they sought wealth and exploited the poor, but because by their dedication to their work they have discharged their duty to love God and serve humanity. People are rich because they are virtuous. Likewise people are poor because they are slothful. Poverty is the just reward of their vice. Such views change the operations of the market from a tool of exploitation into the instrument of divine judgment. The invisible hand of the market is revealed as the hand of God.

The Protestant ethic thus makes work part of one's duty to God. In the secularized variant of this concept, productive work is held to be the primary means through which people discharge their duty to their fellows. Thus any form of productive labor has dignity since it contributes to the wellbeing of others. The nature of the work, the quality of the task, matters little so long as the task is faithfully discharged and the end is some useful or needed good or service. The lowliest janitor need not feel inferior to the highest executive if he performs to the best of his ability. Menial laborers are entitled as anyone else to feel the satisfaction and the dignity which result from a job well done, from a faithful discharge of their duties, and from performing a valued service.

This view of the dignity of work involves a recognition of the fact that the basic value of human beings should not be linked to the value of their personal services on the market or to the status of their occupation. It focuses attention instead on a set of moral qualities such as willingness to serve and devotion to duty. Indeed the view seems to recognize that in some important way human beings are of equal worth and that it is therefore objectionable to have self-esteem linked to occupational status. Hard work may not always lead to a high level of affluence, but it can lead to a high sense of one's own worth. There are positive aspects of the work ethic.

This view is deficient in not seeing any link between the dignity of a task and its quality. The work ethic supports the values of efficiency over those of the quality of work. It makes the value of work depend on things external to the nature of the task—primarily faithfulness in doing one's work and the social utility of the job. These values, in turn, function to create a moral obligation on the part of the worker to be as productive and thus as efficient as possible. There is no sense that the value of work should be sought in the quality of human relations it generates or in its capacity to develop and permit the expression of human talents and capacities. *The Protestant ethic consequently is consistent with the values concerning work implicit in empiricist psychology. It focuses attention on efficiency and external ends and detracts from interest in the quality of work and its capacity to promote individual growth.*

C. LIBERALISM AND THE VOCATIONAL ROLE OF SCHOOLING

We have now detailed the concepts necessary to clarify liberalism's ambivalence about work and about the vocational role of schooling. On the one hand liberals have good reason to see economic competence as a central purpose of public schooling. This in itself is not problematic, for the vocational role of schooling can be conceived in a way which is quite consistent with the more basic role of the school to promote rationality.

On the other hand, if the vocational role of schooling is to be consistent with the broader function of producing rational citizens, this will require a view of work in which work itself is conceived as potentially promoting growth. It is unlikely that the vocational role of schooling will be understood in a way which encourages the growth of the capacity for intelligent and creative thought, unless the values of intelligence and creativity are seen as important aspects of work and as requirements for genuine economic competence.

Here, then, is the problem. Liberalism is linked with views which dissociate work from the values of rationality and creativity. Empiricism and the Protestant ethic generate a view of work which emphasizes efficiency and external rewards and which tend not to see work as a means to promote individual growth. Moreover these ideologically rooted values for work seem to provide support for what is in fact the current state of affairs, because our society surely does generate many types of work which may be long on efficiency, but which are short in their capacity to promote creativity and intellectual growth.

Given this ideological ambivalence and the character of work in America, it would be surprising if schools had a clear view of the vocational role of schooling. That they do not is evidenced by the inclusion of the vocational curriculum within the comprehensive high school, by the continuing debate about the relations of vocational and liberal or general education, and by the continuing charges that the vocational role of schooling is performed in a way which reflects more the class structure and nature of work under capitalism than it does the emphasis on individual growth and rationality which are central to a humane liberalism.

Recent neo-Marxist writers have made much of the idea that there is a tendency for the social relations of the school to mirror the social relations of work. In the literature on the topic[4] this notion is generally referred to as *the correspondence principle.* Consider Bowles and Gintis: "The educational system helps integrate youth into the economic system, we believe, through a *structural correspondence between its social relations and those of production.* The structure of social relations in education not only inures the student to the discipline of the work place, but develops the types of personal demeanor, modes of self presentation, self-image, and social-class identifications which are the crucial ingredients of job adequacy."[5]

This is more nearly a thesis about what might be termed the hidden curriculum than the official curriculum. It assumes that such features of the school as its structure of authority or its tracking system constitute more than simple devices to expedite the teaching function of the school. They also teach a variety of lessons to the student. They function as a model of the life in the world of work. The correspondence principle also has implications for the official curriculum. What is officially taught must be consistent with the demands of the workplace.

The content of the hidden curriculum embedded in the social relations of the school includes a large affective component. The school will provide those cognitive skills which are needed by the world of work and withhold those which are not, but it must also properly mold the students' attitudes and expectations to their future economic niche. Indeed this is viewed as its primary function.

What are the social relations of work? In contemporary American society most work is done in large bureaucratic organizations. Work in such organizations is hierarchically ordered. Policy- and decision-making are done at the top and executed at the bottom. People at the mid-level are responsible for translating general policies into specific tasks and seeing that these tasks are carried out by their subordinates. Work is motivated by external rewards—primarily wages. Efficiency expressed in terms of the maximization of profit is the primary value attached to work. At the bottom of hierarchies, the demand for efficiency leads to highly fragmented tasks. Work is broken up into basic components, each of which is performed by individuals who do little else. Finally work is competitive. Since incentives and ability are attached to productivity, workers will compete with one another for such gains as salary increases and promotions. The correspondence principle suggests that such features of work are reflected in the structure of schooling. The school is hierarchical in structure. The authority relations among school board, administration, teacher, and students mirror the relations between management and worker in the corporate hierarchy. Work in the school is also motivated largely by external rewards—chiefly grades. Learning tasks in the school are fragmented in much the same way as work is fragmented. Division of labor is reflected in academic areas of specialization, and it is hard to imagine a more nearly perfect analogue of a task divided into its constituent components than a curriculum divided into behavioral objectives. And schools are highly competitive institutions. Students compete for grades much as workers compete for wages. Such common features of school life mean the alleged correspondence between the social relations of school and work is plausible.

But the correspondence principle also requires schools to provide students with differential experience according to their anticipated niche, for the job market requires different characteristics of individuals, depending on their location in the hierarchy. Jobs low in the hierarchy require only modest degrees of cognitive attainment, but are likely to put a premium on such traits as the willingness to obey rules and a tolerance for routine tasks. Mid-level jobs require a higher degree of internalization of the norms of the organization. High-level jobs require a genuine capacity for creative thought, at least in achieving organizational goals. They also permit a fair amount of autonomy and require the ability to use it.

Schools provide differential experience reflecting these sorts of occupational niches, largely by such devices as ability grouping and tracking. At the postsecondary level the requirements of the world of work are also reflected in differences between institutions. These sorting mechanisms allow schools to provide experiences suitable to the students' projected economic niche. Thus students in the lower tracks are taught routine skills and are subjected to a rigid and authoritarian regimen. Students at the top of the heap, however, are given a curriculum placing more emphasis on creativity and critical thinking, and they are granted more discretion in their personal conduct.

I will not evaluate this thesis in detail, but make several claims concerning it and suggest the kind of evidence which can be advanced for each. That there is some form of structural correspondence between the structure of work and the structure of school has a good deal of plausibility. Indeed, it would be surprising if this were not the case. Other things being equal, it is quite reasonable for a society to expect its schools to educate students to function within its economic system. A structural correspondence between schooling and work becomes problematic only when a society's economic system is unjust.

We must also acknowledge the plausibility of much of the critique of the organization of work in America. Certainly work is commonly carried out in large bureaucratic organizations in which power and autonomy decrease with distance from the top of the hierarchy. Certainly also our society generates numerous jobs whose capacity to promote growth is negligible. Blue-collar jobs often involve qualities which Marxist critics rightly regard as miseducative.

We must also admit that there is much about schooling which reflects the organization of work. The very existence of distinct vocational and academic tracks makes sense only if we assume that the world of work is characterized by a division into one set of jobs which require some form of academic training and another set for which the student can be trained without additional preliminaries. It also seems reasonable to suppose that the lower tracks are more involved with transmitting skills and less concerned with transmitting ideas and the capacity to judge them than the academic tracks. Finally the common perception that students are assigned to lower tracks because they have exhibited a lack of ability or a disinclination for academic work rather than because they are positively inclined to do the jobs to which lower tracks lead is almost surely true.

All of these factors indicate that, in the tracking system at least, structural correspondence exists between work and school. Moreover it seems inescapable that we have such tracking in schools because it is believed that academic subject matter is unrelated to some types of jobs and that it is inappropriate for some types of people. Vocational tracking thus appears based on a set of assumptions which, like empiricism and the Protestant ethic, see at least some types of work primarily in terms of efficiency and which divorce work from its capacity to promote creativity and intellectual growth.

It is a mistake, however, to see the structural correspondence of schooling and work as the entire story or to see the vocational components of schooling as resting entirely on such unpleasant assumptions. The tracking system normally applies in the comprehensive high school. The system is so embedded because many Americans have wished to ensure that vocational training is linked to a broader and more general education and because they believe that children with diverse economic backgrounds and economic futures will profit by going to school together.

Many vocational educators see vocational education as more than job preparation. They argue that vocational education involves a significant intellectual component and that it can function as a mechanism for transmitting cognitive skills to students who often do not function well in more traditional and formal institutional situations.

The existence of the comprehensive high school and the aspirations of many vocational educators assume an ideology which sees a more intimate connection between work, vocational education, and intellectual growth than the view which seems to underlie the existence of tracking. Nor can we assume that the comprehensive high school is simply a fraudulent smokescreen designed to obscure the class structure of schooling or that the sentiments of vocational educators are disingenuous. It is more reasonable to hold that the correspondence between schooling and work is not as tight as the Marxist critique would indicate or that the structure of work is not as dehumanizing as the critique would suggest. Possibly both are true. So far as schooling is concerned, I believe both current thought and current practice reflect ideological confusion about the vocational role of schooling. The current state of affairs is a compromise between one ideology which sees the vocational role of schooling as a mere extension of the school's general role of promoting the growth of the individual's capacity for rational self-governance and a second ideology which dissociates work and intellectual growth and consequently dissociates the vocational role of schooling from schooling's intellectual functions.

That the current system reflects such a compromise is easily seen in the historic debate which surrounded the emergence of the comprehensive high school and the current tracking system. Consider these comments by influential figures during the period at which the explicitly vocational curriculum was being developed. The first was written in 1908 by Charles W. Eliot, president of Harvard University:

How shall the decision be made that certain children will go into industrial schools, others into the ordinary high schools, and others again into the mechanic arts high schools? Where is that decision to be made? It must be a choice, or a selection. Here we come upon a new function for the teachers in our elementary schools, and in my judgment they have no function more important. The teachers of the elementary schools ought to sort the pupils and sort them by their evident or probable destinies. I am afraid that strikes you at once as an undemocratic idea, but let us see whether it is undemocratic or not....

If democracy means to try to make all children equal or all men equal, it means to fight nature, and in that fight democracy is sure to be defeated. There is no such thing among men as equality of natural gifts, of capacity for training, or of intellectual power....

Here is the teacher's guide in sorting children. Each child must be put in that work which the teacher believes that child can do best.[6]

The second passage, also written in 1908, by Edward C. Elliot.

Until we possess reliable data upon which to base a rational scheme of reorganization, the public schools cannot hope to become instruments for "industrial determination"; neither will they cease to prevent the present positive mis-selection of individuals for their proper station of efficiency and happiness. For a rightful selection must precede and underlie the maintenance of the educational equilibrium of democracy.[7]

These statements reflect a clear sense of an occupational world divided into two qualitatively different sorts of tasks, some of which demand low cognitive skills. These men insist that schools should rank people on the basis of intelligence and assign less able students to an education suitable to their low intelligence and their future economic role. The desire to make the curriculum correspond to the nature of the available work is historically part of the ideology behind tracking.

This view of the vocational role of schooling was, however, aggressively opposed by another. Consider John Dewey's assessment of a proposal before the Illinois legislature to establish independent vocational schools.

Those who believe in the continual separate existence of what they are pleased to call the "lower classes" or the "laboring classes" would naturally rejoice to have schools in which these "classes" would be segregated. And some employers of labor would doubtless rejoice to have schools supported by public taxation supply them with additional food for their mills. All others should be united against every proposition, in whatever form advanced, to separate training of employers from training for citizenship, training of intelligence and character from training for narrow industrial efficiency.[8]

Dewey here projects a view of the vocational role of schooling as integrated with and consistent with its other functions. It thus seems that *historically and currently schools are a compromise between an ideology which seeks to track students according to their I.Q.'s and provide them with an education suitable to their niche in the class structure and a view which seeks to promote the democratic distribution of intelligence.* The comprehensive high school thus does not reflect a consistent view of the vocational role of schooling. Instead it exhibits a conflicting set of practices which themselves reflect a tension in liberal attitudes toward the values of work and intelligence.

Liberalism does not consistently view the vocational role of schooling. The view which interprets the vocational role of schooling as part of the democratic distribution of intelligence is compromised with another which tends toward the result that the structure and organization of schooling is to some extent dominated by the structure of work in our society. The correspondence of school and work functions to generate differential environments matched to the needs of the labor market and to restrict the schools' emphasis on rationality, creativity, or critical thinking in ways that are consistent with the needs of the labor market but are inconsistent with the broader needs of a democratic society. The lower tracks of the schools' curriculum can have an antirational character, with minimal emphasis on developing a capacity for critical thought. They emphasize, instead, training and the development of character traits consistent with the station of the laborer. This emphasis is based on the notions that the students assigned to such tracks are capable of nothing better and that this is the training required for their future economic role. It represents a dissociation of work and intellectual growth of the sort legitimized by empiricism and the Protestant ethic.

D. SUMMARY AND CONCLUSIONS

The thesis of section II is that public schools in a liberal society can be expected to have difficulty transmitting values. Let us see how the argument of this chapter relates to that thesis.

A focus on rationality permits a consistent view of how three classes of educational goals can be simultaneously pursued by schools. A school should help the individual to achieve a rational set of preferences, should promote political competence, and should promote economic competence. Each of these goals can be held to be promoted by a curriculum which focuses on the acquisition of the means to obtain information (basically literacy) and on what I have called transcultural rational enterprises. Liberal ideology thus prefers basic disciplines and basic skills although it assigns to them a largely instrumental character. This curriculum facilitates each goal because it develops the individual's rational capacity. Peoples' rational capacity in turn is a means whereby they can develop a rational set of preferences, function as enlightened citizens, and promote their own economic well-being.

The difficulty with the second concept of the vocational role of schooling which has emerged is that it divorces vocationalism from the development of rationality. We have generated a concept of the vocational role of the school which emphasizes training to execute specific tasks and which assumes that blue-collar and clerical workers have a limited capacity for critical thought. Workers need to tolerate routine tasks and need to be subservient to authority since it is their role to execute the decisions of others.

Such a conception of the vocational role of public schooling is at odds with the other functions of schooling. When we do not seek aggressively to develop the rational capacities of our youth we should not be surprised if they fail to develop rational and sophisticated systems of preference. It should not come as a shock that many students' preferences are more influenced by advertising and their peer culture than by the arts and sciences; nor should we be mystified that youth are more attuned to beer and disco music than to burgundy and Beethoven. If schools are ambivalent about the value of rational preferences, we must expect students to exhibit preferences which are easily manipulated and which exhibit few signs of developed taste.

Likewise, if we are ambivalent about the value of rationality, we should not be too surprised if the political judgment of students is immature and is easily manipulated by political advertising and by peer influence. And, while the vocational curriculum may seek to induce docility and subservience to authority, we should not be startled that when students fail to be properly subservient, they rebel in irrational ways.

In short we have evolved a concept of the vocational role of the school which runs counter to other roles of the school. Insofar as it fails to promote the rationality of students and even finds critical thinking counterproductive, the attempts of the school to create economic competence will undermine its attempts to produce students who are competent citizens with rational preferences.

The chief villain in this scenario is work as it has developed under our highly centralized form of industrial capitalism. Work, especially as it exists at the bottom levels of corporate hierarchies, represents a triumph of efficiency over quality. Such work is efficient, but it contributes little to the realization of human capacities. When the need for individuals with skills and attitudes suitable to the demands of such work becomes a significant factor in what we do in schools, then education comes to represent a triumph of means over ends. Not only do we generate educational tasks which reflect the instrumental character of work and which thus exhibit the same lack of quality as their counterparts in the world of work, but we undermine the system of ends to which work is supposed to be a means. For work, even if it cannot be experienced as intrinsically worthwhile, ought at least to be a means whereby people gain the resources to achieve their preferences. But if the view I have presented is correct, the nature of work leads to a conception of vocational education which is inconsistent with the education necessary if students are to develop a rational set of preferences. In short, schools can become places where preferences get scaled down so as to be consistent with the demands of the means for realizing them. When work debases people or fails to promote their growth, it will also influence the kinds of preferences they will have. When schools become part of the mechanism for matching people to economic niches, they become a part of this debasement of preferences. They thus come to represent a triumph of means over ends.

While this thesis applies most straightforwardly and most forcefully to students pointed toward blue-collar industrial jobs, it is not limited to these students. Even an academic curriculum can suffer from being excessively vocationalized. When the academic curriculum is dominated by a concern for college admissions and is seen largely as a means of acquiring the educational credentials necessary in order to obtain managerial, professional, high-level clerical, or technical positions, the curriculum can be inched away from any serious concern with those activities which promote rational capacity in cultural or political matters. Such jobs require that individuals have certain cognitive skills. But such jobs do not necessarily require sophisticated ability in more than a narrow range of intellectual skills. The student who is to become a skilled engineer need not have refined taste in music or be an astute judge of political events. Rationality is not one thing; it is many. To the extent that there is little transfer from one kind of rational activity to another, an individual who is capable of being rational in one area need not be assumed to have the same capacity in other areas. And to that extent, an excessively vocationalized education can generate skilled leaders and professionals who are nevertheless narrowly trained and who thus may not succeed well in other areas. Vocationalism can then be incompatible with the goals of developing rational preferences and rational citizens even in those areas of the curriculum which seem concerned to develop the students' capacity for critical thinking.

The solution to these problems in education is not to reject the vocational role of schooling but to reassert the more traditional liberal view of that role. The vocational role of the public school should be discharged by teaching students to have the rational capacity and knowledge to make their own way in the world. Such a view does not require the schools to avoid preparation for particular kinds of occupations, but it requires them to locate such occupations in a larger intellectual and cultural context. Nor does such a view require the school to avoid useful knowledge. It merely requires applied fields to be taught broadly and to be rooted in the principles which govern them.

The key to generating a conception of vocational education which focuses on the expansion of the rational capacities of the individual is to generate a higher appreciation of the qualitative aspects of work. Inevitably the nature of work in our society will be a factor in determining our concept of the vocational role of education. It is thus likely that our concept of vocational education will focus on the development of the rational capacity of individuals when work is organized so as to permit and even require individuals to exhibit a wide range of judgment and skill. A suitable view of work and of the vocational role of schooling therefore requires us to take seriously a set of values for work which are more like the set described at the beginning of this chapter than the set pointed to by empiricist psychology and the Protestant ethic. We need to value the quality of our activities as well as their efficiency.

When I began section II I claimed that public schools in the liberal state cannot properly educate students because they cannot solve the problem of how to transmit values. This thesis has developed into a number of subtheses concerning different kinds of values.

1. Liberal public schools cannot find a way to teach values which express fundamental convictions. Such private values will be excluded from the public school and will have to be pursued in a private context. The extensiveness of public education, however, limits the ability to pursue values through private means.

2. Liberal public schools will have difficulty transmitting those private values which are not linked to fundamental convictions. Private preferences are by definition not part of the public function of public education. Enterprises which are intended primarily to develop rational or sophisticated preferences will become implicitly or explicitly extracurricular. Moreover the fact that adults in schools will not share a common set of preferences will prevent the school from being united in the pursuit of common values. This failure to achieve a sense of community in the school will weaken the influence of adults and strengthen the influence of the peer group. Students thus are denied an important human resource for developing rational preferences. Finally the vocational role of public

schooling has evolved in a way as to weaken the commitment of schools to develop the rational capacity of students.

3. Liberal public schools have difficulty transmitting liberal political values. The reasons are that the lack of community limits the ability of adults in transmitting liberal values to students, and the conception of vocationalism weakens the commitment to the development of a rational citizenry.

All of these claims are speculative and controversial and require debating at length far in excess of the space I have given them. The virtues I claim for my presentation are to have rendered them plausible and to have shown how these problems represent the outworking of the social logic of liberal ideology concerning public education. If I am right, we have good reason to be concerned for the future viability of public education in the liberal state.

III

Equal Rights and Equal Opportunity

That all men are created equal and as a consequence have equal rights is a concept located at the center of a liberal viewpoint. Yet it is a puzzling doctrine. People may be equal, but they are not the same. How are they equal? And people may have equal rights, but few liberals have found equal rights to be inconsistent with the notion that it is permissible for some to be rich and others poor. In what, then, does having equal rights consist?

Liberals have traditionally answered such questions with a view of equality which treats equality as fair competition. Life is a race. The state's role in the race is not to alter the outcome, but to see that the race is fair. The race may have winners and losers, but the track should be the same for everyone. No one should have a better chance to be a winner than anyone else.

The doctrine of equal rights thus has as its end to specify what counts as fairness in the race for private goods. The state is made the referee in life's race—the enforcer of the rules.

Concepts such as "one man one vote" give content to the notion of equal rights. The idea is that everyone should have the same ability to influence the outcome of public decisions. The underlying doctrine is that all people have the same prima facie right to have their wants and needs met.

The doctrine of equal opportunity is likewise part of the larger notion of equal rights. Here the idea is that everyone is entitled to fair treatment in the marketplace. The rewards generated should be attached to skill and hard work, not to irrelevant factors such as race or sex. The race should go to the swift. If that is to be the case, the track must be the same for everybody.

Public schools have been seen as the device through which the track of life is to be made the same for everybody. Children are supposed to get the same chance to learn and thus to acquire skills they can cash in for social rewards, regardless of their social origins. Then the race of life will in fact go to the swift.

In the previous sections I have argued that rationality has a special place in the curriculum of the public schools. Rationality is assumed to be an important component in political and economic competence and in the development of reasonable preferences and personal autonomy. Liberals view rationality as a kind of universal instrumentality. This has led to the conclusion that the central public function of the school is the fair distribution of rationality. The two previous sections have analyzed the idea of rationality and argued its centrality in a liberal view of schooling. Here we have to determine what counts as its fair distribution.

To do this I shall examine in detail the concept of equal opportunity and the capacity of schools to succeed on this ideal. I shall use this discussion to develop a broader doctrine of equal rights. This last task is the culmination of the entire enterprise, for it will allow the formulation of an adequate view of liberal justice and thus provide a formulation of liberalism by which a view of the public role of schooling can be developed. That will permit me to recapitulate many of the themes of this book in the concluding chapter.

CHAPTER 9

I will not live my life for another nor ask another to live his life for me.

—AYN RAND

The Ideology of Liberal Equality

A. EQUALITY AS FAIR COMPETITION

How do liberal societies distribute their goods? A traditional answer might be: *Liberal societies should reward merit as expressed in productivity and as measured by free markets.* People are entitled to what they earn.

Many liberals have believed that people's rewards should reflect their contributions to the well-being of others as expressed by the free choices of others. In a liberal society one is supposed to be able to pursue one's own conception of the good without social or governmental interference so long as the manner in which the good is pursued does not harm others. It follows from this logic that individuals ought to be free to spend their money or trade their work or its products as they wish.

Consider what results from free choice by consumers. Suppose I wish to buy a recording of Mozart's four horn concertos. And suppose that there are only a few in stock. In a liberal society I will be free to pay what ever I wish to obtain the record, and the seller will be free to charge whatever he or she wants. Since I love Mozart I will be willing to pay more than my fellow consumer to obtain the record. If there are a large number of Mozart fans and a small number of Mozart records, the people who sell records will do well for themselves because they will be able to get a good price for their records. Of course, if they do well, others will begin to make Mozart records. Then the supply should increase and the price drop.

Thus in a liberal society the free choices of consumers determine what persons will make. They will offer their work, ability, and products on a market. What they will get in exchange will depend on how free people choose to express their preferences. The results of such a system should be that those whose ability enables them to provide goods for which others are willing to pay will do well.

In a society in which the well-being of individuals depends on their ability to enter into voluntary exchanges with others, wealth may be unevenly distributed. Is this fair? Are the results of free choices of consumers just when the results will be that some will have much more than others?

We can address this by asking under what conditions would such a system be unfair. Consider one possibility. Suppose someone who had a skill or a product to sell was arbitrarily prevented from doing so. Suppose, for example, a society feeling that Mozart should only be played by Germans or Austrians prevented people with English names from making Mozart records. Here presumably is an injustice. People with the talent and desire to do well in the Mozart business are prevented from doing so on the irrelevant grounds that they are not German.

Despite the fanciful example this is a real and current problem. This kind of unfairness occurs everytime someone is denied a job or excluded from producing or selling because of race, religion, sex, or some other feature irrelevant to ability. The injustice consists in unfairly denying someone the opportunity to compete in the market for talent. The norm involved is that economic opportunity should be made available on grounds of ability. John Rawls calls this principle "careers open to talents."[1] It is one major aspect of the concept of fair competition.

Suppose rather than denying people the opportunity to sell their skills on the open market we denied them the opportunity to acquire skills. Feeling strongly that non-Germans ought not to play Mozart horn concertos, we simply exclude non-Germans from horn lessons or provide such poor lessons that Germans will have no problems defeating them in later competition. And we do these things regardless of any aptitude a non-German person might show for playing the horn.

It seems clear that this policy also is unfair. Persons cannot compete in a free market when they are arbitrarily prevented from selling their talents and when they are arbitrarily prevented from developing talents to sell. Thus the idea that liberal societies should provide for fair competition includes not only the notion of positions open to talents but also the notion that people should have a fair chance to acquire a talent. This aspect of fair competition might be labeled fair or equal opportunity.

A society which wishes to provide for equal opportunity will find it has good reason for establishing public schools. Unless society undertakes to provide a free education for its children, opportunity will tend to depend not on ability, hard work, and integrity but on parental wealth. Public schools in liberal societies then have as a major function the elimination of any dependency between opportunity and family background.

This position is crucial. I shall state it as a paradox consisting of the following claims:

1. Liberal societies attempt to have rewards reflect individual contributions as measured by consumer preference expressed in free markets.
2. Fair competition for such rewards involves having positions open to talents and in having a fair chance to acquire talents.
3. Inequalities in rewards which result from fair competition in free markets are just, but inequalities resulting from unfair competition are unjust. The traditional liberal norm concerning justice in distributing social goods can thus be expressed: *Given fair competition, the distributive effects of free markets are just whatever they are.*
4. Free markets may not distribute rewards equally.
5. Opportunities have a cost. (Education must be paid for by somebody.)
6. Children of people who do less well than others in the competition for social rewards will be less able to afford the cost of opportunities than the children of the affluent.
7. Such children will thus not have a fair chance to develop talent in that their opportunity to do so will depend on the irrelevant factor of parental wealth rather than relevant factors such as native ability, initiative, and willingness to work hard.

There is thus a problem to be solved if liberal norms are to be successfully realized in society. *The liberal society must permit rewards to reflect ability in one generation and at the same time prevent the resulting inequalities from causing rewards to fail to reflect ability in the next generation. A liberal society is committed to reconstructing its reward structure each generation. It thus must prevent inequality from being inherited.*

What seems required is some mechanism that makes opportunities available to everyone regardless of the wealth of his parents. Everyone should get roughly the same opportunities and should receive them regardless of ability to pay. It seemed obvious to many early liberal educational reformers that what was required was a free common education—one where everyone was exposed to the same curriculum and could profit from it as ability allowed.

This argument provides a plausible theory of why a liberal state needs public schools. The argument has difficulties and complexities.

One can question the adequacy of the liberal norm of distributive justice. Are the distributive effects of free competition fair whatever they happen to be? If the effects are extreme, is it fair to have people living in poverty because they cannot compete in a free market? Don't people who are handicapped still deserve a decent life? Why should we adopt a view of justice which rewards ability? Are people deserving of more because they came into the world better endowed than their fellows? Why not reward something else—such as need? Most contemporary liberals, while still subscribing to the basic tenets of a free-market society, also believe that human beings deserve a minimal level of support independently of what they earn in the market. On what basis can people be entitled to something they haven't earned?

We should also ask if it is inevitable that free and fair competition leads to inequalities in the distribution of wealth. Consider that Adam Smith, capitalism's patron saint, believed that free competition tended toward equality. "The whole of the advantages and disadvantages of the different employments of labor and stock must, in the same neighborhood, be either perfectly equal or continually tending to equality. If in the same neighborhood, there was any employment evidently either more or less advantageous than the rest, so many people would crowd into it in the one case, and so many would desert it in the other, that its advantages would return to the level of other employments."[2] Do significant inequalities therefore mean that competition is not fair, or does fair competition lead to inequalities because there is substantial difference between the native ability of individuals? If there are significant differences in ability between individuals, is this compatible with the empiricist view that the mind is a blank tablet and that individual differences are environmental? Do schools have any responsibility to compensate for individual differences in ability acquired in preschool years? What are the reasons that there is inequality? What obligation does the school have to do something about it?

We also need to know how schools actually affect the distribution of social rewards. Do schools now function as liberal theory suggests they should? Do they neutralize irrelevant factors of background and permit students to advance as their individual ability makes possible? Or, as many argue, are schools actually part of a system of discrimination? Do schools make opportunities available on irrelevant and discriminatory grounds? Perhaps schools have become part of the problem they were intended to solve. Or perhaps schools are inconsequential. After all, the attempt to achieve fair competition through schools is based on the assumption that what schools teach is relevant to success in life. Perhaps that is not true. Perhaps the liberal assumption that rationality is the element crucial to success is mistaken. Some recent critics of education have so argued. Or perhaps rationality is crucial, but schools do not teach it.

The final set of issues concerns what constitutes relevant and irrelevant grounds for dispensing opportunities. The discussion has assumed that it is objectionable to dispense educational opportunity on criteria such as wealth or family background. Race, sex, ethnic or religious background can also be presumed to be irrelevant to distributing educational services. But it seems reasonable that need and ability are relevant grounds for different treatment by schools. Mentally retarded students and high I.Q. students should not have the same educational program. But why are race and wealth irrelevant to distributing educational opportunities, but not need and ability? How do we know this? How are ability and need relevant? Should persons of high ability have a better claim because they are more educable or a lesser claim because they are better able to learn on their own? Might not race and wealth be relevant to some issues about educational opportunity?

B. THE BACKGROUND OF EQUAL OPPORTUNITY

Let's look at the concept of equal opportunity in more detail. Consider two children, one of whom is of below-average intelligence, and the other of whom is exceptionally bright. What counts as treating them equally? Consider some possibilities:

1. Equality consists in making the same educational experience available to each child, even if each child cannot profit equally from the experiences.

2. Equality consists in making available different educational experiences according to the child's ability so as to maximize the child's capacity to contribute something positive to society.

3. Equality consists in making available different educational experiences according to the child's needs, expenditures being determined by what is necessary to enable each child to achieve his or her potential and have a fair chance at a meaningful life.

4. The first three views are consistent with equality which requires only that educational opportunities not be allocated differentially according to irrelevant criteria such as race or family background.

Only the least plausible of these views assumes that equality entails treating everyone in the same way. The first view permits different results to occur from exposure to the same experiences. The other three all require or permit different treatment of the two children in ways reflecting either ability to profit or need. We can conclude that, first, *in order to treat people equally it is not necessary to treat them in all respects the same.* Second, *issues of equality concern when people should be treated the same and when they should be treated differently.*

In each of these four cases a claim of this kind is made. *Child one and child two differ/are the same in some relevant way, thus, they should be treated differently/the same in some particular way.* The second and third of the cases hold that differences in ability or need justify providing different educational experiences. Case one holds that differences in ability do not justify providing different educational experiences, but do justify permitting different results. The fourth claim holds only that certain differences between individuals cannot be used to justify differences in treatment.

Assumed in these examples is a general rule concerning how people should be treated. I shall state it in two ways. *People who are the same according to relevant criteria should be treated the same.* The negative corollary is: *people who differ according to relevant criteria should be treated differently.* These rules provide one standard of equality. Equality consists in treating those similarly situated in some relevant way the same and in treating those differently situated in some relevant way differently. They tell us what is meant by equality of educational opportunity when the kinds of treatments at issue are educational opportunities.

The trouble with these rules is that they tend to be vacuous. Such rules do not help us to decide what educational experiences to provide for children of different abilities or needs. We need to know what is to count as a relevant criterion. How do we distinguish features of individuals which justify differences in treatment, and how do we decide what kinds of differences in treatment are justified? We need a theory of relevant differences.

Let us start with an intuitive list. Consider the following possibilities:

Reasons for Distributing Educational Opportunities

Relevant	Irrelevant
Ability	Race
Need	Sex
Merit	Religion
Virtue	Ethnic Background
Capacity to contribute to the well being of others	Inherited Wealth

I would suggest that most readers will find this a plausible listing. There may be quibbles. Why did I include virtue? Are ability and need in conflict? Might not one's religion be relevant to admission to a parochial school? But the intuitive listing does not get us far in understanding how some things come to be relevant and others not. Why should ability be relevant to educational decisions—but not race? Nor does the intuitive listing tell us what kinds of decisions should be linked to relevant properties. Granting the relevance of ability, for example, should the student of high ability get more educational resources because he or she can profit from them or less because people of lower ability have greater need?

Let us begin by considering John Locke's views on equality. The initial phrases of the Declaration of Independence lay down a basic democratic creed.

We hold these truths to be self-evident; that all men are created equal; that they are endowed by their creator with certain inalienable rights; that to secure these rights, governments are instituted among men, deriving their just powers from the consent of the governed; that whenever any form of government becomes destructive of these ends, it is the right of the people to alter or to abolish it, and to institute new government, laying its foundation on such principles, and organizing its power in such form, as to them shall seem most likely to effect their safety and happiness.

Jefferson is expressing doctrines best articulated in John Locke's *Second Treatise of Civil Government.*[3] Society, argues Locke, rests on a social contract. The duty to obey a government consists in the consent that people have given to that government. That consent is not unlimited: if violations occur, then it may be withdrawn. The Declaration of Independence is in effect an indictment of King George for breaching the social contract. Since the social contract has been violated, Jefferson asserts, the colonies no longer owe obedience to the English king.

In these doctrines of Locke may be found many of the components of the liberal view of equality. Let us start with the context in which Locke wrote.

In seventeenth-century England a conservative asked to justify political authority might have responded that the king is sovereign because he wields the authority of God. The king is the heir of the authority given by God to Adam to rule over all the earth. Political authority descends from on high to the king through the nobility to the common man. Such authority is inherited, and the aristocracy thus rule by divine right and by birth. The political duties of the common man consist in unquestioning obedience to superior authority which represents the authority of God.

Locke's *First Treatise* is an attack on this doctrine. The *Second Treatise* develops a new view of the right to rule and the duty to obey. Locke's fundamental concept is that legitimate authority does not rest on divine will and the inherited authority of Adam but rests on the consent of those over whom authority is exercised.

Locke's vehicle for developing this view of legitimate authority is his concept of the state of nature. Let us imagine, he suggests, the condition of people in which authority does not exist and ask how and why governments might arise in such a state. People in a state of nature Locke describes as in a *State of perfect Freedom* to order their Actions, and dispose of their Possessions, and Persons as they see fit, within the bounds of the Law of Nature, without asking leave, or depending upon the Will of any other man. A *State* also *of Equality,* wherein all the Power and Jurisdiction is reciprocal, no one having more than another: there being nothing more evident, than that Creatures of the same species and rank promiscuously born to all the same advantages of Nature and the use of the same facilities, should be equal amongst another without Subordination or Subjection. . . . The State of Nature has a Law of Nature to govern it which obliges every one: And Reason which is that Law, teaches all Mankind, who will but consult it, that being all equal and independent, no one ought to harm another in his Life, Health, Liberty or Possessions.[4]

An essential idea is that there is no natural authority. Thus, before people agree on some social arrangements, no person has any inherent right to authority over any other. People live in a state of perfect freedom and equal sovereignty. *Equality in the state of nature is thus equal sovereignty. The essence of the claim is that regardless of how people may differ in intelligence, wealth, or family, they have equal standing so far as the right to command one another is concerned.*

Locke justifies this position both positively and negatively. Implicit in his rejection of any natural right to govern is the view that however people may differ from one another, none of these differences is sufficient to justify the inherent right of one person to authority over another. The positive justification holds that people have rights simply because they are people. Creatures of the same species should be equal to one another without subordination or subjection.

There are other rights which people possess because they are persons. Besides equal sovereignty Locke suggests that each individual is entitled to protection from harm in life, health, liberty, and possessions. Jefferson altered the list to life, liberty, and the pursuit of happiness.

Here we see two more typical liberal themes. The first is that people have certain rights which others may not violate; the second, the moral primacy of persons. Persons are entitled to be treated as ends rather than means. It is persons who are of fundamental value. In conjunction the doctrine of the primacy of persons and the doctrine of rights yield the view that some rights attach to persons simply because they are persons and that these rights do not differ from one person to the next because of any differences in individual characteristics. People equally possess basic human rights.

Locke's image of a state of nature thus expresses his rejection of the medieval doctrine that people are born into a place in a natural social hierarchy. The middle ages had viewed society and social inequality as the natural state of affairs. It was social change which was unnatural and in need of justification. Locke's doctrine, however, announces the view that the individual is prior to society. The natural state of persons is freedom and equality. Therefore authority and social position, even society itself, require justification.

The state of nature also assigns to each person a condition of moral autonomy and individual responsibility to reason and the law of nature. If no one is naturally subservient to the will of another, then people cannot excuse their conduct by saying they were merely obeying the authority of another. Individuals must accept the responsibility for their own acts. Individuals may not do whatever they wish. People are subject to the laws of nature and of reason. They must respect the rights of others and obey the natural law. Moreover in the state of nature each person has the responsibility to enforce the moral law against others. The state of nature is not without sanctions.

Civil authority is necessary because without a threat of force many people will not obey the moral law. Civil authority exists to secure justice. But the real problem in Locke does not concern why authority is necessary, but how it can be justified. If all persons have a moral obligation to take responsibility for their own acts, how can anyone else have a right to tell them what to do?

Locke's response is that individuals cannot have this freedom taken from them, but they may voluntarily give up a part of it. This is accomplished in a social contract through which the members of a society agree to obey a sovereign so long as he respects and protects their rights. People in society are obligated to obey the sovereign by their promise to do so. The authority of the government rests on this promise, on the consent of the governed.

Once people live in civil society, equal sovereignty no longer exists. In civil society the right to rule has been delegated to some authority. What sort of equality exists in civil society? Part of Locke's answer is that in civil society people "are to be governed by *promulgated established Laws,* not to be varied in particular Cases; but to have one Rule for Rich and Poor, for the Favourite at Court, and the Country Man at Plough."[5]

Here Locke introduces aspects of the concept of due process of law. The law must be established and promulgated. Authorities cannot create the law as they go or change it to suit their preference, and the law must be announced to those who are expected to obey it. Locke also views equality as equal protection of the law. Equality in civil society means that the law cannot be formulated or applied differently so as to give an advantage to those who are rich or highborn. The law must be applied equally regardless of social station. The doctrine of equal protection as well as the doctrine of equal sovereignty is rooted in Locke's rejection of any natural privilege or natural superiority. People possess a common humanity and are entitled to equal rights. The government, therefore, may not support the interests of some against the interests of others. Wealth or social standing do not entitle anyone to the special attention of the government.

What does this tell us? *What we know from Locke is that people are naturally equal, and consequently even in society those characteristics of people springing from social position should be irrelevant in a government's dealings with its citizens.* Locke indicates wealth and social class. We may reasonably add race and religion and label these irrelevant features *accidents of birth.* One of Locke's basic contributions is his pointing out that many of the attributes which feudal society had treated as fundamental to how persons were treated are in fact irrelevant.

C. UTILITARIANISM AND CAPITALISM

Not all liberals are Lockeans. Let us look at a different strain of liberal theory, utilitarianism, and its connection to laissez faire capitalism. Utilitarianism provides the moral theory. Laissez faire capitalism provides a view of the economic world which allows the moral theory to be applied.

Utilitarianism is the extension of hedonism into social ethics. Happiness or pleasure is the good. An individual thus determines the desirability of a given act by asking how much pleasure and pain the act will lead to. The best act is that one which produces the highest pleasure.

Utilitarianism is the application of the hedonistic calculus to social ethics. The justice of a set of social institutions is the contribution of the institutions to the greatest good for the greatest number. A society consists of a large aggregate of individuals—each pursuing pleasure and avoiding pain. Should not the justice of a society be decided by determining how well its institutions facilitate the pursuit of pleasure by its members? How else would one determine this except by adding the pleasures of individuals into a grand total? Thus the most just society—the one that succeeds best by meeting this criterion of the greatest good for the greatest number—is the one with the highest total of pleasure over pain, the highest utility.

Well not quite, for utilitarians soon realized that the total quantity of pleasure over pain might be increased merely by an increase in population, although the utility of each person stayed the same or even declined. Thus what we want is not the total utility of a society but its average utility, the total utility of a society divided by the number of its members. Achieving justice, then, consists in discovering institutions which maximize the average utility.

How is the average utility maximized? Many utilitarians in the last century were convinced that the economic system which best maximized utility was a free-market system—one in which the nature and price of goods produced is determined only by the consumers. Among the reasons given are that free markets assure that available goods will go where they are most valued and thus where they produce the highest utility. The person who values something the most will be willing to pay the most for it. Individual preferences—what people actually want—will determine what is produced. In a free-market society production responds only to expressed desires. People thus get what they want and are happier as a consequence. Finally a free market provides incentives for individuals to work for the good of others. Since the price attached to one's work in free markets functions according to the value others attach to it, individuals are rewarded to the extent that they contribute to meeting the desires of others. Despite the fact that a free-market society is highly competitive, it provides incentives for each to contribute to the happiness of all. In Adam Smith's felicitous metaphor, in a free-market society an invisible hand guides society to maximum efficiency, productivity, and happiness. The norm of distributive justice—that the distributive effects of free markets are fair whatever they happen to be—finds easy justification within utilitarianism.

Equality too is justified in these terms. Both equality of opportunity and positions open to talents can be justified because they promote the ability of individuals to make a contribution to the well-being of others. When we give a person a job on grounds other than the ability to do it, we fail to use available talent so that people can contribute most. When we deny people equal opportunity to develop their talents we fail to use human resources best. In short, equality is justified because it is efficient.

These arguments lead to a meritocratic view of social rewards and of the allocation of educational resources. From a utilitarian viewpoint rewards and opportunities are allocated to maximize the average utility. Given free market assumptions, income will be a function of social contribution as measured by free markets. Educational opportunities will be allocated on grounds of ability to profit. The assumption is that the people chosen will be the most productive. Ability will be understood as the capacity to develop talents which markets reward.

The argument thus points to ability to profit as the central relevant feature for the distribution of educational opportunity. Utilitarianism thus gives us a criterion for distributing educational resources: *Ability should be rewarded with opportunity in such a way as to maximize the average utility.*

The views of Locke and utilitarianism thus provide a reasonable picture of a liberal theory of what count as relevant and irrelevant grounds for allocating educational opportunity. The Lockean view and the utilitarian view are united in holding that characteristics linked to social position are irrelevant. This conclusion is derived differently within each viewpoint. Locke's argument is linked to the idea that the natural state of persons is freedom and equality and that social distinctions are unnatural and must be justified. Utilitarians by contrast object to discrimination by arguing that responding to such background characteristics is inefficient. Utilitarianism moreover leads to the notion that educational opportunity should be provided to maximize the average utility. Therefore the relevant criterion for allocating education opportunity will usually be ability to profit. The liberal consensus thus appears to be that social position or other accidents of birth are irrelevant to allocate educational opportunities and that ability to profit is the relevant criterion. Such are some of the basic assumptions which define fair competition in a liberal society and which constitute the context in which a liberal view of educational opportunity must be developed.

D. EQUAL OPPORTUNITY AND SCHOOLING

These assumptions do not sufficiently generate a view of schooling's role in promoting equal opportunity. We must examine what additional assumptions are required to create a reasonable view of schooling and to examine areas of potential disagreement among liberal viewpoints. Let us first recapitulate the argument to perceive the role schooling will be expected to play in a liberal theory of fair competition. These views govern the role of schooling vis-à-vis equality.

1. The basic role of the state in a liberal society is promoting fair competition for private goods.

2. In a society which distributes its goods largely by a free-market system, part of fairness in competition consists in ensuring that the opportunity to acquire a marketable talent is not achieved by social rank. Fair competition requires equal opportunity to acquire the means of competition.

3. To give substance to the idea of fair competition and to equal opportunity, one needs a theory of what counts as relevant and irrelevant reasons for treating people differently. Liberals have generally argued that properties which can be termed accidents of birth—such as family, social class, and race—are irrelevant. Utilitarian liberals have also advanced the thesis that what is relevant needs to be determined by the criterion of the maximization of the average utility. For education this usually means that educational opportunities will be distributed according to the ability to profit.

These notions do not tell us much about what kind of schooling we ought to provide to whom. Indeed thus far I have been assuming that it is reasonable to regard schools as the basic social institution in which opportunities to develop marketable talents are distributed. That assumption is not self-evident. If liberals consider schooling the primary vehicle of equal opportunity, they assume that the kinds of talents which are important in economic competition are the qualities effectively taught by schools.

Liberals do make such an assumption. The essence of the reasons for the liberals' focus on schooling as the primary dispenser of opportunity inheres in the idea that rationality is primary. Rationality is the primary means whereby people get what they want. For many empiricists rationality is the capacity to effectively relate means to ends. Knowledge is power. Rationality accordingly is the primary commodity in being able effectively to compete for private goods. Opportunity then essentially entails the opportunity to become rational. Equal opportunity thus involves the fair distribution of rationality. These ideas do not entail that schools are the primary social institution for providing opportunity. That argument necessitates the additional assumption that rationality is best distributed in formal educational settings.

Liberals thus see rationality as a mediating variable between schooling and social benefits. If one is willing to substitute the phrase *cognitive skills* for the word *rationality,* it turns out that a good deal of research has been done on the distributive effects of schooling, research which reflects a liberal view concerning how schools are supposed to function. Such research normally involves the connection between educational resources, cognitive skills, and some class of social benefits, predominantly income.

This research is inconclusive at best. Some of it, however, suggests that rationality may not be connected either to schooling or to social benefits, as liberals are inclined to assume. Christopher Jencks and others, in an influential book entitled *Inequality,*[6] argue what is popularly called the "schools don't make a difference thesis," holding that schooling accounts for little of the variance in cognitive skills and that differences in cognitive skills are only loosely connected to income. (If the Jencks thesis is correct, my argument might seem to suffer the worst fate which can befall a philosophical thesis—irrelevance.) The thesis that schools don't make a difference does not assume that cognitive skills and/or rationality are not acquired in schools. Instead it holds that schools do not account for the *differences* in achievement. Surely no one would dispute the claim that many students learn to read, write, and compute in schools. Schools account for achievement, but not for differential rates in achievement. It is, of course, different rates of achievement which are interesting vis-à-vis equality of opportunity.

We must recognize that income is only one social benefit. Rationality, however, is the key to both personal and civic competence. It is also an intrinsic good. Thus, in order to know how rationality and schooling are connected to a properly large class of benefits, we need to understand such matters as how they affect citizenship, how they affect the capacity to formulate and execute successfully a rational life plan, and how they enhance the quality of experience. Income is part of this package, but it is far from the entire package. In much of what follows I shall, by following the currents of research, perhaps seem overly preoccupied with income, but we should not be seduced in giving income a larger role in social theory than it deserves.

Finally let it be clear that the liberal view of the place of rationality in the distribution of social benefits represents an ideal, not a description. If it should turn out that rationality is not connected to income as liberals suggest, the conclusion may be that society should take steps to restore it to its proper role. Jencks appears to conclude from his work that educational reform is not a viable means to promote equality and that we should look elsewhere. I believe it is fair to conclude that extraschool paths to equality are in order and perhaps required. To conclude that we need no longer be concerned with schools, however, is to forget that education should constitute more than a means to a good job. Such thinking ultimately neglects the central role of rationality in a liberal view of the world.

To explore two additional assumptions which can be important in developing a fuller view of equality is useful. These assumptions are that people are roughly equal in their capacity to acquire rationality and that schools have the duty to compensate for differences in ability to acquire rationality which are a function of extraschool inequalities.

These assumptions lead to a radically egalitarian view of society. If individuals are equal in the ability to acquire rationality and if the opportunity to acquire rationality is equal, it is reasonable to suppose that people will emerge from schools with equal ability to compete. This viewpoint does not assume that everyone will acquire the same type or amount of education, since aspirations may differ; but it does suggest that it should be difficult for individuals with similar aspirations to gain a significant competitive edge on one another. This is particularly true if schools are responsible for compensating for differences in ability to learn which are acquired from extraschool sources.

If people are equal in their ability to compete, free-market assumptions suggest that they will also achieve rough equality as they compete for social goods, for free markets will reward a given talent disproportionately only on the assumption that it is scarce. In a society composed of persons of equal ability, however, no talent should be scarce—or if scarce should not remain so long. Thus, given these assumptions, a society which provides fair competition at all levels should also generate equal results. Such results are not required by liberal views of justice. Liberal justice permits any outcome if it results in fair competition. But, if competition is fair and if persons are equal in ability, similarity of results is what we should expect. If such results do not obtain, we can reasonably suppose either that people are not equal in ability or that the system is unjust.

These two ideas also generate some expectation about schooling. They do not require that schools generate a common curriculum, but they do suggest that the variations in curriculum which do exist be justified by differences in aspirations. Conversely they would preclude diversification of programs based on the assumption that people differ substantially in ability. Thus, while diversification according to vocational preference might be expected, vocational tracking when students are tracked more according to ability than aspiration would not. If people are incapable of doing normal work, that is grounds for compensatory education, not for creating a separate curriculum for those judged incompetent.

The denial of these two assumptions results in quite a different set of social outcomes and a different view of schooling. A society in which people vary widely in terms of native ability and which fails to compensate for environmentally induced inequalities can be expected to have notable inequalities. These inequalities in its reward structure reflect the need for jobs requiring high educational attainment and the scarcity of adequately capable people. Thus it is likely that in this society competition for the educational slots leading to elite positions will be intense.

In such a society curriculum in schools will be diversified more according to capacity than to aspiration. Offerings will be categorized according to the degree of intellectual ability judged necessary for success. Students will be placed according to their degree of ability appropriate to the offerings, not because they prefer the offerings or want the social niches to which the offerings lead. Schools will have a high degree of vocational tracking which is strongly linked to the idea that the occupational structure should reflect intellectual competence.

Despite the potentially high degree of social inequality and of vocational tracking, such a society can nevertheless logically claim to provide equality of educational opportunity. It can do so because its jobs are awarded according to demonstrated merit and because opportunity to develop the talent to get these jobs is awarded owing to demonstrable ability to profit. Social background is never recognized as a relevant basis for decisions. If able parents can pass on their ability to their children without the involvement of the school, that is not society's responsibility. Such a society need only prevent able parents from using their wealth or power to gain enough control over schools so that the children of the able are given favorable treatment regardless of their own ability.

We thus conclude that the concept of equality of educational opportunity does not by itself require any particular view of education nor of

the anticipated results of such opportunity. A complete view of equal educational opportunity requires other assumptions. I have noted two central
issues: one concerns whether people are roughly equal in their capacity to
develop rationality, and the other concerns whether schools have a compensatory role to play in promoting equality. These issues are pivotal in
understanding current debates about equality and schooling, and they are
deeply embedded in the views I will argue. Consider how these issues fit
into the broader liberal context.

When equality of natural ability is at issue, liberals, being empiricists, tend to prefer the view that people are at least roughly equal in their
ability to develop rationality. They are thus inclined to see individual differences as a function of environment, not heredity. But deeper reasons
for liberals to assume rough equality of intellectual capacity also exist.
Liberal views of liberty and democracy assume that the capacity to govern
one's affairs competently and to participate competently in collective
decision-making is widely distributed in the population. The degree to
which the vast majority of humanity is incapable of rational choice is the
degree to which liberal views of society and government are unwarranted.

Such views do not preclude differences in native capacity, but they do
preclude differences in native capacity which are great enough to warrant
the conclusion that many people are not fit to manage their own lives and
that other people are inherently suited to govern.

Such ideas suggest why liberals have focused on educational solutions to social ills. A functional democracy requires an educated citizenry.
Moreover such inequality as exists will tend to be seen as having environmental causes and thus as having educational solutions. A focus on
educational solutions to poverty and inequality is deeply rooted in a liberal world view.

The idea of rough equality can be applied in two ways—to individuals and groups. When applied to groups the assumption of rough equality of capacity holds that, whatever the differences which may obtain between individuals, the distribution of capacity does not vary between
groups. This claim is thus weaker than the claim that there is equality between individuals. It can admit of substantial variation between individuals, insisting only that the range of capacities among people generally is
proportionately represented in each relevant subdivision of humanity.

Concerning these issues first, I assume, that although there are variations among individuals, these differences are not so large as to render liberal views concerning liberty and democracy unwarranted. The vast majority of humanity can achieve the capacity for individual and collective
self-government. Second, I assume that there is strict equality of capacity
between relevant social groups. Whatever differences in capacity which
may exist between individuals are proportionately distributed among rele-

vant groups. I cannot defend these controversial assumptions here. The plausibility of much of what I shall henceforth argue assumes I am right.

One's opinion concerning the duty of schools to compensate for inequalities rooted in a student's background becomes important to the extent that one begins to see family or community as part of a child's opportunity and as potential sources of inequality. I believe there are excellent reasons to view family and community in this way, and I shall argue that schools have a duty to compensate for such differences in background.

For liberals a compensatory role for schooling becomes problematic because it can lead schools to distribute resources in apparently unequal ways and because it can lead to expanding the role of the state in education, an expansion which may threaten other liberal views.

These issues will be dealt with later. At this point we have sketched the philosophical background of liberal equality and introduced some issues in an abstract way. We now need to see how these matters work out in some current educational issues.

CHAPTER 10

It's fun to eulogize the people you despise, as long as you don't let them in your school.

                                                              —TOM LEHRER

Applying Liberal Equality: Desegregation

My argument in chapter 9 assumes that schools ought to function as this diagram illustrates:

Student Characteristics   Schooling   School Outcomes   Relevant Social Outcomes

Background ——— Rationality   Achievement   Income, status, etc.

Ability ———

The lines and arrows indicate direction of causality. The diagram indicates that schools should function so that ability, not irrelevant background characteristics, determines achievement understood as the development of rationality. Rationality, in turn, is assumed to determine social outcomes (although it is also a relevant outcome in its own right).

This model assumes that the basic concern of equal opportunity is to achieve fairness in the distribution of social good. We therefore need to ask what results schools should produce and how these results are relevant to judging fairness in educational arrangements. Should we be interested primarily in how school affects the distribution of income, jobs, or status? Or should we look at other factors such as how schools affect self-respect? Moreover can we use results in such matters to judge the fairness of schooling? Should schools be responsible for producing a certain distribution of results? Or are schools only responsible for allocating their resources in nondiscriminatory ways? If liberals treat equality as fair competition, doesn't that mean that outcomes are irrelevant to deciding if educational opportunity is equal?

Another assumption is that schools are relevant to the distribution of rationality and that rationality is the basic end of competition. Both assumptions are controversial. I wish to look primarily at the link between schooling and achievement. Here we must know how schools function in producing whatever effects they produce. Do material resources such as buildings, books, or libraries make a difference? Or do the quality of teachers or something about the mix of students make a difference? Are whatever differences in achievement which schools produce a function of cognitive factors—the ability to learn—or are they the result of affective differences—motivation or differing educational values? Most important, how does schooling interact with students' backgrounds in producing results? These last questions are empirical ones, the stuff of sociology or economics, not philosophy; but the relevance of different answers to them is a major philosophical question.

These various sets of issues are posed in the legal and social science literature on desegregation. Desegregation is therefore a handy vehicle for examining the assumptions of liberal equality and for working out in an important context some of the details of its application.

A. BROWN AND DESEGREGATION

The fourteenth amendment to the Constitution of the United States says that no state may deny to "any person within its jurisdiction the equal protection of the law." This amendment was added to the Constitution in 1868. Its intent was to secure political rights for recently freed slaves.

The amendment is normally interpreted as insisting that states must not employ inappropriate classifications in its dealings with its citizens. That is, states may not treat individuals differently because of their race or because of any other irrelevant factor. Thus the basis of classification employed or assumed by any action of the state must have a plausible relationship to some legitimate state purpose. Otherwise the action of the state is unconstitutional.

The equal protection clause therefore bears a clear relationship to the liberal doctrine that governments may not treat people differently owing to accidents of birth. Because of its history the suspect classification in a paradigmatic sense is race rather than wealth or social position. Nevertheless the underlying philosophical point is the same. Governments may not create or apply laws in such a way as to treat people differently because of irrelevant features of their background.

The crucial case in applying the fourteenth amendment to education is *Brown* v. *Board of Education* (1954)[1]. The *Brown* decision is commonly held to have repudiated the separate but equal doctrine announced in an 1896 case, *Plessy* v. *Ferguson.*[2] This case upheld the constitutionality of a Louisiana law requiring railroad companies to provide "equal but separate accommodations for the white, and colored races.''[3] Justice Brown in his majority opinion in *Plessy* noted that separate schools had long been the rule and have "been held to be a valid exercise of the legislative power even by courts of States where the political rights of the colored race have been longest and most earnestly enforced."[4]

The attacks on school segregation, conducted largely by the NAACP, were initially designed to show that facilities provided for blacks were separate, but not equal. Early cases concern admission to professional schools which were largely unavailable to blacks, and it was therefore easy to show that facilities were unequal. One case, *Sweat* v. *Painter,*[5] focused on the comparative quality of the University of Texas Law School and the newly created black law school. In that case the court considers both tangible facilities and intangibles such as faculty quality and prestige in determining the inequality of Texas's separate legal education. Most cases before 1954, however, are dominated by a concern for equality in material and human resources.

Brown concerns elementary and secondary education and struck at the heart of the system of racial segregation. In rejecting *Plessy* v. *Ferguson* the Court first pointed out that the importance of school to success in life had changed substantially since 1896. Chief Justice Warren observes:

In these days, it is doubtful that any child may reasonably be expected to succeed in life if he is denied the opportunity of an education. Such an opportunity, where the state has undertaken to provide it, is a right which must be made available to all on equal terms.[6]

Warren then quotes with favor these remarks from a lower court:

Segregation of white and colored children in public schools has a detrimental effect upon the colored children. The impact is greater when it has the sanction of law; for the policy of separating the races is usually interpreted as denoting the inferiority of the negro group. A sense of inferiority affects the motivation of a child to learn. Segregation with the sanction of law, therefore, has a tendency [to retard] the educational and mental development of negro children and to deprive them of some of the benefits they would receive in a racial[ly] integrated school system.[7]

On this basis Warren states the conclusion of the Court—that "in the field of public education the doctrine of 'separate but equal' has no place. Separate educational facilities are inherently unequal."[8]

What is the moral point of *Brown*? Granted that segregation is evil, in what does its evil consist? What wrong was *Brown* intended to redress? I want first to look at a group of interpretations which treat the stigmatizing effects of segregation as central to its evil. Let us call them stigma theories. The first of these theories sees the stigmatizing effects of segregation as an intervening variable in a causal chain which produces low achievement and poor chances in life for black children.

Let us suppose *Plessy* v. *Ferguson* holds that segregation is permissible unless it can be shown that harm results to the segregated group. Separate facilities may be considered equal, however, when no significant harm is done to any group thereby. *Brown* then can be read as attempting to establish that segregated education inevitably harms black children in that segregated schools damage their prospects.

The argument to demonstrate this assumes that the relevant features of an educational environment, so far as equality is concerned, are those which are causally linked to the significant outcomes of schooling and achievement. It is these causally relevant features which must be equalized. But, Warren suggests, *the fact that a school is a segregated school is itself a causally relevant factor.* By stigmatizing black children, segregation inhibits their desire to learn. And since segregation is the cause of educational harm to Blacks, segregated schools are inherently unequal. Since segregation is a causally relevant variable and since it produces an unequal distribution of educational and social results, it is illegal. In this interpretation the Court suggests this chain of causality: segregation leads to feelings of inferiority which cause low motivation, which results in low achievement and then in low success in life.

The Court's theory in *Brown* is that *because of the stigma of inferiority implied by segregation, the ability of black children to succeed in school is impaired; and in consequence of this impairment, black children are at a competitive disadvantage in pursuing various social goods.*

The interpretation of *Brown* has been controversial partly because it appears to make the illegality of segregation depend on sociological or psychological claims. The noted legal scholar Edmond Cahn thus wrote concerning the testimony of social scientists in *Brown:* "I would not have the constitutional rights of Negroes—or of other Americans—rest on any such flimsy foundations as some of the scientific demonstrations in these records."[9] It is crucial here that the need for such social-science data is a consequence of the notion that the illegality of segregation depends on segregation damaging the life prospects of black children. The Court is read as saying "No harm no foul." Social science is needed to document the harm.

Are there readings of *Brown* which rely less on complex causal models concerning the effects of segregation? Such an interpretation can be developed by returning to *Plessy* v. *Ferguson*. One of the arguments advanced there held that segregation was objectionable because it was based on the presumption of the inferiority of blacks. The Court dismissed this argument. "We consider the underlying fallacy of the plaintiff's argument to consist in the assumption that the enforced separation of the two races stamps the colored race with a badge of inferiority. If this be so, it is not by reason of anything found in the act, but solely because the colored race chooses to put that construction upon it.''[10]

Judge William Doyle picks out this link between segregation and the assumed inferiority of blacks as the crucial element in *Brown*. "No person would argue that any race or group is inferior to another, that it is to be considered unworthy to associate with the excluding groups. I submit then that this is the actual key to the *Brown* decision. . . . *Brown* (and others) were not predicated on the studies of sociologists and psychologists. They are all based on the fundamental invalidity of isolating a people from other people."[11] Doyle sees the majority opinion in *Brown* as based on the fact that segregation is rooted in the presumption that blacks are inferior. *Segregation is a state-imposed insult to the dignity and worth of black people. That is why it is immoral and illegal.*

This interpretation has two variants. The first focuses on the psychological harm resulting from this state-imposed insult. Blacks are assumed to internalize this public judgment of their inferiority. Segregation thus is destructive of the self-respect of black children. *It is this psychological damage itself which is the basic evil of segregation.* Perhaps, however, the psychological effect of this state-imposed insult to Blacks is not crucial. Instead it may be the fact of the insult itself or, more accurately, the principle expressed by the insult. What then is the principle affirmed by the institution of segregation?

Doyle suggests that principle is the inferiority of blacks. But if segregation is based on the assumed inferiority of blacks, this inferiority must be fundamental. Mere empirical differences between groups of people cannot be the basis of a denial of equal rights to any group. Nor can they be the basis of the refusal to associate with any group. If it were the case that blacks were on the average less intelligent than whites that would not constitute grounds for segregation or the denial of any other civil rights. Whites have not felt any urge to segregate themselves from other whites on a criterion of intelligence. To put the point more philosophically, the liberal ideal that people have equal rights is based on the Lockean concept that regardless of individual differences there is a sense in which all persons are equal. Rights are rooted in the mere fact that one is a person. Moreover everyone is fully and equally a person. There are no variations in the property of being a human being such that these variations justify a denial of equal rights.

If this is correct, then someone who wished to justify segregation on the grounds of the alleged inferiority of blacks would have to claim that blacks are less human than other persons and as a consequence are not entitled to the same rights as other persons. Such a person would in effect be denying the essence of the liberal doctrine of equality—that all men are created equal. Such a person would also be affirming the rationale, if not the institution, of slavery, and he would consequently be denying the moral point which it was the purpose of the fourteenth amendment to affirm.

Perhaps then what the courts find objectionable in the institution of segregation is that the institution denies a fundamental principle of liberal societies. *Segregation rejects the principle that all men are created equal and consequently have equal rights. It affirms instead that blacks are somehow less human beings than whites.*

We have seen three versions of the stigma theory. Each makes the stigma or insult involved in segregation central, but each differs according to the harm attached to the stigma.

1. *The distribution theory:* The evil of segregation inheres in its damaging the achievement and life prospect of blacks. It is a mechanism for the unequal distribution of social rewards.

2. *The self-esteem theory:* The damage to the self-esteem or self-concept of blacks is the chief harm of segregation.

3. *The Lockean theory:* Segregation is noxious because it denies the fundamental principle that all persons are equal and thus have equal rights.

These theories are not inconsistent. Segregation may be objectionable for all these reasons. And each view seems consistent with the general liberal theory of equal opportunity in that each sees segregation as either a denial of a central liberal doctrine or as a maldistribution of some social good. Thus there is no compelling reason to choose between them. Moreover, at first glance, they seem to have the same implications. Each treats the stigma of segregation as central. The obvious remedy is to eliminate the stigma. That presumably could be done by a racially neutral policy of assigning pupils. Such a view of segregation need not result in racial integration. *In stigma theories the harm of segregation does not result from the fact that blacks attend school only with blacks. The harm results from the fact that blacks are compelled to go to school only with blacks.* Removing the compulsion need not lead to any given racial mix.

The major difference between these views is that the first two treat segregation as objectionable because of its consequences. They thus seem to require empirical evidence to demonstrate that segregation has such consequences. The distribution theory requires a more complex defense; however, both views open the Court to the objection that its opinions depend on dubious social science. These views also raise the question of what follows if the social-science facts alleged about the psychological harm done by segregation to black children are wrong or incomplete. Since these views make some factual assumptions, it appears that they could be challenged on the facts.[12] The third view, however, assumes nothing about the consequences of segregation. It only holds segregation to be based on an unpermissible moral claim.

Having decided *Brown,* the Court received a variety of cases stemming from attempts to evade desegregation which required it to refine its view of what counted as a segregated school system and what remedies were required. Prince Edward County, Virginia, closed its public schools and provided tuition grants and tax credits to finance private schools.[13] Only white students availed themselves of these grants. A more common strategy was to create freedom of choice plans.[14] Students were assigned to the schools they had previously attended unless they expressed a choice to attend different schools. The predictable outcome was that white students elected to continue to attend the former all-white school while black students continued to attend the former all-black school. The freedom of the latter to choose otherwise was suspect. State-sponsored segregation was thus replaced by a system in which it just so happened that whites and blacks attended separate schools.

Such attempts at evasion led the Court to an expanded definition of illegal segregation by which segregation was defined as racial imbalance which is the result of some state act. Public officials cannot act so as to tend to produce white schools and black schools. Where they have done so, it is not sufficient merely to cease or to remove the offending statute. Instead officials must eliminate dual school systems. They must create a unitary system where some schools are not identifiably white and others identifiably black.[15] The state continues to be important in defining segregation. Presumably it is not the racial imbalance but the fact that the state created it which conveys the stigma of segregation.

B. THE COLEMAN REPORT

Would our thinking about desegregation be changed if we accepted a different view from the one in *Brown* of how schools affect achievement and life prospects? Just such a different view was provided in 1966 by what is popularly known as the Coleman report.

In 1964 the U.S. Office of Education under congressional direction commissioned James Coleman to undertake a survey to ascertain the "lack of availability of equal opportunity." This large-scale survey (data was collected for over a half-million students), officially known as the *Equality of Educational Opportunity Survey,*[16] contains some surprising results. The differences in material resources available to white and minority students were found to be small, although they favored white students. The usual school-related variables—class size, facilities, and curricula—did not explain much about the substantial differences in achievement between minority and white students. On the other hand, the variable which best predicted a student's achievement was his socioeconomic background. Finally the school variable which seemed most to affect a student's achievement was the socioeconomic status of his classmates. Coleman sums up these results as they pertain to black students: "The magnitude of differences between schools attended by Negroes and those attended by whites were as follows: least, facilities and curriculum; next, teacher quality; and greatest, educational backgrounds of fellow students. The order of importance of these inputs on the achievement of Negro students is precisely the same: facilities and curriculum least, teacher quality next, and background of fellow students, most."[17]

The maldistribution of educational resources, according to the Coleman report, is not a significant part of the explanation of inequality. Schools, however, do appear to distribute one educationally relevant factor unequally. That factor is their students. The socioeconomic background of the school makes a significant difference for achievement. It would appear that an obvious policy implication of the Coleman report is that a major path to equality of opportunity is socioeconomic and racial integration. For it appears that black students learn more when they attend school with white students, and it appears that low SES students learn more when they attend school with high SES students. Indeed, some have claimed that there is an optimal balance.[18] When the racial or SES mix in a school is 70 percent white and 30 percent black or 70 percent middle class and 30 percent lower SES, it appears that blacks and lower SES students make educational gains while the achievement of the white and affluent does not suffer. Students, therefore, can be considered an educational resource to be equitably distributed. *This line of reasoning has had an interesting effect on the attitude of many educators concerning desegregation. They have come to see desegregation as a vehicle for achieving the desired racial or socioeconomic mix, rather than as a vehicle for eliminating a social stigma unjustly attached to Blacks.*

What difference does this make? To answer this question, let us try to reconstruct *Brown* as though the social-science information referred to in the case was James Coleman's work on the effects of socioeconomic background on achievement rather than Kenneth Clark's work on the effects of segregation on the self-image of black children. To do this, we will have to assume a view of *Brown* which regards segregation as evil because it results in maldistributed achievement and social outcomes. Assuming this approach, we might then argue that the Court's opinion in *Brown* incorporates the wrong causal chain. Rather than a causal chain linking segregation to feelings of inferiority and ultimately to low achievement and income, we need a causal chain that links segregation to race and to social class. The problem with segregation is that it results in the maldistribution of a school-related variable which has been shown to correlate significantly with student achievement—the racial and socioeconomic composition of the student body.

Such a view generates an account of the nature of segregation and what action is necessary to remedy it which significantly differs from the one which results from stigma theories. Let us call this second theory the SES theory. Compare their implications.

1. The agency of the state is an important aspect of segregation in stigma theories, but not in the SES theory. Stigma theories focus on the insult done to blacks by segregating them in separate schools. An insult requires an insulter. Thus it is not the fact that blacks happen to attend schools which contain only other blacks which is problematic. It is the fact that blacks are intentionally excluded from attending schools with whites which defines illegal segregation. In stigma theories the emphasis is on the motivation for segregation, not the resulting racial mix in schools. There is no reason here to view an *accidental* racial imbalance as either illegal or harmful since the fact that the imbalance is unintentional removes the aspect of insult and stigma from the situation. But on the SES theory it is the racial or socioeconomic imbalance itself which is harmful and which should therefore be illegal. The SES theory does not, however, provide any reason to assume that the agency of the state is important to the consequences produced by racial or socioeconomic imbalance.

2. The stigma theories tend to view the educational harm done to black students as a direct consequence of overt discrimination. They thus suggest that the harm of discrimination should disappear with the discrimination. Stigma theories therefore view desegregation as a means to eliminate the stigma of segregation and consider this action sufficient to eliminate the harm of segregation. The SES theory views desegregation as a device to overcome deficiencies in a student's background. It tends to shift emphasis away from eliminating overt discrimination toward eliminating the effects of poverty. Perhaps the most significant thing about the Coleman report is that it, unlike the stigma theory, suggests that the harm of discrimination will not disappear with the discrimination. The reason is that Coleman's results suggest that socioeconomic disadvantagement is self-perpetuating, even when overt discrimination is absent. In this view the children of lower socioeconomic groups tend to do less well in school than the children of higher socioeconomic groups. If one's educational attainment is a major cause of socioeconomic status, the children of low SES parents will tend to occupy lower socioeconomic niches themselves. Poverty begets poverty. Affluence begets affluence. The SES theory thus makes it the responsibility of the school to compensate for background deficiencies, not simply to avoid discrimination.

3. The remedies indicated by the SES theory are potentially more extreme than those indicated by stigma theories. The stigma theory requires

the elimination of dual-school systems. (A dual-school system is one which contains identifiably black and identifiably white schools.) This elimination may be accomplished by having the racial composition of each school in a district reflect the racial composition of the district at large. Desegregation may thus be accomplished even in a district which is dominantly black. Here desegregation requires only the elimination of identifiably white schools. But desegregation requires no particular racial balance. It is compatible with the existence of schools in the same district having a significantly different racial composition so long as this results from a racially neutral pupil-assignment policy. Segregation consists in having schools which are intentionally made black schools and white schools, but not in having schools which differ in the percentages of blacks and whites which happen to attend them. The SES theory, however, requires a certain racial and socioeconomic balance. It follows that desegregation cannot be accomplished in districts which contain too few white or high socioeconomic students. Desegregation efforts based on the SES theory thus will sometimes seek to combine school districts or bus children from the inner city to the suburbs and from suburbs into the inner city. The SES theory turned into judicial policy can require courts to order some Draconian measures, the most obvious being metropolitan desegregation.

Federal judges have apparently resisted the urge to read the Coleman report into the Constitution. The opinion of Judge Sobeloff responding to the testimony of Harvard's Thomas Pettigrew provides one illustration of what seems the dominant judicial view.

[The] central proposition is that the value of a school depends on the characteristics of a majority of its students and superiority is related to whiteness, inferiority to blackness. Although the theory is couched in terms of "socioeconomic class" and the necessity for the creation of a "middle class milieu," nevertheless, at bottom, it rests on the generalization that, educationally speaking, white pupils are somehow better or more desirable than black pupils.

The . . . proponents of this theory grossly misapprehend the philosophical basis for desegregation. It is not founded on the concept that white children are a precious resource which should be fairly apportioned. . . . Segregation is forbidden simply because its perpetuation is a living insult to the black children and immeasurably taints the education they receive. This is the precise lesson of *Brown*.[19]

The reluctance of judges to view segregation and desegregation in the way which seems suggested by the Coleman report has had its most noteworthy outcome in the refusal of the Supreme Court to accept metropolitan desegregation. The key case is *Milliken* v. *Bradley*.[20]

This case concerns Detroit, a city with a substantial and growing black majority in its public schools. The city is, however, surrounded by suburbs with largely white schools. A federal district court ordered a remedy to segregation in Detroit which required the integration of the Detroit school population with that of the surrounding suburbs. The court appeared motivated by the consideration that it is difficult to have integrated schools when the white population is a substantial minority and by the consideration that a Detroit-only desegregation plan would be likely to hasten "white flight" to the suburbs, thus hastening the emergence of Detroit as an all-black city.

The Supreme Court, however, rejected this interdistrict remedy. The essential reason given was that the scope of the remedy cannot exceed the scope of the violation. Since in the opinion of the Supreme Court, the violations leading to segregation in Detroit did not involve the suburbs, the suburbs could not be included in the remedy for Detroit segregation. A second reason given by the Court was the importance of local control over schools. School districts are not just arbitrary lines on a map to be capriciously redrawn on the slightest pretext. They are the means by which the local citizenry can participate in the education of its children and by which education can be made to reflect local concern. There are other democratic values at stake here, the Court intimates, in addition to equal opportunity. The Court thus ordered the implementation of a Detroit-only remedy. The essence of the remedy which has resulted is the elimination of any identifiably white schools.

The results of *Milliken* v. *Bradley* show all the signs one would expect if the Supreme Court was appealing to some form of stigma theory. The agency of the state is important in determining the existence of a violation. The mere existence of a racial imbalance is not sufficient to determine the existence of illegal segregation. The remedy in turn does not require any particular racial or socioeconomic mix; it does require the elimination of identifiably white and black schools in a district. That such a remedy may produce schools which are now largely black and which may shortly become almost entirely black is not problematic. The stigma of segregation is not carried by the maintenance of schools where black students happen to attend school largely with one another. One only begins to link remedies and violations to the actual percentages of blacks and whites who go to school together when one tries to read a sociological theory such as Coleman's into the Constitution.

D. OUTCOMES AND EQUAL OPPORTUNITY

The fact that stigma theories and SES theories have significantly different implications for policy makes a prima facie case that the Supreme Court's views on desegregation and the view suggested by the Coleman report are incompatible. They differ on how schools affect inequalities and (depending on the particular stigma theory at issue) they differ on the relevance of outcomes for judging inequalities. The Lockean variant particularly does not seem to require desegregation to produce any particular consequences. Its concern is to prevent the state from enforcing any policy based on the notion that blacks are less fully persons than whites. The other views assume the relevance of outcomes to judgments of fairness and make some assumptions about how schools produce outcomes, assumptions which differ from the Coleman report.

We do not have a clear view of the sources of this incompatibility. Nor have we examined the possibility that one or more versions of the stigma theory may be consistent with the claims of the Coleman report. To address these issues we must examine each of the three variants of the stigma theory.

The distribution variant of the stigma theory has an incorrect or incomplete view of the facts. It assumes that it is the point of desegregation to create an educational system which gives all students an equal opportunity to achieve and to succeed in life. Segregation is illegal because it has objectionable consequences for how achievement and ultimately social goods such as income and status are distributed between blacks and whites. It is this empirical connection between segregation and achievement and success which makes segregated schools unequal schools.

This view rests in part on a philosophical point about what counts as having an opportunity. For a situation to be an opportunity for something, it must be a potential means to that thing.[21] We would not, for example, count systematic differences in the color of walls between white schools and black schools as an inequality of opportunity unless we believed that the color of walls had something to do with achievement. If wall color is not connected to the relevant outcomes of education, then it is not part of educational opportunity. It follows that differences in wall color cannot constitute an inequality in opportunity. For something to be an opportunity it must make a difference. To be an inequality it must also be differentially available on some irrelevant criterion.

The distribution variant of the stigma theory treats segregation as an inequality because it views segregation as connected with achievement and life success. Moreover it is the stigmatizing aspect of segregation which is the causally relevant factor. The inequality of opportunity involved in segregation is thus that black children study under emotionally debilitating conditions whereas white students do not.

The Coleman report challenges this view of the facts. We can agree that what counts as an inequality of opportunity needs to be identified in terms of an element that makes a difference in achievement. But the Supreme Court has a wrong, or at least an incomplete, view of the factors in schooling which make a difference. The racial or socioeconomic mix of the school makes a difference in learning. Since it does, it cannot be ignored as a factor in deciding what counts as equality of opportunity and in formulating a concept of desegregation. If it is the purpose of desegregation to provide equal educational opportunity for black students, it is not reasonable to ignore a causally relevant factor, one which may account for some of the differences between black and white achievement.

If Coleman's facts are correct, they do not clearly demonstrate that the facts assumed in *Brown* are false. It is possible that black achievement suffers from both the stigma of segregation and the racial or socioeconomic homogeneity segregation produces. The truth of Coleman's claims entails only that the assumptions of *Brown* are incomplete. We should not forget, however, that this incompleteness in *Brown* is of potentially great significance, for it permits what is in effect a distinction between desegregation and integration to be made. Stigma theories do not forbid schools which are racially or socioeconomically homogeneous. They only require that the homogeneity not be an intentional product of public policy. Thus the current trend of many urban school systems to become populated largely by minorities and the poor is not forbidden. It now seems possible to have desegregated city schools which are almost entirely black surrounded by nonsegregated suburban schools which are almost entirely white.

If we must form our concept of desegregation in terms of facts about what features of schools make a difference and if the racial and socioeconomic composition of schools makes a difference, then we will need a concept of desegregation which involves genuine integration. Desegregation will require that black and white students actually go to school with one another.

The distribution version of the stigma theory therefore cannot be defended if it is true that racial and socioeconomic mixes make a difference. The view is essentially correct concerning how to decide on what counts as an inequality of educational opportunity but is based on an incomplete view of the facts.

These arguments assume that it is achievement and ultimately social variables such as income and status which are at stake in schooling and that the difficulty with the Court's policy is that it assumes a dubious theory about how schools distribute these variables. Suppose, however, that achievement and income are not the socially relevant variables at stake in schooling. One might take the simpler view that desegregation is aimed at creating an equitable distribution of self-esteem. The moral offense of segregation is that it represents an attack on the self-esteem of blacks. This is not objectionable primarily because a maldistribution of self-esteem leads to a maldistribution of achievement and income. It is objectionable because self-esteem is itself a socially relevant variable of considerable importance.

There are excellent reasons for considering self-esteem as a socially relevant variable deserving consideration in a liberal theory of distributive justice. Self-esteem is an important component of the individual's happiness. Moreover self-esteem, like income and rationality, has the character of a universal instrumentality. It is a psychological and logical requirement for taking one's other goals and plans seriously.[22] People can only feel that their personal desires have a claim on being fulfilled if they believe themselves to be of sufficient worth that their happiness matters. The focus of Supreme Court policy on the stigmatizing consequences of segregation is thus justified because of the paramount moral value of self-esteem.

This argument is plausible, but it too assumes a naive sociology concerning the origins of self-esteem. Perhaps self-esteem in our society depends on achievement and income. Americans tend to define themselves in terms of their current or anticipated occupational role. This habit of identifying one's self with one's job is perhaps to be lamented, but it is real, and the status of a job correlates with both the degree of educational attainment required and the income involved. Of course one would expect this in a society which professes to reward talent, defines talent in terms of rationality, and believes that schools develop rationality. Moreover clearly our society treats manual labor as suitable for those who have failed to attain a more sophisticated level of talent, and thus it rewards and values such jobs poorly. The cost in self-esteem to the possessors of these jobs is perhaps best reflected in the trend to attach prestigious labels to low-status jobs. What besides self esteem is at stake in making a janitor a sanitation engineer?

A theory which believes that the distribution of self-esteem can be changed without changing the distribution of achievement and income is at best, therefore, incomplete. If society should cease overt discrimination against blacks while leaving the achievement and income levels of blacks as they are, it ought not to expect to change more than the grounds of low self-esteem. *This approach accordingly cannot justify basing desegregation solely on the desire to remedy the loss of self-esteem resulting from the social stigma of segregation. Even if self-esteem is of paramount moral importance, it is unlikely that it can be disentangled from how other social goods are allocated.*

Consider the third variant of the stigma theory. In the Lockean reading segregation is objectionable because the institution constitutes a denial of the principle that all men are created equal. Segregation rests on the implicit assumption that blacks are less nearly persons than other human beings. Thus segregation is an affront to the central principle of a liberal democracy—that however people may differ, everyone is fully and equally a person and entitled to equal rights.

This line of argument is, I believe, fundamentally correct. Segregation does imply that the segregated group is somehow less than human and is not entitled to full and equal rights. Clearly the practice is intolerable. Moreover it ought to be crucially important to expunge from public policy any hint of the idea that some people are inherently less worthy of fair and decent treatment than others. What I wish to deny, however, is that this view can be used to justify either the notion that the consequences of desegregation are not pertinent to determining what counts as desegregation or to justify any distinction between desegregation and genuine integration.

The supposition underlying the suggestion that the consequences of desegregation are not pertinent to determining what counts as desegregation must be that state-mandated segregation conveys a rejection of the full dignity and humanity of the groups segregated, but a practice which permits members of that group to go to schools where the human resources for learning are not equally available to them does not similarly convey a rejection of the full humanity and dignity of that group. I believe this view is also incorrect. *The maldistribution on racial or socioeconomic lines of the resources for learning also implies that the group thereby prejudiced is inferior and not entitled to equal rights.*

How are we to determine whether or not some public policy or practice implies the rejection of the full humanity of some group? First, we might simply inquire into the motives of those who make or support the policy. A second approach is to ask whether a rational person would be entitled to conclude on considering a policy that it can only be justified by the assumption that the group affected was less worthy of fair treatment than other groups. This second approach has the advantage over the first of being less subjective since it does not require us to guess about complex motives. More important it allows us to recognize that a policy can be unjust even if that is not what is intended. A society might adopt a policy which would as a matter of logic assume the rejection of the principle that all men are created equal without recognizing or intending that. Justice is not simply a matter of good intentions.

Suppose that our society permits the inequitable distribution of the human resources for learning by permitting racially or socioeconomically homogeneous schools to exist while knowing that the racial and socioeconomic mix of schools has important consequences for learning and for the distribution of other social goods. Can we infer that such a policy would be reasonable only if those disadvantaged by it were less than fully entitled to be treated as persons with equal rights?

Such an inference is warranted. The basic conception of liberal equality suggests why. Equality is fair competition. Individuals are entitled to an equal chance to pursue their own goods because they are persons and because all persons are equal. This doctrine requires that the means of competition be equally available to everyone or more precisely that differences in availability must be justified on some relevant grounds. If the means for competition, society's opportunities, are not equally available, we can conclude that the persons who are thereby deprived are being treated as though they are not equal.

A policy which results in the unequal distribution of some resource which is known to be connected with achievement does precisely what is forbidden. Thus, *if current desegregation policy does not remove such inequalities in opportunity or if it permits them to increase, such a policy implies the lack of humanity of those who are at a disadvantage.*

These arguments can be applied to desegregation in a slightly different way. Suppose we take the position that the sole consideration in determining what are to count as segregation and desegregation is that public policy should clearly express the Lockean notion of fundamental equality, and suppose we hold that this can be accomplished without any concern for the effects of policy on achievement. Policy, we insist, should be intended to affirm our basic moral commitments, not to produce some set of consequences. This view is tantamount to claiming that desegregation need not be concerned with producing equal opportunity.

To see why, we need to reaffirm the point that one can only determine what counts as an equal opportunity by considering the connection between potential opportunities and desired outcomes. If any state of affairs is to count as an opportunity, it must be a potential means to a desired end. The opportunities for obtaining an end are what makes a difference for that end. If a policy is to be justified without a consideration of its consequences, that policy cannot reasonably be concerned with equal opportunity. A policy about equal educational opportunity must be concerned with equalizing the resources on which relevant outcomes depend.

That desegregation is not concerned with equal opportunity is unacceptable. That we can affirm the ideal of fundamental equality while being uninterested in equal opportunity is self-contradictory. In liberal theory the claim that people are entitled to equal opportunity is one of the logical consequences of the concept that all persons are equal and have equal rights. One cannot consistently affirm the principle while denying or not acknowledging its consequences. *The Lockean interpretation of the stigma theory, therefore, makes an important point—that public policy can convey moral commitments; and it is important that justifiable and humane commitments be conveyed. This position, however, rather than providing a rationale for an approach to desegregation which is independent of the consequences of desegregation requires us to take these consequences into consideration.* Thus this argument, like its predecessors, shows that a concern to equalize the resources on which achievement depends flows from a commitment to the basic equality of persons. Any policy which shows a disregard for the equitable distribution of these resources implies a lack of commitment to basic equality.

To see the philosophical implications of these arguments, reconsider the remarks of Judge Sobeloff concerning Thomas Pettigrew's views. Pettigrew argued for a desegregation plan which generated an optimal racial and socioeconomic mix. Judge Sobeloff's response is that Pettigrew does not appreciate the philosophical basis for desegregation. Desegregation, says Sobeloff, is not based on the idea that white children are a resource to be equitably distributed, but it is based on the idea that segregation is an insult to black children and thereby taints their education.

The above arguments show, however, that the considerations in question cannot be separated as Judge Sobeloff assumes. If the racial or socioeconomic mix in a classroom does make a difference in the achievement of black and disadvantaged students, then failure to provide an optimal racial or socioeconomic mix can also be reasonably construed as a living insult by those thereby put at a disadvantage. It can be so construed because the idea that all persons are equal generates a reasonable expectation that the educational resources that matter will be equitably distributed. When resources are not equitably distributed those who are thereby disadvantaged are entitled to feel that they are being treated as though they were somehow less worthy of fair and equal treatment than others. In short the failure to distribute equally an essential resource is wrong. It differs from deliberate segregation only because it is more subtle and less obvious.

The central claim of liberal justice is that all persons are equal. This central claim is actualized as a theory of fair competition. Basic equality leads to an insistence that persons have equal rights when they pursue their own notion of the good. People are entitled to equal political rights, an equal chance to influence collective decisions, and an equal chance to compete in the marketplace. Liberal equality is concerned for fairness in the social mechanisms through which social goods are distributed. It should thus be obvious that a commitment to fundamental equality will lead to a concern for knowledge about how the mechanisms for distributing social goods actually work. Without such knowledge one could not decide in any given context whether fairness actually obtained.

We should therefore affirm the belief with which this section began. Stigma theories of desegregation are incompatible with the claims of the Coleman report because they have an incorrect or incomplete view of the facts or because they incorrectly assume that such facts are not relevant to justice.

A rational view of desegregation means that desegregation policy should meet three criteria. 1. Policy should affirm in theory, pronouncement, and practice that all persons are equal and are entitled to equal rights. 2. Policy should exhibit a concern that everyone be treated with dignity and respect and should promote enhanced self-esteem. 3. Policy should be concerned to effect a fair distribution of the educational resources on which achievement depends. These arguments indicate that each criteria implies the other. It would be difficult to deny one without undermining the rest.

What kinds of policy do they actually justify? Certainly they preclude separation of the races as a matter of public policy. But current policy largely fails to meet the third criterion. Therefore I believe that these criteria require policies designed to create real racial and socioeconomic integration. They particularly require policies which function to reverse the trend of the concentration of minorities and the poor in urban centers and which result in schools which are racially or socioeconomically homogeneous.

The reasons for this last judgment are essentially those of the Coleman report. I do not place great confidence in this study; instead, the Coleman report is an instance of a fundamental fact. *People learn primarily from other people; thus what they learn and how well will be significantly dependent on the quality of human resources available.* It thus seems inconceivable that schools and communities populated largely by people who are economically deprived and who have been the victims of centuries of discrimination will be equal in the quality of human resources to the schools and communities of the privileged and affluent. I am not disparaging the humanity and value of minorities and the poor— quite the contrary. But the human worth of individuals does not make them educational resources of high quality; nor does a history of discrimination and deprivation.

We have been considering two questions: How are outcomes relevant to judgments about fairness and how do schools function in producing their outcomes? The major point concerning outcomes is that liberal views of justice are concerned with the fair distribution of social goods. This concern requires a knowledge of how institutions actually function in allocating goods. The concept of what counts as an educational opportunity has to be decided by what kinds of educational resources actually make a difference in achievement.

When we ask how schools work, the major point to be stressed is that the student's racial and socioeconomic background is a determinate of learning. Since the individual student's background is significantly related to his or her learning, the school's racial and socioeconomic mix is among the relevant school resources and thus counts as part of the opportunity schools provide. I have tried to generalize about these claims by noting the importance of human resources in the school and community for learning and achievement. These views lead to a rejection of what I have called stigma theories of desegregation and to the conclusion that desegregation policy needs to be guided by a concern for genuine integration and the fair distribution of human resources.

CHAPTER 11

The evil that men do lives after them.
—SHAKESPEARE

Applying Liberal Equality: Compensatory Programs

In the last chapter we saw that outcomes were relevant to deciding what counts as an opportunity. This thesis does not, however, require schools to produce outcomes of any particular character. One might argue that having identified what is to count as an opportunity, the school's obligation is to provide these opportunities so that members of different racial or socioeconomic groups have precisely the same opportunities. When this has been done, outcomes should be left to take care of themselves. Given equal opportunity, any student should achieve results reflecting his ability, aspirations, and effort.

This position permits achievement to differ in ways which are related to background. If school opportunities are equal, then the results of schooling should be affected primarily by such characteristics as ability and willingness to learn. But if poverty, let us say, affects the student's ability or willingness to learn, then equal schooling will result in unequal achievement. Poor students will do less well than their affluent peers because they are less capable of profiting from the opportunity. The result of equal opportunity is that those who enter school behind will leave it behind.

Liberal theory thus has to resolve a paradox. The role of schooling vis-à-vis equality is to ensure that opportunity to succeed does not depend on irrelevant background characteristics. But what does this require of schools? Shall schools equalize inputs and allow outputs to differ in ways which will correlate with race and socioeconomic status, or shall schools attempt to equalize achievement and allocate resources unequally so as to compensate for the inequalities in students' backgrounds? Neither position seems satisfactory.

I shall argue that liberal views on justice require schools to produce equal outcomes. The demand is for equal results among social groups, not among individuals. The distribution of black and white achievement should be the same, and the distribution of achievement among rich and poor students should be the same. The demand is for parity among groups defined by some irrelevant background characteristic.

This demand requires compensatory education. We must overcome whatever incapacities for learning children acquire from their background. I shall complicate the matter by also arguing that it is unlikely that this obligation can be met. We thus will have to assess the implications of the inability of a society to succeed on the requirements of its view of justice.

A. HEAD START AND SESAME STREET

Assume that children from lower SES families come to school with affective or cognitive handicaps to learning and that we are obligated to prevent these handicaps from affecting life prospects. We will want to intervene at some point so that such disadvantages are compensated for and their effects are eliminated. But when will we intervene and how?

Liberals will be reluctant to tamper with employment or income very much. The liberal assumes that people should earn their jobs and their income. If, however, we start assigning jobs or income in order to compensate for a disadvantaged background, we will simultaneously be assigning them in a way which fails to consider merit or talent and in a way which is therefore socially inefficient. We will then want an educational solution. What?

Suppose we decide that the most sensible thing is to begin early . Let's take disadvantaged students before they go to school and see if we can overcome their educational handicaps. Then they can compete on an equal basis with their counterparts who have greater advantages. The parents of higher SES children might complain that it is unfair that more educational resources are being spent on the children of the poor than on their children. Compensatory education could thus be viewed as discrimination against the rich. No doubt the objection would be pressed strongly if compensatory education proved effective.

Compensatory education may also be seen as unwarranted encroachment on the rights of parents to oversee the education of their children. It is in the early years that children acquire their basic character and their basic values, but these areas are not proper objects of the state's concern.

If we want to have early compensatory education, we will have to contend with such arguments. What we will do is make some compensatory programs available to everyone, trying to make them more attractive or appropriate to disadvantaged children. We will also allow more affluent parents to pay for other programs similar to those available free of charge to poor parents. Perhaps we will also subsidize such programs for the rich. Finally we will avoid encroaching on the child's early years. Instead we will have institutionalized programs only for children nearly old enough to enter school. If we have other programs, we will take them to the children in their homes.

This is roughly what has been done in two major compensatory programs, Head Start and Sesame Street. Sesame Street is available to anyone with a television set, and it does not encroach on family prerogatives. Head Start, on the other hand, is for poor children about to enter school. Preschools or nursery schools (sometimes publicly subsidized) are readily available to more affluent parents.

Consider another approach. Suppose we do not have early compensatory programs for some or all disadvantaged children or that those we do have are failures. We might reason that if a disadvantaged student has not done as well as his or her peers with more advantages, he or she nevertheless may be as able as someone who has previously exhibited some success. Furthermore, since it is not the fault of the disadvantaged students that they are disadvantaged and since we wish to promote an equal chance for them, let us make available to such students opportunities for further education which would not be available to other students with similar qualifications. If we follow this line of argument, we will then seek to attract and admit disadvantaged students to colleges and graduate schools and will perhaps lower admission standards to do so. Furthermore, in order to make it possible for disadvantaged students to finance their education, we must provide much of our financial aid on the basis of need, not achievement. We will thus seek to compensate at the other end of the educational spectrum.

Again there are objections. It might be held that those so admitted still cannot compete with those admitted according to the normal criteria either in their studies or in their chosen occupation.[1] Moreover such a practice could constitute reverse discrimination by discriminating against students on irrelevant criteria such as being affluent, white, or male.

To avoid such charges we will provide remedial education to those we admit. And the prudent among us will avoid admission quotas and harsh labels such as *reverse discrimination*. Instead we will talk about goals and affirmative action and will try to pretend that we can admit more disadvantaged students while not harming the interests of the other students and not increasing the number of students admitted.

The basic point is this. *Any compensatory program can be charged with being itself discriminatory simply because it allocates resources and opportunities on criteria of wealth or minority status.* Such programs thus accomplish in the name of equal opportunity what the doctrine of equal opportunity intends to exclude. Compensatory programs also may be charged with encroaching on other rights, such as the right of parents to spend their wealth on the education of their children or the right to determine the nature of the education of their children. We must examine such programs to see if they are justified.

Programs such as Head Start and Sesame Street on one hand and affirmative action on the other represent the options available in providing compensatory educational opportunities to the disadvantaged.

Head Start and Sesame Street are grounded in the belief that disadvantaged children do less well in school than their counterparts because they begin school having acquired fewer of the cognitive and affective prerequisites for educational success than their middle-class peers. This being the case, programs designed to provide the children of the poor with the cognitive and affective prerequisites to learning, available automatically in middle-class families, ought to permit poor students to enter school at the same level as their more advantaged peers and, thus, to profit equally with them in school.

The justification for both enterprises is succinctly stated in an evaluation of Head Start. "The rationale for Head Start, then, follows this line of reasoning: The poor are educationally disadvantaged. Their disadvantaged status is caused by experiential handicaps imposed by poverty. Therefore, compensatory education ought to effect a cure."[2]

The cure envisaged is developing resources designed to provide those cognitive and affective skills thought appropriate to school success. Sesame Street focuses on counting, recognition of letters, and positive attitudes towards learning. It is placed in an inner-city context in order to relate effectively to the experience of poor children.

Head Start adds to this diet instruction not easily accomplished on television. Students are presented with a schoollike institutional setting and are taught skills such as how to button coats and tie shoes. Head Start is available largely to disadvantaged children while Sesame Street is available to anyone with access to television.

Head Start appears to have performed poorly both as an educational endeavor and as a compensatory program. Students appear to have failed to profit significantly from Head Start. Sesame Street in contrast has been a smashing success as an entertainment endeavor, and it is reasonably successful educationally but is a failure as a compensatory program. Children like it and learn from it, but it does not narrow the gap in achievement between poor children and affluent children.

Perhaps the best statement of the overall impact of Head Start can be taken from an evaluation conducted jointly by the Westinghouse Learning Corporation and Ohio University. The report concludes:

In sum, the Head Start children cannot be said to be *appreciably* different from their peers in the elementary grades who did not attend Head Start in most aspects of cognitive and affective development measured in this study, with the exception of the slight but nonetheless significant superiority of full-year Head Start children on certain measures of cognitive development.

A variety of interpretations of the data are possible. . . . It is conceivable that the program does have a significant impact on the children but that the effect is matched by other experiences, that it is contravened by the generally impoverished environment to which the disadvantaged child returns. . . . or that it is an intellectual spurt that the first grade itself produces in the non-Head Start child.[3]

Head Start has failed in its attempt to put disadvantaged children on a par with their affluent peers, and no one knows exactly why. Other evaluations of Head Start have produced results which differ in some particulars from this one. A few are more positive. I tentatively accept the view which, if not clearly correct, has at least been widely believed: either Head Start fails to produce any advantage for its pupils over other disadvantaged children or the advantages are dissipated by the end of elementary school.

Sesame Street has generated better results. Evaluations have indicated that children who watch Sesame Street benefit in ways which enhance their ability to profit in elementary schools.[4] Unhappily there is a catch, for it seems that children profit from Sesame Street roughly in proportion to the amount of time they watch, and while children from all classes watch the program, affluent children watch it more. Cook summarizes the finding of a group who had reanalyzed data from several studies concerning Sesame Street's effect on the gap in achievement: "The data that we have examined were not of high quality for ascertaining how one season's viewing of "Sesame Street" is affecting the national preschool gap in prereading skills. The data consistently suggested, however, that (1) "Sesame Street" is not narrowing the gap; (2) if it is affecting the gap at all, it is widening it, especially in letter-related skills; but that (3) the magnitude of gap-widening may not be of great social significance in a single season."[5] The anomaly is that while all children profit from Sesame Street, the gap in achievement between disadvantaged and advantaged children increases. In short Sesame Street functions as school does. Children from all groups profit, but children from affluent families may profit more. Sesame Street thus seems a successful educational enterprise but a failure as a compensatory educational enterprise.

Results such as these are bewildering. They do not show that compensatory programs cannot work. Sesame Street does at least indicate that disadvantaged children can profit from preschool instruction. Moreover the earlier evaluations conducted for Head Start and Sesame Street did not consider the nature of the instruction provided. Thus they were not in a position to suggest what did or did not work or to suggest ways of making the programs more effective. Recommendations concerning Head Start were thus global, including suggestions to extend programs "downward toward infancy and upward into primary grades"[6] and to concentrate on remedying specific deficiencies.[7]

If we look at the results in a broader context, a good deal of cynicism regarding the effectiveness of programs to enhance the comparative educational attainment of lower SES children is warranted. Let us recapitulate the evidence. The Coleman report can be regarded as supporting these conclusions: 1. There are mechanisms other than overt discrimination which function to transmit inequality across generations. Inequality therefore cannot be expected to disappear when overt discrimination ceases. 2. Two general educational strategies might be expected to lessen the tendency for socioeconomic disadvantages to be inherited—racial and socioeconomic integration and compensatory education.

In the last chapter I argued that the U.S. Supreme Court has adopted a concept of desegregation which focuses on eliminating overt discrimination rather than in creating broad racial or socioeconomic integration. Unless the Supreme Court has a change of heart on this stand, meaningful and extensive racial and socioeconomic integration is unlikely. It is not self-evident that such integration would substantially aid disadvantaged students. The evidence on this is mixed.[8] It seems unlikely, however, that courts will give us the opportunity to find out. Compensatory programs appear to be impaled on the horns of a dilemma. Those programs which have been directed largely toward disadvantaged students have not worked. Programs which have produced meaningful educational gains have not been directed solely to disadvantaged students. This may be an insoluble dilemma, for it is hard to see how it would be politically feasible to withhold a successful preschool program from the children of the affluent.[9] One would need to discover a pedagogy which helped only if one was poor. Moreover successful compensatory programs will probably have to be more extensive and therefore more expensive than those previously attempted. Public support seems remote.

We can conclude that *educational programs which might overcome the educational handicaps of the disadvantaged are politically unfeasible, and that politically feasible educational programs will not work*. The requisite kind of integration will probably not be ordered by the Court, and its advocacy is political suicide for any white politician. Compensatory programs which do work will not long remain the property of the disadvantaged. Anyone who wishes to use education to promote equal opportunity must discover an educational strategy which actually works and must discover incentives sufficient to persuade society's more affluent members to permit it and not to appropriate it. That we can do either of these is not clear. That both can be done simultaneously is doubtful.

B. AFFIRMATIVE ACTION

Most American colleges and universities have programs designed to increase minority representation. Such programs involve admission, financial aid, and hiring. Because these programs take into account race, minority status, or affluence in allocating scarce positions, they seem offensive, given prevailing liberal theory which holds that accidents of birth should be irrelevant to how people are treated.

Consider how such programs function in admissions. Admissions for most university programs are conducted by a ranking which orders applicants according to performance. The essential criteria are grades at the student's previous school and scores on examinations such as the SAT, GRE, or LSAT. Interviews, recommendations, and (occasionally) having a relative who is an alumnus or a donor are also considered. Once a ranking of applicants is established, a cut line is drawn which will reflect the spaces available and the institution's sense of the kind of students it wishes to attract. Students above that line will be accepted while students below it will be rejected.

The justification of this procedure is that the student's ranking on the institution's scale predicts academic performance. Students with high SAT scores, for example, tend to get higher grades. Institutions thus regard their ranking primarily as an ordering of students according to their ability to do the work expected of them and to profit from their experience. It is also assumed (at least in professionally oriented programs) that those who will do well in their academic work will be the same people who do well in their professions.

The usual admissions procedure can be easily stated to render it consistent with liberal equality. It is a competitive procedure. The criteria used are relevant to legitimate institutional and social purposes. Irrelevant criteria such as race or socioeconomic class are not considered. Moreover the procedure can be justified as an efficient use of social talent. Resources are allocated to develop the talents of those most likely to make effective use of them. The procedure thus contributes to over-all social welfare.

Affirmative action requires that such procedures must be modified for minority admissions. The controversial Bakke case is illustrative. Bakke, a white applicant, was rejected by the medical school at the University of California at Davis. Davis normally admitted one hundred students per year. Of these one hundred positions, sixteen were set aside for minorities. Applications accordingly were sorted into two groups. Minority applicants were compared only with one another in making selections for the sixteen positions. Nonminority applicants likewise were compared with one another, not with minority applicants. Bakke was rejected even though his scores exceeded those of all of the minority students admitted. Bakke consequently sued for admission to Davis medical school, claiming that he had been discriminated against owing to his race. The California Supreme Court agreed with Bakke and ordered him to be admitted. The U.S. Supreme Court also rejected the Davis procedure and ordered Bakke to be admitted, while permitting procedures using race as a criterion so long as minorities and nonminorities were considered in a common pool so that everyone could compete for every position.[10]

The Bakke case illustrates features typical of affirmative action enterprises. Affirmative action programs provide preferential treatment for minorities in that minority status is used as a criterion for admission. This need not result in the admission of unqualified people, but that is beside the point. Minorities so admitted are less qualified according to the institution's standards than nonminority students who are displaced. Moreover, without affirmative action programs, minority presence in graduate and professional programs and in the professions in America, will be reduced. Hence the dilemma. Rapid movement of minorities into the mainstream of American life from which they have been long excluded requires that usual standards of evaluation be altered and that standards which employ criteria of race or family background be followed.

Can such a procedure be justified in a society committed to equal opportunity? Equal opportunity excludes using criteria of race or family background, does it not? Can equal opportunity be suspended to achieve other social goals, no matter how praiseworthy? The arguments on the topic are numerous and complex.[11] I will not try to cover them all. Instead I will explore the nuances of one successful argument that favors affirmative action. Its chief merit is to exhibit more of the structure of liberal equality and the consequences of its failure.

I assume that the fact that minorities do not compete favorably in most admissions programs is a function of inequality and the failure of attempts to overcome it. The educational failures of minorities are generally traceable to low socioeconomic status, and the low SES of minority families in turn springs largely from a long and dishonorable history of discrimination. Because the inability of minorities to compete favorably results from prior inequality, a certain unfairness obtains in the impartial enforcement of admission standards. Doing so seems to perpetuate the injustice.

The task is to bring philosophical substance to such sentiments. The first step is to look at social opportunities not as isolated units but as a package. Consider a standard path which divides opportunities into preschool, elementary school, high school, and college (or postsecondary education). Standard procedure has involved attempting to equalize opportunity at each point in the path. Head Start and Sesame Street may be regarded as attempts to equalize preschool environments. Public schools (equally financed and suitably integrated) are society's major attempt to equalize environments. Color-blind admissions policies represent equal opportunity at more advanced levels.

Assume, however, that divisions between opportunities are morally arbitrary. That being the case, let us explore what happens if we ask not about the equality of the parts but of the whole. Let me put the point schematically. Let us take groups A and B and opportunities x, y, and z.

The usual view seems to require that x, y, and z be independently equalized for A and B. Thus

Opportunity for	A	=	B if
Opportunity	x_a	=	x_b
	y_a	=	y_b
	z_a	=	z_b

expresses the moral ideal for equal opportunity. To treat opportunities as a package alters the demand to:

$$A = B \text{ if}$$
$$A(x, y, z) = B(x, y, z)$$

Thus, *in this approach, society is not required to equalize opportunity at every point. Its obligation is to equalize only the over-all availability of opportunity to As and Bs. Society's obligation is to provide equal opportunity, not equal opportunities.*

Why make this move? First, it is permissible. There is nothing I can see which is morally at stake in how society slices its opportunity. The approach has practical advantages over the other view by allowing us to concentrate effort where success is most likely or least costly in moral or social terms. The first view requires equality at every point regardless of society's ability to provide it and regardless of social cost or conflict with other values. The second view, however, permits us to compensate for some intractable inequality by an opposite inequality somewhere else. Thus it provides for more flexible policy. Finally the view allows us to express a morally defensible interpretation of affirmative action. Affirmative action is an attempt to balance earlier inequalities with later inequalities so that the over-all system of opportunities might be more nearly equal.

This last point is easily related to the legitimacy of employing criteria of race or background in admissions. If our standard is that the over-all system of opportunities be equal, then opportunity may not be allocated by criteria of race or background. But if at some point some particular opportunity is allocated by such criteria, then it will be permitted to allocate some other opportunity intended to cancel out the inequality on similar criteria. *Opportunities may be allocated according to race or background if the purpose is that opportunity be allocated in a way not reflecting such criteria.*

One difficulty with this approach is that it makes it virtually impossible to judge whether equal opportunity obtains by seeing if inputs are equal. We can no longer decide if equal opportunity obtains by seeing if the amount of x available to A is the same as the amount of x available to B or if As are admitted to z on the same standards as Bs. Moreover it is difficult to see how we can rationally determine how much increase in opportunity y equals some deficit in opportunity x. Input standards for equal opportunity make no sense here. Thus, if we are to accept a "package" view of equal opportunity, we will need a different standard for determining when we have achieved it.

We therefore ask whether equal opportunity permits an output criterion. Note that liberal theory suggests some reasons for thinking that justice should not be defined by means of results. I expressed the liberal norm of justice as the claim that the distributive effects of free markets are fair, whatever they are, if equal opportunity obtains. This maxim seems to indicate that justice in a liberal society is not determined by any feature of the actual distribution of social goods except its history. A liberal society should regard its social allocations as just when they are the result of a history of fair competition. Given a history of fair competition, any resulting allocation is permissible and consistent with the demands of justice. The utilitarian version of liberal theory is an exception to this. Here justice is defined by a feature of outcomes, the maximization of satisfaction. But even utilitarianism is not concerned with how satisfaction is distributed among individuals or groups. The sole concern is the maximization of the average satisfaction.

Thus liberal theory is disinclined to define justice by means of any feature of the distribution of outcomes. It provides little apparent support for defining equal opportunity in terms of parity among social groups. Perhaps, however, instead of asking whether liberalism defines justice by means of any pattern of outcomes, we should ask if it *predicts* any pattern of outcomes. For if the principle of equal opportunity does predict something about outcomes, then that predicted feature of outcomes could be used as a *measure* of whether equal opportunity is obtained. *A just social system has some predictable outcomes. These outcomes do not define justice, but they can be used as a measure to determine whether or not justice obtains.*

Consider a simple model of such a prediction. Let us suppose that some social reward, R (income perhaps), is a function of the total system of opportunity, O, consisting of particular opportunities x, y, and z, plus native ability, N, and Motivation, M. Thus

$$O \ (x, y, z) + N + M = R$$

Let us further suppose that for groups A and B we know: (1) that the distribution of native ability is the same for A and B, and (2) that either the distribution of motivation is the same for A and B or such differences as there are are a function of inequality. These assumptions allow us to remove M and N from our equation so far as contrasting A and B is concerned. Thus, if M and N are identical for A and B, then differences in R between A and B must be a function of some difference in O.

Given this line of analysis, we may use equality of outcomes to measure equality of opportunity. If social rewards are not evenly distributed among social groups, we know that some inequality of opportunity obtains, although we do not know where in the system the inequality is located. The package view of opportunity, however, does not require us to know where the inequality resides in our system. But it does require us to adjust the components of the system until equality of outcomes results.

A rationale for affirmative action can now be stated. We know that minorities have not obtained equal opportunity because while members of minority groups are endowed with equal ability and motivation when compared with nonminorities, they nevertheless receive a substantially smaller portion of social rewards as measured by family income or almost any other index of social welfare. That is sufficient to establish the case. We are obligated to adjust the structure of opportunity until parity in social rewards is achieved. Affirmative action can be treated as such an attempt.

We can object to this view because it results in the allocation of positions to persons who are less capable of making good use of them than those who are excluded. Let us take Jones, a member of group A, and Smith, a member of group B. Suppose that Jones is more talented than Smith, who because of his membership in group B has received educational opportunities superior to those of Jones. Smith thus achieves a higher score for university admissions. We must decide whether to admit Smith or Jones.

Here the argument I have given indicates that we should admit Jones over Smith on the grounds that had equal opportunity obtained, Jones would have done better than Smith and admitting Jones is necessary to equalize the over-all opportunity of Smith and Jones.

The objection holds that, regardless of the history of the qualifications of Smith and Jones for university admission, Smith is, nevertheless, the more qualified. And being the more qualified means that Smith will profit more from the experience than Jones and that he should make a more substantial social contribution than Jones.

If our criterion for determining the justice of social institutions is utilitarian, Smith ought to be admitted, for admitting Smith is more likely to maximize the average utility than admitting Jones. Perhaps if Jones had had opportunities equal to Smith's, then he would have been the more qualified. But if justice requires us to maximize over-all social welfare, we should admit those who *are* the best qualified, not those who might have been.

This line of argument undercuts my view since it suggests that the history of a person's qualifications is not morally relevant to how we respond to them. The only relevant considerations are the consequences of how we deal with current qualification. (Utilitarian arguments are always future-regarding; the past is morally dead.) My view treats the history of opportunities as relevant to how current opportunities are to be allocated. Doing so leads to inefficient use of current human resources. Therefore the only rational (efficient) approach is to adjust inequalities where they occur.

I reject this argument because it is utilitarian. In the next chapter I offer a general refutation of utilitarianism which will demonstrate that considerations of fairness cannot be overturned by considerations of efficiency as this line of argument proposes.

Consider a further objection. It is easy to imagine Smith claiming that he was entitled to be admitted over Jones since by virtue of his having attained qualifications superior to those of Jones, he had earned the position. Smith might further argue that although he had superior opportunities to those of Jones, it was not his doing. Since he is not responsible, there is no reason that he should be denied the fruits of his achievement.

Smith's argument challenges the assumption that college admission can be treated simply as an opportunity. That (unlike elementary and secondary education) a university education is not automatically available to everyone, that admission is competitive, that admission must be justified in terms of academic success and talent, and that education can be considered of intrinsic worth as well as instrumental value all suggest that university admission can be treated as a social benefit or reward. That one can reasonably claim to have *earned* admission to a university when the claim to have earned admission to elementary school is senseless confirms the judgment. "Now," Smith might argue, "it is all well and good to manipulate society's opportunity structure in order to promote equal opportunity. But what grounds do liberal theories of justice provide for tampering with social rewards? If there are inequities in the system of opportunities leading up to university admissions by all means let them be corrected, but what grounds are there for withholding from someone the benefits he has earned?"

Smith's objection also implies that an injustice in the comparative histories of the qualifications of Jones and Smith for university admission would only warrant a denial of Smith's claim in favor of Jones if the injustice has been perpetrated by Smith. "Let us suppose," Smith claims, "that my opportunities to become qualified for university admission were unfairly superior to those of Jones. That is hardly my fault. Why then should I be punished for a situation I didn't create?''

Granting that university admission is a benefit, how are claims to some benefit justified? Consider a simple rule: one is entitled to a given benefit only if he or she earned the benefit justly. The rule borders on being self-evident. Norms of justice are norms of entitlement. When the manner in which a society distributes its benefits violates basic norms of distributive justice, the claims of individuals to be entitled to what they have gotten become suspect.

The traditional liberal norm is that the distributive effects of free markets are just, whatever they are, if fair competition obtains. The corollary is that if fair competition does not obtain, entitlements to what one gets in economic competition are suspect. The application to Smith's objection is straightforward. If university admission is a benefit and if there is some unfairness in the manner in which Smith obtained qualifications superior to those of Jones, then Smith's claim to be entitled to the benefit is weakened. Moreover, nothing here depends on whether or not Smith perpetrated the injustice. The only relevant fact is that he benefited from it. Smith's advantage over Jones is analogous to someone who has found a bag of stolen money. The fact that he did not steal it does not void his obligation to return it.

This objection to my views on affirmative action, while not successful, is most revealing concerning the dilemmas of liberal equality. The confusion over whether to treat a university education as an opportunity or a benefit—it is, of course, both—reveals a significant dilemma. The claim that the distributive effects of free markets are just if fair competition obtains assumes a reasonable capacity to distinguish between the conditions of competition and the results of competition—between opportunities and benefits. If opportunities and benefits are either identical or highly dependent on one another, a view which demands equality of one but not the other is incoherent. This is the most general way to formulate the inadequacy of liberal equality. Suffice it to say for now that affirmative action personifies the difficulty of distinguishing opportunities and benefits.

The discussion also suggests that the failure to achieve liberal equality tends to undermine liberal society's structure of rewards. Insofar as university admission is a benefit, any argument to justify affirmative action must cast doubt on the right of the more qualified to the benefit. The argument clearly has broader application. So long as a society has significant inequalities of opportunity, persons in that society lack a firm moral claim on what they consider theirs. Thus the implications of failure to achieve equality are profound and disturbing.

Unhappily liberal norms suggest little guidance as to how to respond to these dilemmas except that society should try harder to achieve equal opportunity. Traditional liberalism has an obvious and strong preference for creating equality by manipulating opportunities but not rewards. But the last two chapters suggest the futility of continuing this approach. But what other approach is there? The dilemma of liberal equality generates significant incentives for reconsidering the traditional liberal norm.

C. THE EMPIRICAL DEMISE OF LIBERAL EQUALITY?

In the last two chapters I have discussed some of the problems and research which suggest that the public schools cannot succeed in the task which liberal political theory assigns to them. They cannot prevent inequality from being inherited. Of course I have not proven this. The topics I have discussed will demonstrate that the traditional conception of the schools' role in promoting equality both underestimates the task and overestimates the capacity of instruction to accomplish the task; but they do not show that it is unattainable.

In retrospect the role assigned to the school by liberal theory can be viewed as based on these assumptions: 1. Free markets govern social rewards and do not generate excessive inequalities in wealth. 2. Markets reward ability, and the specific ability most likely to be rewarded in modern society is rationality. 3. Schools are the primary distributors of rationality. 4. Such inequalities of opportunity as exist can be traced to overt discrimination.

Our discussion has cast doubt on these assumptions and has suggested reasons to believe that: 1. Achievement (and the social benefits which depend on it) appears to be attached to factors other than ability, some of which reflect race or social class. 2. The family and the community, in addition to schooling, are important distributors of achievement. Moreover, differences in family and community background largely account for differences in academic achievement. 3. Compensatory education programs are insufficient to overcome the educational effects of family background.

Although I have not argued against free markets, the claims concerning free markets are doubtful. Thus *the outcome of these considerations is that our society generates inequalities of such magnitude that schools cannot be expected to overcome their effects on the distribution of achievement and social rewards in the next generation.* But so what? I have already suggested part of the answer. *To the degree that liberal equality has not been realized, the legitimacy of the current distribution of social rewards is in doubt.*

Other problems flow from the fact that we do not know that liberal equality is unattainable. We merely have some grounds to suspect it. What if liberal equality is unattainable? Does that refute the norm? Do the moral demands of a social ideal become diminished if it is difficult to attain? Perhaps all that means is that we should try harder.

The unrealizability of a norm does count against it. Norms of social justice are justified in a social context. They are intended to govern the relations among members of society on the assumption that these relations have a definite character. Norms of justice thus will have psychological, economic, and sociological assumptions built into them. The liberal norm of justice makes sense only in a society whose economy exhibits significant division of labor and whose members obtain most of their goods by trading with others. Liberalism has tended to assume a psychology in which an individual's notion of the good is personal and private and in which the individual is motivated largely by self-interest. The problems a theory of justice is intended to solve differ if the desires of individuals can be created by the social system or motivated by the well-being of others. Norms of justice thus depend on empirical as well as philosophical assumptions. These assumptions often govern the selection of appropriate means for implementing the norms. If the norms cannot be achieved, one properly suspects that the norms rest on false empirical assumptions.

The discussion of implementing liberal equality permits us to focus on one such assumption. *The claim that if fair competition obtains, the effects of free markets are just, whatever they are, assumes that the basic social conditions of competition are, or can be made, distinct from society's reward structure.* Suppose, however, that what is being distributed by society—its particular rewards—is the basis of the conditions under which the next generation will compete. The result is that the liberal norm proves inconsistent since it requires competition to be fair and at once permits the unequal distribution of the means of competition.

Since we are interested in equal opportunity, let us spell out the difficulties concerning this notion. Here the assumption is that society's opportunities and its rewards are, or can be made, distinct. If opportunities and rewards overlap or turn out to be much the same, then the liberal norm of justice requires both that society equalize its opportunities and that it permit inequalities of opportunity.

That one generation's rewards are the next generation's opportunities is hardly surprising. Affluent parents can, by passing on their money to their children, pass on financial opportunities. (Some liberals therefore have been hostile to inherited wealth.) And affluent parents can provide their children with a superior education. Indeed the demand for free public schools can be regarded as rooted in the observation that one generation's reward is the next's opportunity. It is the point of the schools to drive a wedge between reward and opportunity by making the conditions for acquiring marketable talent independent of wealth.

This theory, however, fails to confront how strong the connection between the parents' rewards and the child's opportunities is. This traditional liberal view assumes that the educational advantage of the rich consists in either the power of wealth to buy a superior education or in its political power to prevent disadvantaged groups from gaining an equal share of education resources. The argument of the last two chapters suggests that this view is simplistic. The children of the poor do less well than the children of the affluent, even on those rare occasions when they obtain a higher share of educational resources. It appears that the affluent succeed in passing on their advantages to their children before they reach school.

This suggests that the connection between the parents' rewards and the children's opportunities is far more intimate than liberal educational policy assumes. Neither the purchasing power nor even the political clout of the affluent is decisive. Instead it appears that inequality is part of the air that children breathe in their homes and communities. What ensues is that the parents' reward is the child's opportunity in a way that is not readily susceptible to social intervention. And what follows from this is that *the liberal norm of justice is inconsistent. That norm requires opportunities to be equal but permits rewards to be unequal. Rewards and opportunities, however, turn out to be nearly identical.* This inconsistency counts substantially against acceptance of the norm. At the very least liberal theory will need to be modified so as to deal with this problem.

But we merely suspect that schools cannot succeed in establishing equal opportunity: we do not know that. None of the research which links inequality in achievement and income to social class is beyond challenge. The research is highly controversial. Moreover the research, if correct, only establishes that current efforts have not succeeded. The reports do not show that some future effort cannot succeed. There is always that next innovation just around the corner—the breakthrough that will show us how to resolve the educational problem of disadvantaged students and which will set us on the path to equality.

The uncertainty of our opinions on such important matters itself becomes a significant problem. How does one decide what to do in the face of uncertainty? Should one act on what seems to be the general drift of the research? Or should one stand pat on liberal ideals until it becomes clear that they will not work? Surely we ought not to engage in anything so revolutionary as rejecting the norms of justice of one's society unless we are sure that they are wrong. But can we ever know this?

The considerations of this chapter thus leave us with a perplexing list of unresolved questions. Recent research on how schooling affects achievement and income suggests that schools cannot perform their role as it is seen in liberal theory. Moreover, the inability to create equal opportunity tends both to refute the liberal norms of justice and to undermine the legitimacy of society's reward structure. The grounds on which these judgments are made seem far from certain, however.

These problems of liberal theory stem from a common source. Liberal equality does not permit us to create equal opportunity by direct manipulation of social rewards. In the next chapter I argue that equal opportunity should be interpreted as implying a constraint on the variance in social rewards permitted. I will argue that this modification of liberalism solves all of the foregoing problems. That it does solve them, however, is only a part of its justification which should be stated first in philosophical terms. We can reexamine the role of schooling in a liberal society when we have developed a philosophically adequate variety of liberalism.

CHAPTER 12

A person's a person, no matter how small.

—DR. SEUSS

Liberal Equality and Equality of Persons

In the last chapter I asked whether liberal equality could be achieved. But if we could achieve it, would we want it? One way to ask this question is to see if we can imagine a society which succeeds in achieving liberal equality but seems abhorrent. If we can do this, then we have some reason to doubt that liberalism can be the basis of our moral judgments. Our moral intuitions may thus lead us to a more detailed philosophical critique of liberal equality and a more adequate view of justice.

A. UTILITARIAN JUSTICE

A major strain in liberal thought is represented by utilitarianism. In this section I shall develop a more persuasive conception of liberal justice from a critique of a utilitarian formulation.[1]

Utilitarianism holds that the justice of social institutions is to be decided in terms of the capacity of institutions to maximize the average utility—the total satisfaction divided by the population. Under utilitarianism, rights must be justified in terms of their contribution to the average utility. Characteristically liberties such as freedom of opinion are justified because they promote rational decision-making. Equality of opportunity is justified since it leads to efficient use of talent. Both rational decision-making and efficient use of talent are held to promote the average utility.

One objection to utilitarianism is that it is possible to imagine cases which satisfy the criterion of maximizing the average utility but at the same time are otherwise morally noxious. If utilitarianism can be shown to run counter to our basic ethical intuitions, this provides excellent grounds for rejecting it.

A strategy to show that utilitarianism can lead to noxious consequences results from noting that the justification of rights under utilitarianism depends on the *empirical* connection of rights with the average utility. Thus rights can be undermined if the facts are different than utilitarians imagine. If it should happen that freedom of expression leads to rational decision-making only when it is restricted to an intellectual elite, then utilitarianism will restrict liberty to an elite. Or if it should turn out that racial bigotry reduces inflation and maximizes the average utility by keeping a small part of the population unemployed, then utilitarianism can justify racial bigotry. It is not hard to imagine conditions under which slavery might maximize the average utility.

A related objection is that utilitarianism can justify the exploitation of one individual or group by another because utilitarianism is concerned with the maximization of the average utility, not its distribution. Compare the distribution of satisfaction in the two two-person societies compared in the following diagram.

	Society	
Persons	I	II
1	30	16
2	2	15
Average Utility	16	15.5

The units measure satisfaction. Utilitarianism selects society I as the most just because it has a higher average utility than society II despite the fact that the distribution of satisfaction is more nearly equal in society II and regardless of how the distribution in I came about. Indeed utilitarianism is capable of justifying a society in which some members fail to have enough for bare survival. One need show only that when wealth is transferred from the most productive to the most needy that the average utility decreases.

These points illustrate the ways in which utilitarianism fails to accord with commonplace beliefs concerning how persons should be treated. To generate a better conception of justice, we must find reasons to support our rejection of these consequences of utilitarianism. The basic reason is that these consequences of utilitarianism are incompatible with how persons should be treated. Basic principles of justice must be grounded in what it means to be a person. We can approach this by considering the conception of justice forged by Rawls as an alternative to utilitarianism.

The center of Rawls's theory, which he calls justice as fairness, consists in his two principles of justice.

FIRST PRINCIPLE

Each person is to have an equal right to the most extensive total system of equal basic liberties compatible with a similar system of liberty for all.

SECOND PRINCIPLE

Social and economic inequalities are to be arranged so that they are both: (a) to the greatest benefit of the least advantaged . . . and (b) attached to offices and positions open to all under conditions of fair equality or opportunity.[2]

These principles are ordered so that the first principle is prior to the second and in the second (b) is prior to (a).

The first principle is designed to protect basic freedoms such as freedom of conscience and political rights—for example the right of majority rule and one-man vote. The second principle governs the distribution of economic goods. It requires equal opportunity. Rawls adds what he refers to as the difference principle, the first part of the second principle, which requires inequalities to work to the benefit of all, particularly the least advantaged members of society.

These principles solve the problems of utilitarianism. Justice as fairness does not view justice as a matter of maximizing satisfaction or anything else. Consequently the rights claimed under justice as fairness cannot be rejected on empirical grounds. One cannot argue for empirical reasons that justice as fairness can lead to slavery or other noxious institutions. Justice as fairness also specifies the distribution not only of the several liberties but of economic and social goods. By requiring inequalities to be to the advantage of the least advantaged it precludes social systems in which some people can benefit by the misfortune of others or in which basic needs are not met despite society's capacity to produce enough for all.

Some of the features of justice can be grasped by considering further the difference principle. Inequalities are permitted only when they are to the advantage of the least advantaged members of society. The point of permitting departures from simple equality is that there are conditions under which it is to everyone's advantage to do so. By permitting income to vary according to ability and social contribution we can increase productivity so that even society's least affluent members are better off than they would be under an equal distribution of goods. Such arguments have a faintly utilitarian ring to them, but they operate under a different criterion. Utilitarianism permits the inequalities which maximize average utility regardless of how satisfaction is distributed, while justice as fairness permits only those which increase the well-being of the least affluent.

Justice as fairness also differs from some versions of liberalism in that it regards individual talents as social resources rather than as private possessions. It thus permits superior ability to be rewarded only when it is used to the advantage of everyone. One basis for this view of individual ability is that native endowment, just as social circumstance, is an accident of birth. Ability as such reflects no merit on the person who possesses it. Hence there are no moral grounds for permitting a person whom the natural lottery has given superior ability to profit from this ability unless this is for the good of everyone.

Rawls justifies these two principles by claiming that they would be agreed to by rational self-interested persons deciding under impartial circumstances. Rawls describes what he calls the original position—a hypothetical condition under which rational self-interested agents must select principles of justice without knowledge of how their choice would affect themselves. Rational persons choosing in the original position, Rawls claims, would select his two principles.

B. THE RIGHTS OF PERSONS

Let us examine Rawls's argument to illuminate the foundation on which it rests and to clarify its connection with the liberal tradition.

It has been urged that Rawls's argument for his principles of justice uncritically assumes that rational agents avoid risk. Since agents in the original position making choices do not know what social positions they will finally occupy, they recognize that they could turn out to be society's most impoverished. Since they might turn out to be one of society's outcasts, rational agents will choose principles which make this person as well off as possible. Their principles maximize the social minimum. In so acting they show themselves unwilling to accept the risk involved in choosing principles which would be to their advantage if they were not among society's lowest classes.

But why should we assume that rational agents should go to such lengths to avoid risk? Might not rational agents opt for principles more favorable to people with advantages, acting with the hope that they would turn out to be among these classes? People who temperamentally avoid risk may believe principles which fail to maximize the social minimum are imprudent, but it is hard to see what would make those principles irrational.

I thus do not believe that rational and self-interested agents choosing under conditions of impartiality must agree to Rawls's principles. Indeed I do not believe they must agree on any principles since agreement would depend not only on what is rational but on the temperament of the individuals.

The crux of the difficulty is Rawls's stipulation that these principles would be subscribed to because rational people would see them as in their self-interest. They would recognize that it is to their advantage to secure the cooperation of their fellows in an orderly and cooperative society. They would therefore accept principles of justice sufficient to enlist the cooperation of all. But is it obvious that the principles which would be accepted by rational self-interested agents would be just? The discussion of the choices made by persons accepting the risks suggests that this is not obvious. Possibly rational agents who accept risk and who are constrained only by constraints of impartiality and by their own self-interest might accept the risk of choosing unjust principles to increase their social position, should they be among society's upper classes. A rational self-interested person accepting risk might accept the possibility of being a slave to gain the possibility of being a master. Thus the question as to what rational self-interested agents would ratify under impartial conditions is not the same as the question of what is just.

A second view of Rawls's notion of the original position is Ronald Dworkin's.[3] Dworkin argues that Rawls's fundamental value is that all persons are entitled to equal respect and concern. They are entitled to equal respect because they are persons and because every person is fully and equally a person. This right to equal respect does not result from agreement in the original position but is a prerequisite of participating in the agreement. In Dworkin's words "the right to equal respect is not, on his account, a product of the contract, but a condition of admission to the original position. This right, he says, is "owed to human beings as moral persons", and follows from the moral personality that distinguishes humans from animals. It is possessed by all men who can give justice, and only such men can contract. This is one right, therefore, that does not emerge from the contract, but is assumed, as the fundamental right must be, in this design."[4] From this perspective the point of the original position is to test various claims concerning what principles of justice follow from the abstract commitment to equal respect of persons. It does this by forcing people to consider the interests and needs of others impartially.

The argument concerning the choices of persons willing to accept risk suggests that the device is not wholly successful. One can consider one's own interests impartially without considering what is just.

We might, however, consider the issue by asking directly what we think being a person involves and what kinds of rights thereby obtain. Obviously this question cannot be adequately treated in brief compass, but I will make a few observations, hoping that the philosophical roots of my basic commitments can be illuminated.

I make two assumptions about persons: 1. Persons are moral and rational agents. 2. Moral and rational agents are entitled to be treated as ends rather than as means.[5] The first claim means that the central aspect of being a person is that persons are capable of rational thought and of holding and acting on conceptions of what is good and right. The second claim holds that moral and rational agents are of intrinsic value. They are ends in themselves and therefore should not be treated as instruments of others' purposes.

These claims lead to two general moral claims: 1. Each person has the right to be treated as a moral and rational agent. 2. Each person has the right to be treated as an object of intrinsic worth. We should add, with Rawls, that personhood does not vary in degree and accordingly that all rights which persons have as persons they have equally. Thus follows a third principle: Persons possess all fundamental rights equally.

These general ideas can be used to argue for several more specific classes of rights. They contain the makings of arguments for freedom of conscience. Moral and rational agents have the positive duty to act in accord with what they find to be good or right. They are responsible for their own beliefs and conduct. Since they have such duties and responsibilities, they must also have the widest possible liberty to believe and act as their reason and moral sense indicate. As moral and rational agents they have freedom of conscience.

Freedom of conscience can also be seen as a right of privacy or inviolability. Persons normally have some convictions which are sufficiently important to them such that an attack on these convictions constitutes a violation of the individual's sanctity. One cannot consistently affirm that persons are ends in themselves while simultaneously compelling them to act in ways which contravene their fundamental convictions.

The claim that persons are intrinsically worthwhile provides us with reason to believe that the needs, desires, and interests of persons have prima facie validity. Persons are not entitled to everything they want, but the fact that a person wants or needs a thing is a sufficient reason for holding that his or her claim to that thing deserves fair consideration. We cannot consistently claim that persons are ends in themselves and deny that what persons want or need is of concern.

This general idea leads to a concern for ways of collective or public decision-making which gives all persons a fair chance to express and pursue their own wants and needs. That the wants and needs of persons have validity entitles them to a right to public institutions which fairly take their wants and needs into account. The validity of the wants and needs of persons thus generates a demand for institutions in which decision-making is democratic.

A similar demand is generated for fairness in economic arrangements. If the wants, needs, and interests of persons are valid, then those institutions which distribute goods and services must give due regard for fairness in arranging how the resources for meeting the wants, needs, and interests of persons are produced and distributed.

Finally the fact that persons are ends gives everyone a claim on the social means for meeting individual wants and needs. Moreover this claim must be to some degree independent of the individual's productivity or economic contribution. To argue to each according to his productivity is to hold that persons will only be rewarded to the extent that they meet the desires of others. That seems equivalent to holding that persons are to be treated as means and not ends.

The word *fair* has often appeared in the preceding discussion. Its inclusion was meant to stress the idea that since all persons are equal, whatever rights they have as persons they have equally. Obviously the rights we have discussed cannot be absolute since they can conflict. Thus the demand for fairness must be expressed as the rule that however these rights are expressed, there are no grounds for applying them preferentially to any group. All rights must be participated in equally by all.

These considerations can be expressed by enumerating these basic principles of justice:

1. All persons have the right to the greatest freedom of conscience consistent with an equal freedom of conscience for others and the right to their own conception of the good.

2. All persons have the right to have their needs, desires, and their concept of the good considered on an equal basis with everyone else. This right has three parts: a. All persons have the right to decision-making institutions which assign them equal weight in advancing and protecting their interests. (This will guarantee such rights as freedom of expression, majority rule, and one man one vote.) b. All persons have a right to allocating institutions which permit them to advance their interests on an equal footing with everyone else. (This includes careers open to talents and equal opportunity.) c. All persons have an equal claim on social resources for meeting their needs. (This guarantees that material resources, capital, and native ability be viewed as social resources for the benefit of everyone.)

Let me state two rules for applying these rights. I shall call these rules *limiting principles.* 1. No differences among characteristics of persons are relevant grounds for biased application of these rules. 2. Inequalities in these rights are permissible when they are in the interest of those receiving the lesser right.

The first point affirms that there are no characteristics of persons which are relevant grounds for varying basic rights. The second point is a variant of Rawls's difference principle, and it serves the same purpose. It will permit inequalities when they serve the interests of those receiving the lesser share.

These rights are also arranged by priority. Freedom of conscience is primary. Rational agents above all else will want to be able to act in accord with their fundamental convictions. Political rights are prior to economic ones.

The content and application of this system of rights are roughly equivalent to Rawls's two principles. I have reorganized them to clarify what is involved in Rawls's principles. The one substantive difference between my views and Rawls's is that I have separated freedom of conscience from Rawls's first principle. I believe it to be central morally. Hence it should not be conflated with liberties which affirm the right of political participation.

This exposition of rights places Rawls's view and mine in the Lockean tradition of liberalism rather than in the utilitarian strain. Obviously Locke would not have accepted this system of rights and would doubtless be particularly unhappy with the implication for private property. Yet the central values of Locke and Rawls—the equality and intrinsic worth of persons—seem to me similar. These are the fundamental commitments to which a humane liberalism needs to return.

The second of Rawls's principles is of most interest to us, given our concern with equal opportunity. I will show the implication of the priority rules. Rawls's formulation will prove more felicitous than mine.

C. THE PRIORITY OF EQUALITY OF OPPORTUNITY

Rawls holds that his first principle is prior to the second and that within the second principle fair equal opportunity is prior to the difference principle. He attaches a great deal of importance to the priority of the principle of equal liberty over the second principle. The priority of equal opportunity over the difference principle, however, is given minimal treatment. Rawls does not justify his view; nor does he devote much effort to explaining or illustrating it. I believe, however, that the priority of equal opportunity over the difference principle has considerable import for formulating the role of schooling in promoting equality. Why should equal opportunity be prior? Rawls does not say, but let us imagine a system for the distribution of social benefits. The system's first phase is the result of fair competition. It assumes that positions are assigned on the basis of talent and that the opportunity to develop a talent is equal. It also assumes that individuals receive what they earn and that free markets reward people according to their productivity. The second phase is redistributive. Recognizing that fair competition can result in a distribution which is not to everyone's advantage and which can leave some destitute, earnings are redistributed so as to help the least advantaged.

In Rawls's scheme fair equality of opportunity is part of the first phase of distribution. Equality of opportunity is intended to ensure that competition for social benefits is fair by requiring that jobs and educational opportunities are fairly allocated. The difference principle, however, is intended to realign such a meritocratic distribution so that the end result is consistent with Rawls's commitment to fundamental equality.

This way of looking at the matter makes it clear that the coherent application of the difference principle assumes that fair equality of opportunity already obtains. The difference principle should realign the results of fair competition. Its application assumes that the initial phase is in accord with the requirements of fair competition. Fair equality of opportunity is prior to the difference principle, for the simple reason that the coherent application of the difference principle assumes that fair equality of opportunity obtains.

This point can be made more forcefully by looking at it from the perspective of the least advantaged. Let us suppose that equal opportunity has not been achieved, but that the difference principle is being applied. In such a case the least advantaged class of persons may complain that they are being treated unjustly because the fact that they are the least advantaged is a consequence of some failure to provide fairness in allocating opportunity. We should not expect people who are discriminated against to be greatly pleased because the consequences of discrimination are lessened by the difference principle.

We conclude that equal opportunity should be prior to the difference principle and that, in cases where the two principles conflict, equality of opportunity must be satisfied first.

The fact that fair equality of opportunity is lexically prior to the difference principle has the potential consequence of placing a limit on the extent of inequality which can be justified by the difference principle. The difference principle cannot justify any inequality which is great enough to generate social positions which are inherited.

Rawls's initial comments on the matter seem quite compatible with my position. ''Fair equality of opportunity means a certain set of institutions that assures similar chances of education and culture for persons similarly motivated and keeps positions and offices open to all on the basis of qualities and efforts reasonably related to the relevant duties and tasks. It is these institutions that are put in jeopardy when inequalities of wealth exceed a certain limit; and political liberty likewise tends to lose its value, and representative government to become such in appearance only.''[6] Here Rawls generally accepts the view that the distribution of wealth should be constrained by other principles in addition to the difference principle. Differences in wealth cannot be so wide as to undermine equal liberty or equal opportunity.

This is potentially a very radical doctrine. If concentrations of economic power of the kind represented by large corporations are incompatible with equal liberty, then Rawls would require substantial economic decentralization. And if a given distribution of wealth results in unequal opportunity, that distribution is not permitted regardless of whether the difference principle permits it. Variance in wealth must therefore be narrowed to the point where social advantage ceases to be inherited.

There are, however, passages in a *Theory of Justice* which suggest that Rawls might wish to limit the application of this argument. If, for example, an attempt to narrow the variance in wealth resulted in a general decline in opportunity so that those with the lesser opportunity actually got fewer opportunities than previously, Rawls would likely forbid it. He seems willing to accept inequalities of opportunity if the consequence is that the opportunities of those receiving the lesser opportunity increase.[7]

For our purposes, however, the more interesting issue is suggested by this passage:

It seems that even when fair opportunity (as it has been defined) is satisfied, the family will lead to unequal chances between individuals. . . . Is the family to be abolished then? . . . Within the context of the theory of justice as a whole, there is much less urgency to take this course. The acknowledgment of the difference principle redefines the grounds for social inequalites as conceived in the system of liberal equality; and when the principles of fraternity and redress are allowed their appropriate weight, the natural distribution of assets and the contingencies of social circumstances can more easily be accepted.[8]

I have not proposed the dissolution of the family, but it could be argued that my view easily leads to this.[9] Once we accept an obligation to eliminate inequalities which are rooted in family background, it is hard to see how we can stop short of major intervention in family life, perhaps even including the abolition of the institutions of the family.

These Draconian results can be avoided if we hold that fair opportunity requires society only to provide equal educational resources to individuals regardless of family background and to treat inequalities resulting from family background or other contingencies of social circumstance as though they are inevitable, just as one's natural endowment is inevitable. In this case we will treat contingencies of social circumstances just as we do differences in native ability. We do not allow ourselves to be bothered by them because we know that the difference principle ensures that those possessing superior ability or advantageous social circumstances are using these assets to the benefit of all.

I suggest this way of applying the ordering of the sections of the second principle. 1. Fair opportunity is to be understood as equality of input. Persons of similar ability or motivation are to receive similar treatment. No compensation for limits on ability or motivation which have a social rather than a biological origin is warranted. 2. The priority of fair opportunity over the difference principle should be interpreted as a restriction on differences in wealth which lead to unequal input, not as a limit on differences in wealth which lead to inheritable contingencies of social circumstance. In effect only differences in wealth which allow the affluent to purchase a superior education for their children or which generate the political power to achieve a superior education for their children are forbidden. 3. Inequalities resulting from contingencies of social circumstance are treated the same as inequalities resulting from differences in native endowment. The difference principle assures us that they are employed as social resources and work to the advantage of everyone.

This reading of Rawls depends on treating the phrase *contingencies of social circumstances* broadly enough to include all aspects of family background. Rawls, however, suggests a narrower reading. "Even in a well-ordered society that satisfies the two principles of justice, the family may be a barrier to equal chances between individuals. For as I have defined it, the second principle requires equal life prospects in all *sectors* of society for those similarly endowed and motivated. If there are variations among families in the same *sector* in how they shape the child's aspirations, then while fair equality of opportunity may obtain between *sectors,* equal chances between individuals will not" (italics mine).[10]

Here Rawls appears to restrict the phrase "contingencies of social conditions" to the factors which may differ between families in the same sector. What is a sector? Let me assume that a sector will be a socioeconomic, racial, or other relevant social group.[11] This passage extends the application of fair equality of opportunity to include eliminating the effects of family background on life chances when those effects result from a feature of family background associated with membership in a socially relevant group. This view requires the narrowing of the variance of wealth to the point where it does not generate inheritable advantages.

Given this reading, then, *Rawls advances two views concerning how to deal with inequalities of opportunity resulting from family background. When those inequalities are a function of membership in a relevant social group, society has the obligation to overcome these inequalities, including the obligation to reduce the variance in wealth when that is what is required. When these inequalities are episodic in the sense that they do not arise from membership in a relevant social group, then society is not responsible for eliminating their effects on opportunity.* Instead they are to be treated as on a par with differences in native endowment.

Let us suppose this is Rawls's view. Is there any reason to agree with it? One reason is that not accepting it may go a long way to making the notion of equal opportunity vacuous. The research I have cited in the previous two chapters demonstrates that the degree of inequality currently tolerated by Americans is inherited apart from overtly discriminatory practices. If this is the case, a theory of equal opportunity which in effect only equalizes educational input to people of similar motivation and endowment will do little to eliminate the inheritance of inequality.

It is difficult to see why any moral importance should be attached to the distinction between mechanisms for transmitting inequality which depend on overt discrimination and those which do not so far as society's duty to promote equality is concerned. Perhaps the fact that this distinction is thought to be morally significant depends on viewing issues of equality as on a par with a situation of this kind. Let us suppose that Jones and Smith are running a race and that Jones slips, enabling Smith to win. Here the moral verdict and Smith's entitlement to the victory depend substantially on why Jones fell. If Jones was tripped by Smith, clearly Smith's entitlement to his victory is void. If Jones merely got his feet tangled, Smith is still the winner. He is entitled to his victory even if it is clear that Jones would have won had he not tripped.

It is tempting to argue by analogy that the children of the affluent Smiths of the world are entitled to profit from any advantage they have over the children of the poor Joneses unless they engage in the moral equivalent of tripping. The moral equivalent of tripping would presumably be an act of overt discrimination.

This analogy, however, breaks down on several grounds. The effects of socioeconomic deprivation on the children of the poor are not analogous to an accident in a contest. The analogy would be closer if we compared a race in which Smith's side of the track was dry but Jones's was wet and slippery. Here the race is unfair and Smith's claim to his victory would be questionable. The grounds for this do not depend on the condition of the track being Smith's fault. And the moral issue we are considering is not as trivial as the winning of a race. We are discussing the distribution of fundamental human rights. It is not clear that persons can be denied such rights because no one deliberately acted to bring about the conditions which result in the denial. Compare this to the obligation to rescue a drowning man. The obligation of one who can swim to save someone who is drowning does not depend on whether the drowning man fell or was pushed or on whether the person in a position to save him was responsible for his being in the water. Finally it is misleading to compare the relationship between a state and its citizens to the relations between individuals. Individuals do not exist primarily to secure one another's rights, but states—in liberal theory—do exist to secure the rights of their citizens. To claim that states must protect rights only when their loss is threatened by an act of the state is therefore bizarre. Hence the distinction between mechanisms concerning inequality which depend on overt discrimination and those which do not does not relieve society of the duty to compensate for the latter.

The grounds for not extending the principle of equal opportunity to the episodic aspects of social contingencies which may lead to unequal opportunity are that the consequences of doing so are likely forbidden by Rawls's first principle and that many episodic sources of inequality can not reasonably be brought under social control.

The desire to eliminate the episodic causes of inequality leads to the desire to encroach on the family. The effects of socioeconomic differences on opportunity could be eliminated by state rearing of children; they might also be eliminated by reducing variation in wealth. But episodic differences (by definition) will not be so affected. Accordingly more direct intervention into family life seems required, but such intervention into family life is prohibited by the principle of equal liberty. The first principle protects, among other liberties, freedom of conscience in respect to moral or religious matters. The right of parents to govern the education of their children can be considered part of the freedom of conscience of both parents and children. Liberal societies, for example, consider that freedom of religion includes the right of parents to educate their minor children in their faith. It is intolerable for persons of strong moral or religious convictions that the state be permitted to force other principles on their children. Thus state encroachment into family life may be incompatible with equal liberty.

Such state encroachment into family life is probable if we attempt to overcome the effects of episodic differences between families. Such differences include differing attitudes toward the value of education which are rooted in moral or religious values. Similar but less severe difficulties arise from attitudes toward education which are based on occupational preference or style of life. To attempt to counterbalance the educational consequences of these aspects of family life brings the state into conflict with the private values of families.

To attempt to remedy the effects on opportunity of low socioeconomic class is to respond to liabilities that will not have been freely chosen. But to try to overcome differences of an episodic character will bring the state into opposition to values freely chosen. This provides an excellent reason for distinguishing between the socioeconomic and the episodic sources of inequality.

There are, of course, many episodic differences among families which are not of this kind. Being raised in a family in which parents are neurotic, drunken, inept, or antiintellectual presumably can lead to differences in motivation or in ability to profit from education. Such social contingencies can be grouped into two sorts. One class contains cases for which the causes are widespread, the effects understood, and the remedy known. Such contingencies should not be classified as episodic. When society has the capability to alleviate the consequences of some widespread malady, it should. But when the malady is not widespread, when it is poorly understood, or when no treatment is available, it makes sense to consider the matter as differences in native ability are treated. Society has no obligation to alter the matter when it cannot. Such episodic contingencies thus fall under the difference principle. Fairness does not require eliminating the effects of such social contingencies but does require that the talents of those more fortunate work to the advantage of those less fortunate.

We can now adequately support these assertions: *Society has the obligation to overcome inequalities of opportunity which result from membership in a socially relevant group, including the obligation to reduce the variance in wealth to the point that it does not produce inheritable advantages. But this obligation does not extend to eliminating the effects on opportunity of social contingencies not linked to membership in a socially relevant group.*

One more point needs to be considered. How does the difference principle affect our attitude toward the distribution of educational resources? Consider this passage:

The difference principle would allocate resources in education, say, so as to improve the long-term expectation of the least favored. If this end is attained by giving more attention to the better endowed, it is permissible; otherwise not. And in making this decision, the value of education should not be assumed solely in terms of economic efficiency and social welfare. Equally if not more important is the role of education in enabling a person to enjoy the culture of his society and to take part in its affairs, and in this way to provide for each individual a secure sense of his own worth.[12]

The difference principle should be implemented not only by redistributive taxation but by investment in, or regulation of, institutions which govern social rewards, including education. We should also not apply the difference principle to the distribution of too narrow a class of goods.

Here, then, is a comprehensive view of the criteria governing the allocation of education resources. These criteria derive from Rawls's theory. Four suffice: 1. Resources should be committed to educating the children of the least advantaged to the point that inequalities resulting from the application of the difference principle cease to be inherited. The difference principle will not be allowed to cause inequalities in excess of the power of education to eliminate their effects for the next generation.

2. Resources should be committed in relation to ability to profit in the way which is to the advantage of the least advantaged. 3. In cases when 1 and 2 conflict, 1 takes precedence. 4. The class of social outcomes which the principles govern should include goods such as cultural appreciation and self-respect as well as income.

The third principle reflects the priority of fair opportunity over the difference principle. Imagine a case in which the children of the disadvantaged are receiving a higher-than-average share of resources in compliance with 1 and when the difference principle requires students with high native endowment to receive less than an average share of resources. How are we to treat a student of high native ability who has a disadvantaged background? The priority of 1 over 2 indicates that this person will be entitled to the share of resources allocated to the disadvantaged.

Liberal equality requires that schools overcome the socioeconomic effects on educational opportunities so that one's opportunity to succeed does not depend on social origins. I have suggested reasons to believe that the extent of inequality is too great and the power of schools too small to succeed in this task. Indeed, the strong possibility that the social class of one's family is a significant determinant of educational attainment—that the parents' rewards are the child's opportunities—shows the liberal norm to be inconsistent. This left us with three difficulties. 1. The failure of schools to create equal opportunity undercuts the social reward structure. When equal opportunity does not obtain, claims of entitlement to social rewards are suspect. 2. The liberal norm suggests no rational alternative to achieving justice other than to succeed in creating equal opportunity via schooling. The liberal norm provides no grounds for direct manipulation of social rewards. 3. The empirical grounds for our pessimistic view of liberal equality are uncertain, but liberal equality suggests no way to respond to uncertainty.

Concerning the second point Rawls's theory provides a rational approach to providing equal opportunity other than increasing the power of schooling to overcome the effects of socioeconomic class. That alternative is to reduce the variance in wealth to the point that schools are capable of dealing with it. Two consequences of interest follow from this. The restriction implied by fair equality of opportunity on the degree of inequality which will be permitted to result from application of the difference principle will be directly proportional to the capacity of education to prevent the advantages of affluence from being inherited. A society in which schools do make a difference is one that can enjoy the full range of benefits of the inequalities tolerated by the difference principle. (Recall that these inequalities are to everyone's advantage.) Conversely a society in which schools are impotent in dealing with inequality will require a more nearly equal distribution of (reduced) wealth. That the legitimization of inequality depends on achieving equal opportunity provides incentive for the affluent to promote the potency of schools. It might be worth discovering how effective schools can be in dealing with the disadvantaged when it is in the interest of the advantaged for schools to succeed. In any case we do have a rational alternative to education in pursuing equal opportunity.

Rawls's views solve the first problem as well. They do not permit inequalities to exceed the capacity of schools to compensate. Thus the legitimization of the social reward structure does not depend on any particular degree of educational potency.

The third difficulty is also solved in part. We are not put in the position of knowing how to act in the face of uncertainty. In effect we are required to reduce the variances in wealth to the point that the schools can manage its consequences. This does not require us to know a great deal about the mechanisms which cause inequality or require us to anticipate or hope for the next educational innovation. It merely entitles us to respond to successful innovation when it occurs by adjusting the distribution of wealth to the increased power of schools.

The need for accurate social-science data remains. We need to be able to judge when the effects of socioeconomic class on education have been eliminated, and this is not an easy task. Nevertheless our view does not generate the indecisiveness which results from uncertainty about the actual or possible effects of schooling under the liberal norm.

Thus, in achieving fairness, the role of schooling parallels that under the traditional theory. Schools exist to promote fair competition by creating equal opportunity. The significant difference is that legitimacy of social rewards does not depend on the power of schooling as it does on the traditional view. Furthermore, the schools cannot be assigned tasks beyond their power. Because such justice has alternatives to creating equal opportunity besides education, schools can succeed in their social role.

D. RAWLS AND MARX

Rawls's theory of justice stands well within the liberal tradition. Despite the fact that it involves substantial modification of classical liberalism it nevertheless falls within the definition of the liberal state and thus does not represent a radical departure from the American political tradition.

For Marxists the cause of social woes is the private ownership of the means of production; therefore the cure for social woes is the public ownership of the means of production. Private ownership leads to un-democratic, unequal, and exploitive relationships both in the social organization of production and in political arrangements.

In an economy in which goods are produced by large organizations rather than by self-employed persons, the private ownership of produc-tion will make the distinction between owner and employee the basic fact in determining the social relations of work. This tends to divide people in the workplace into those who make decisions and those who execute the will of another. By virtue of owning the means of production, capitalists are entitled to make decisions about how production will occur. Workers in turn are expected to execute these decisions as a condition of receiving their salaries. For the worker the job ceases to be an occasion for develop-ing or employing intelligence and creativity. Because workers have no power of decision over their labor, work becomes repetitive, meaningless, and dehumanizing. The workplace becomes a place where human poten-tials atrophy, not grow.

Ownership also gives capitalists power to appropriate an unfair share of the wealth generated by production. When workers are employees, part of the value produced by their labor will go to the owner as profit. This income to owners exceeds whatever value may have been created by owners by their work in planning or administering production. Profit therefore is ill-gotten gain and represents the exploitation of the labor of workers. Moreover, because ownership of the means of production gives the capitalist superior bargaining power over the worker, he or she may be exploited severely. Because workers do not own their own tools and because they can easily be replaced, they have little choice but to accept whatever wage the employer will pay. The employer in turn will have little incentive to pay more than is necessary to enable the worker to continue to work. Thus, under the social relations of capitalism, the few get richer and the many poor are reduced to the level of bare subsistence—or so the theory goes.

The undemocratic character of the social relations of production ac-counts for other injustices as well and is readily translated into the political arena. For example the desire to maximize profit by keeping wages down will lead capitalists to keep unemployment high, since an oversupply of labor will hold down the cost of labor. Discrimination against women and minorities can cause a similar effect by creating in-dividuals who are willing to do meaningless work at a low wage.

In the political area the power of capitalists allows them to make meaningless the political rights and liberties valued by liberal de-mocracies. Politicians and government are easily controlled by a wide variety of devices. Rights such as free speech and press also can be rendered harmless by the control of media and education. Newspapers and television networks are owned by capitalists. Liberal and democratic institutions thus serve the interests of the dominant class. Indeed, by serving the interests of the dominant class while appearing to serve the interests of all, they tend to legitimize to the masses the society which oppresses them.

Marxists are inclined to ascribe several functions to schools in maintaining the capitalist order.[13] Schools indoctrinate students in the official ideology of liberal democracy and thus help maintain capitalist supremacy. Schools transmit the social relations of work, essentially by organizing the school along the same undemocratic lines as the workplace.

Finally schools enable the dominant class to transmit its social position to its children. Schools do this by tracking and sorting children along class lines. Thus the children of the elite are given an education suitable to their position as are the children of the nonelite. The rhetoric of equal opportunity serves the interest of the social elite by disguising the actual nature of the transmission process and by legitimizing its results to its victims.

The potential connection between the Marxist accounts of work and equality is important. Part of the thesis concerning work is that the structure and organization of work entails educational consequences. Fragmented, authoritarian, dehumanizing work detracts from the quality of experience and leads nowhere. It may well negatively influence the capacity of parents to function as educational resources for their children.

Consider that thus far the description of how inequality of opportunity originated has emphasized that the distribution of human resources is important in accounting for inequality and that the role of social class in understanding inequality is essential. The conjunction of these two factors leads us to ask: What is it about social class which affects the ability of individuals to function as educational resources?

Marxist commentaries may provide fruitful hypotheses. Marxists believe social class does not primarily concern income. The central reality for Marxists involves the relation of individuals to the means of production and the power (or lack thereof) which results. Differences in social class translate into difference in the character, conditions, and organization of work as well as difference in income. Class manifests itself in a structure of work which is miseducative, particularly for those on the bottom of corporate hierarchies. And, in suggesting a connection between social class and the educational potential of the work that people do, Marxist views also suggest hypotheses concerning how social class affects the ability of people to be educational resources. If the work that some people do retards their growth, it may also limit their ability to help in an educational sense.

The reader may or may not accept the Marxist account, but it should at least suggest that we should not treat the educational consequences of social class as involving only differences in income. Moreover, if we treat the educational consequences of class as a function of matters other than income, we may have to change the previous section of this chapter. There I claimed that the priority of equal opportunity over the difference principle could result in limits on permissible variance in wealth when such differences proved inheritable. This assumes that it is differences in income which are the relevant factor leading to inequality of opportunity. If, however, inequality should also be a function of the structure of work, the same priority requires that work be reorganized to promote equal liberty or equal opportunity. Rawls's theory of justice linked to a different set of facts may prove very radical.

The solution Marxists prescribe for all these ills is the abolition of the private ownership of production. When the workers own the means of production, then the undemocratic organization of work and all the other evils which flow from the power of private ownership will presumably cease, including those which beset the schools.

This account of Marxism is traditional. It does not measure the power collective bargaining has given labor or the ability of capitalists to understand that a degree of affluence and decent working conditions inhibit the desire to revolt. This formulation fails to distinguish between ownership of the means of production and control of the means of production. The ills Marxists trace to private ownership probably are traced more appropriately to centralized control over production. This is true both in western nations where ownership of stock is increasingly dispersed but where control is increasingly concentrated in the hands of professional managers and technicians. It is also true in the Soviet Union and much of Eastern Europe, where ownership is public but where control resides in a bureaucratic elite.

Can justice as fairness respond to any of these problems? Rawls holds that public ownership of production is consistent with his position so long as goods are distributed by free markets. This acceptance of free-market socialism suggests that there is nothing foreign to justice in socialist solutions to social ills. We must also distinguish the two principles of justice from Rawls's views on what is required to implement them. It is possible that justice as fairness is quite defensible while Rawls's views on what kind of society realizes justice as fairness are wrong on empirical grounds. And it is arguable that if Marxist empirical claims concerning the results of private ownership or concentrated economic power are correct, then justice as fairness may require a society organized along Marxist lines. At least, however, one ought not to reject justice as fairness because the institutions Rawls imagines do not appear to realize it.

Rawls does recognize that concentrations of wealth and power can be incompatible with justice as fairness. "Compensating steps must, then, be taken to preserve the fair value for all of the equal political liberties. A variety of devices can be used. For example, in a society allowing private owership of the means of production, property and wealth must be kept widely distributed and government monies provided on a regular basis to encourage free public discussion."[14]

Here Rawls suggests that justice as fairness countenances manipulation of the economic structure in order to achieve justice. Devices to distribute wealth and property adequately are in order, although little guidance is given on what counts as adequate. Rawls also attaches importance to liberal reforms which are intended to limit the transformation of economic power into political power. His chief suggestions involve public funding of the political process.

We should view the extent of economic decentralization or reorganization required by justice as depending on the capacity of the liberal reforms discussed to prevent the translation of economic power into political power. If effective safeguards can be designed, then high concentrations of economic power may be made compatible with equal liberty. If such safeguards cannot be designed, then equal liberty will require some form of economic decentralization. Indeed, if the Marxist facts are right, justice can lead to socialist solutions.

Rawls's view has a plausible response to the claim that the concentrations of economic power permitted in liberal capitalist societies are incompatible with liberty or equality. The response is simply that such concentrations of power which exceed the remediable capacity of liberal reforms, such as public funding of the political process or of schooling should not be permitted.

It also has a way of responding to the charge that private ownership leads to the exploitation of workers and to other ills such as unemployment. The response is that these problems are managed by the difference principle. In a society regulated by the difference principle, we know that individual talents and personal resources are used to the good of all, not just for the good of their possessors and that the least advantaged in society are as well off as they can be.

Perhaps the greatest weakness of Rawls's view vis-à-vis the Marxist critique is that it does not explicitly recognize as a problem the character of work which results from private ownership. The two principles do not seem to preclude the loss of worker autonomy or the existence of dehumanizing or miseducative work. Justice as fairness does not, however, prohibit the recognition of the social organization of work as a serious problem or prevent its pursuit as a legitimate political objective. Moreover, if the undemocratic organization of work is in fact a serious problem, then in a society in which the fair value of equal liberty is maintained, change should be forthcoming. Finally I have just explored a line of argument which could show the organization of work to fall under the principles of justice. If any autonomy over one's work or work which allows for development and employment of intelligence and creativity is important in promoting equal liberty, equal opportunity, or self-respect, this should relate the social organization of work to the basic principles of justice. To regulate the structure of work by Rawls's principles, one must show that the work has consequences for implementing the principles. To be entitled to justice is to be entitled to these social conditions which realize it.

These remarks can engender optimism about the possibility of educational reform in a liberal state. Perhaps one of the virtues of the Marxist critique of schooling is to remind us that schools are as likely to be the social tail as the social dog. Liberals who fail to recognize that schooling is as inclined to reflect society as to change it have assigned excessive social obligations to schools. One of the virtues of justice as fairness is that by indicating other devices for curing social ills, it reduces the responsibility of the schools. We may add to this the Marxist insight and hold that society which has succeeded in creating a measure of social justice apart from school reform will find it easier to reform schools to reflect the needs of a just social order.

If my arguments are correct, there are good reasons to urge the orientation suggested by justice as fairness against more radical Marxist positions. This is the case even if the Marxist facts are largely correct. Incorporating the Marxist facts within the moral framework of justice as fairness results in making reform more probable by arguing for it along lines consistent with our liberal political traditions and by curbing the excesses of power and the erosions of liberties to which Marxist views frequently lead. Even granting for the sake of argument the Marxist critique, humane reform seems far more likely in the intellectual and institutional context of liberal democracy.

E. SUMMARY

I have argued that liberal conceptions of justice are more persuasively argued in the context of the rights which attach to being a person than they are in terms of utilitarianism. I have held that Rawls's notion of justice as fairness is a reasonable rendition of what constitutes fair treatment of persons. Justice as fairness was shown to provide a suitable context for thinking about the role of education in a liberal society in that by providing means for achieving equality other than education, it assigned to schooling a role in which it could reasonably be expected to succeed. Finally I argued that justice as fairness provided a more suitable context for conceiving social and education reform than Marxism even if many of the facts of a Marxist critique are correct.

We need to view these results in light of the argument of the entire third section. In chapter 9 I reviewed the philosophical background of liberal equality. I held that traditionally for liberals equality has meant fair competition, a major component of which is equal opportunity. In chapters 10 and 11 I weighed evidence suggesting that liberal equality is unlikely to result either from eliminating overt discrimination or from instituting compensatory education. These conclusions are indicated both by the fact that the extent of inequality exceeds what was envisaged by some liberal economists and by the discovery that the effects of social class on educational attainment exceed the power of schools to overcome them. The results of the inability of schooling to promote equal opportunity call into question the reward structure of liberal society.

In this chapter I argue that these defects of liberalism could be overcome by modifying liberal norms so as to reduce variation in wealth and economic power to the point where it is within the power of schools to overcome the inheritance of what social advantage still remains.

While I have not argued any case concerning exactly what degree or type of economic changes are in order, it is quite possible that the achievement of the goals of equal liberty and equal opportunity require economic and political decentralization. Liberty and justice for all may not thrive, given the current tolerated degrees of concentrated power and bureaucratic control. The development of ways to organize production which are consistent with both justice and efficiency therefore must be treated as a high social priority.

A program of liberal reform needs to focus on three questions. 1. How can we increase the capacity of schooling to overcome the effects on opportunity of the degree of inequality required to maintain reasonable levels of economic efficiency? 2. How can we prevent the concentration of economic power necessary to maintain reasonable levels of economic efficiency from being translated into political power of the sort which undermines equal liberty? 3. How can we organize an efficient economic system which does not generate differences in wealth or power in excess of what can be managed by education and by reforms divorcing political and economic power?

In my opinion much of the failure to achieve liberal justice stems from the unwillingness of liberal societies to address the third question. This unwillingness is motivated in part by a concept of justice which restricts social intervention to manipulating social opportunities. Thus a considerable advantage of justice as fairness over the traditional liberal theory of justice is that it permits a broader range of approaches to achieving justice.

CHAPTER 13   *Social development moves with a logic whose in-*
                  ferences are long delayed.

                                                      —R.H. TAWNEY

Conclusion

We now must take stock of the various lines of
argument developed in this book. Perhaps, then, we should end where we
began—with a discussion of the nature of a liberal state. We can thus see
what light has been shed on either the nature of a viable conception of liberalism or on the role of public education in a liberal state.

A. THE MORAL BASIS OF LIBERAL EDUCATIONAL POLICY

For liberals the state exists to regulate the competition among individuals for their private goods. The problems considered in this book are
rooted in this view. The liberal conception of the state forbids the state
from having a public notion of the good or from using its power to impose
some concept of the good on its citizens. The legitimate role of the state
must be understood in terms of regulating the competition among individuals for private goods. The theory of justice of a liberal state is intended to
formulate the basic rules which govern this function of the state. Such a
theory specifies what is to count as fairness in the rules according to which
individuals cooperate and compete with one another in pursuing their
own ends.

These notions suggest several things concerning education in the
liberal state. Initially we must distinguish between the public and the
private sphere in education. Some aspects of education are attached to the
individual's private sphere. Concerning these, the state's primary duty is
to avoid encroachment. Public schools in the liberal state should not
become vehicles for imposing a private concept of the good on individuals. Nor should public schools erode the ability of individuals to
pursue their own private goods.

The basic determinant of the public role of the school will be the conception of justice, for it is the theory of justice which describes rules which govern the activity of the state. The theory of justice is basic in determining the character of the public sphere.

In the second and third sections of this book, I suggest primary public functions which should be performed by schools: the school should promote citizenship, economic competence, and equal opportunity. Consider, then, how these notions fit into the conception of justice developed in chapter 12.

My formulation of the basic principles of justice is:

1. All persons have the right to the greatest freedom of conscience consistent with an equal freedom of conscience for others and to their own conception of the good.

2. All persons have the right to have their needs, desires, and their conception of the good considered on an equal basis with everyone else. This right embraces three subrights: a. All persons have the right to decision-making institutions which assign them equal weight in advancing and protecting interests. b. All persons have a right to allocating institutions which permit them to advance their interests on an equal footing with everyone else. c. All persons have an equal claim on social resources for meeting their needs. This view suggests much about how we should conceive the public role of the school and the private aspects of education as well.

The first principle suggests areas which lie outside public schools. Public schools are not permitted to encroach on a person's fundamental convictions or a person's conception of the good. The first principle also suggests that there will be educational endeavors which are in principle private. Such endeavors pertain to the transmission or evaluation of fundamental convictions or will concern the transmission, development, or evaluation of a person's conception of the good. Public schools will be obliged either to avoid dealing with private matters or to find neutral ways of dealing with them. They must not monopolize educational resources to a point which erodes the capacity of private educational endeavors, and they must not pursue their public functions in ways which unnecessarily conflict with the private sphere.

The second principle suggests why I have treated citizenship, economic competence, and equal opportunity as the basic public tasks of schools. Consider first citizenship. Part (a) of the second principle means that all people have a right to institutions which give them equal weight in pursuing their interests. Some of the typical institutions of a democratic society—such as representative government, one man one vote, and freedom of expression—are justified in that they serve this objective. There are educational conditions which must be met if these rights are to have any value. Individuals must possess certain competencies if their political rights will allow them to pursue their interests. They must be able to evaluate and formulate political arguments; they must be able to function within political institutions designed to realize these rights; and they must be able to judge where their interests lie. When people fail to develop such abilities they are unable to pursue their own interests. In sufficient numbers they can undermine the efficacy of political rights, even for those who possess suitable political skills. The school should ensure that the cognitive resources on which the exercise of rights depends are fairly distributed. In Rawls's terms, schools should help to maintain the fair value of equal liberty. And schools should ensure a great enough distribution of political skills to protect democratic institutions against political incompetence.

If a society is to regulate its affairs by these principles of justice, it should promote a reasonable degree of acceptance of the principles among its citizens. This is a suitable public task for a public school. A final responsibility of the school regarding citizenship is to promote the development of a sense of justice.

Part (b) of the second principle provides for fairness in competition for economic resources. Fairness entails allocating positions on relevant grounds—i.e., careers open to talents—and in allocating opportunity to develop talent on relevant grounds—i.e., equal opportunity. Providing equal opportunity should not be the exclusive task of the school. Nevertheless promoting fairness in the arrangements whereby marketable talents are acquired is clearly a central public function of the school.

The claim that a public function of schooling is to promote fairness in the acquisition of marketable talent assumes that part of the school's role is to promote economic competence. Including economic competence among the public functions of schools can also be argued in terms of part (c) of my second principle. There I have argued that all persons have equal claims on social resources for meeting their needs. I have held that the fundamental property which entitles persons to a share of social wealth is being a person. Social productivity is a relevant basis for rewards when that is to everyone's advantage, but it is not morally fundamental. I also have held that a consequence of this view was that productive resources, including an individual's talents, must be considered to be social resources.

Consider now the argument that one of the public functions of schooling is protecting people from the economic incompetence of their fellows. Against this claim one might argue that the consequences of economic incompetence can be made private. Why is it a matter of public concern when individuals are economically incompetent? Is it because they may resort to violence or theft to survive? But here we may oppose such activities by making them illegal. It is no more permissible to compel people to attend school so that they will not become criminals than it is to enact a general prohibition against alcohol to prevent drunken driving. Perhaps, then, we should require economic competence because people who are economically incompetent must be supported at public expense. But the response here is that people who are economically incompetent need not be supported at public expense. We could permit them to undergo the consequences of their own failure.

It is important to see that part (c) of the second principle gives everyone a claim to economic resources. People are entitled to a fair share regardless of their ability to be productive. We are morally precluded from allowing people to undergo the consequences of their own economic incompetence. Part (c) of the second principle thus makes economic competence a public concern.

The person's economic competence is also a public concern in a second way. Part (c) of the second principle makes a person's native ability a public resource. The failure of an individual to develop his or her abilities to the point of being minimally self-reliant therefore can be viewed as the squandering of a public resource.[1]

The view of justice developed in chapter 12 provides a general way both to view the public function of schooling in a liberal society and to formulate the constraints which should be imposed on it. This view can be summarized as follows: 1. The liberal state must recognize a private sphere of educational endeavors. The public schools must avoid encroaching on or undermining this private sphere. Insofar as they seek to enable individuals to pursue private educational goals, they must do so in a neutral way, largely by developing the individual's capacity for rational autonomous choice. 2. Public schools should as part of their public function, promote citizenship. This includes the fair distribution of the skills for political participation, protection of democratic institutions against political incompetence, and the development of a suitable sense of justice. 3. As part of their public function public schools should promote equal opportunity. Equal opportunity requires schools to eliminate any connection between achievement and irrelevant background factors and thus requires schools to compensate for inequalities rooted in background factors. 4. As part of their public function public schools should promote economic competence.

I have argued that liberals have seen rationality as the key component to achieving each of the public functions of schooling. I have also argued that an emphasis on rationality is required if schools are to promote the individual's development of rational preferences in neutral ways and if schools are not going to retard the development of sophisticated preferences. Finally I have claimed that rationality is best produced by an emphasis on basic skills and basic disciplines. A liberal view of public schools which incorporates this set of ideas can be expressed this way: *If public schools in the liberal state are to perform their public function while not encroaching on the private sphere, they should focus on the fair development of political and economic competence by developing the individual's rational capacities through an emphasis on basic skills and basic disciplines.*

B. AN AGENDA FOR LIBERAL EDUCATIONAL POLICY

Policies are not usually determined by a moral point of view. Even a policy designed to implement some moral ideal will have its character determined not just by that ideal but by the particular way in which the current state of affairs falls short of that moral ideal. Policies are often a form of troubleshooting; therefore we now need to take inventory of our shortcomings.

Section I: Here I dealt with the liberal's view of the nature of rationality. The critique generated of traditional empiricism can be summarized in three parts.

1. Empiricism assumes that people learn directly from experience. Against this notion I have argued a view which holds that learning is a process of modifying current concepts in the light of experience. A corollary of this view is that learning is highly social. The quality of education depends on the quality of the human and social resources available. Empiricism makes the quality of experience basic to learning. My view emphasizes the quality of conceptual and human resources, although it does not make experience incidental.

2. Empiricism has evolved so as to undermine a set of values linked to the central value of rationality. A liberal orientation supports both individual autonomy and participatory collective decision-making. A core value of liberalism is thus the democratic distribution of rationality. Behaviorists, however, have generated a theory which undermines the commitment to rationality and which promotes hierarchical and bureaucratic forms of authority.

3. Empiricism makes rationality into a purely instrumental commodity, a means to maximizing pleasure. I have argued that rationality can also be intrinsically worthwhile.

Section II: Here I distinguished between public and private educational values and asked how our current way of doing business affects the latter.

1. Public schools have contributed to the erosion of private educational endeavors by both the dominance of time and resources and by the

tendency of the public to identify education and schooling. A range of educational values exists that is not well served by public schools and not well served by private endeavors because of public schools.

2. Public schools cannot be united by a commitment to a shared set of private values. They fail therefore to generate communities in which students view themselves as junior members being initiated into common values and in which pedagogical relations are characterized by trust and intimacy. This state of affairs generates a society in which student values are formed more by peers than by adults and erodes the schools' capacity to transmit even those liberal values which are clearly public.

3. Public schools have developed a conception of their vocational role which conflicts with the personal and intellectual development of their students.

Section III: Here I criticized the notion that the distributive effects of free markets are just, whatever they are, if fair competition (including equal opportunity) obtains. I held that this view was not adequate on philosophical grounds and that it permitted social structures and a distribution of goods which make equality of opportunity unrealizable and thus assigns an impossible task to public schools.

1. The liberal norm is objectionable because it is philosophically unsound and because it is unrealizable. It is philosophically unsound because it rejects any direct manipulation of social rewards, and it is unrealizable because it assumes that opportunity and rewards can be distinguished and that schools can equalize opportunity regardless of the incquities which obtain in rewards. Against the first point I have argued principles of justice much like Rawls's difference principle. Against the second I have argued that society is obligated to reduce inequality of rewards and to manipulate social structures in order to put equal opportunity within the capacity of schools.

2. Schools under current conditions cannot achieve equality of opportunity because human resources in society are maldistributed. Equal opportunity thus requires a more equitable distribution of human resources. Various lines of argument in this book suggest three hypotheses concerning the sources of the maldistribution of human resources.

a. Income inequalities: Poverty limits the access of children to human and cultural resources, many of which have a cost.

b. The nature and organization of work: Modern work is bureaucratically organized, atomized, and done in large-scale organization. It can, therefore, be miseducative, particularly for those on the bottom of hierarchies.

c. Segregation: The scale and mobility of modern society not only permits but encourages living patterns which are racially and socioeconomically segregated. Those whose income and work deny them access to educative human resources are thus cast together in a common living space.

The agenda of problems sketched above suggests six primary goals for contemporary educational policy:

1. *The development of a healthy private sector in education must be promoted. A liberal society must recognize that some educational endeavors are inherently private and are not effectively pursued in public schools.* The development of a healthy private sector means a public commitment to the support and encouragement of youth groups. It means using social agencies, such as hospitals, as educational means by providing opportunities for youth to volunteer for responsible and socially useful work. It means reviewing a wide range of public policies for their effects on the family and the families' capacity to educate. It means protecting and enhancing the educational capability of religious organizations and other groups which promote various fundamental beliefs, and it means reducing the role of public schooling to its public functions, and reducing the scope of schooling to make space for private educational endeavors.

2. *We need to recognize the educational importance of communities united by shared values and thus to support the development of such communities and to attach significant educational functions to them.* This requires a higher degree of diversity in public schools and a more significant place in our educational system for private ones. Public schools might allow more diversity among schools or among different programs within schools such that students, parents, and teachers with shared educational values can be free to band together and make available a program reflecting these values. Each school district might well encourage the development of traditional and open elementary schools. High schools should permit students to make a stronger commitment to a particular area of interest. The availability of a private-school education should not be contingent on the ability to pay. The selection of a private school serves a basic liberty in our society. The choice should be available independent of wealth. This requires a public commitment to financing private schools. I have mixed emotions about voucher systems: they can exert too heavy a price on the public functions of schooling, but a properly conceived voucher system would have the significant merit of promoting most of these objectives.

3. *We need to pursue the equitable distribution of human resources.* The discussion in section III shows that while this goal may involve school desegregation, it is also a matter of economic policy. We should make educative work generally available and reduce the variations in wealth. We should also devote considerable energy to finding more imaginative ways of promoting racial and socioeconomic integration in schools than

mass busing, and we need to focus on looking for paths to equality which are consistent with pluralism and smallness, rather than ones which promote bureaucracy and large centralized programs. Magnet schools seem the right sort of thing. They need more emphasis and commitment than we have given them. A properly regulated voucher system also has potential. In the best of all possible worlds integration would result from a proper range of strong educational offerings and the free choices of parents. Finally we need to recognize that school segregation is now a product of social inequality and residential segregation. Social equality and residential diversity are the bottom line in the equitable distribution of human resources.

4. *We need to develop social organizations (including schools) which are smaller and more intimate and in which authority and the organization of activity is more democratic and less bureaucratic.* Effective education depends on intimacy and trust between teacher and learner. Such conditions are not readily promoted when students move from class to class and when teachers may deal with hundreds of students a day—students who will be replaced by other hundreds at the end of the semester. It is ironic that stable and intimate contact between student and teacher is most available in graduate school, where it is probably least required. It is least available in high school and college, where the guidance of a trusted adult may be most important. We need to reorganize schooling so that students spend more time with fewer adults in more personal settings. This need not require abandoning large institutions, but it will require their subdivision into smaller components so that all students have a niche complete with nontransient adults to call their own.

5. *We need to make a liberal theory of justice the central value served by educational policy.* Perhaps the foremost need currently is restoring citizenship to its role as the predominant public task of the school and reducing the subservience of schools to the values of economic efficiency. This is not just a matter of doing a better job teaching civics. It is a matter of making public concerns part of the warp and woof of educational programs, much in the way in which career education often seeks to weave vocational concerns into all aspects of the curriculum. If, as many claim, contemporary students see schooling as fundamentally a means to a job and are less than concerned for public affairs and matters of justice, the explanation may be nothing more complex than that they are learning what they are taught.

6. *We need to develop a pedagogy consistent with the values of liberal democracy.* This means we need to see learning in terms of an epistemology which emphasizes acquiring the conceptual tools for critical thought, instead of an epistemology which emphasizes behavioral change. This means that teaching must be seen primarily as a process of

considering reasons and of deliberating ideas. Good teaching consists in building a rational connection from a students' current concepts to an adequate and justified set of concepts, and it requires the teacher to be a model of rationality.

A few observations will help join some of these themes. Liberal ideology and society and thus schooling in liberal America have been beset by two complementary failings of ideology.

Liberalism has had an inadequate concept of rationality. Rationality, I have repeatedly urged, is among the basic values of a liberal society. Liberals have traditionally been empiricists. Empiricism, however, has proven inconsistent with other liberal values. It has evolved in such a way that it has become mechanistic. In its behavioristic form it has eroded the very notion of rationality itself and consequently has undermined views of authority to which rationality is central, supporting more bureaucratic and hierarchical notions.

Moreover the emphasis on learning directly from experience has contributed both to failing to understand the importance of communities for learning and to failing to understand that equal opportunity requires first and foremost the equitable distribution of human resources. Empiricism therefore has contributed to the inability of schools to develop rational preferences and to our failure to see that schools cannot overcome the effects of large extraschool inequalities.

Finally empiricists have viewed rationality as of merely instrumental value. Empiricists have thus not had a viable concept of an intrinsically worthwhile activity and have thereby contributed to a concept of work and of the vocational role of schooling which is inconsistent with other liberal values.

Liberalism also failed to regulate its economic life with acceptable ideals of justice. Thus we now produce goods and services in large hierarchical, bureaucratic, and socially segregated institutions. The organization of work and the division of wealth, power, and human resources make it difficult for people to develop rational preferences. Schools reflect these failures. Economic efficiency is the dominant value expressed in educational policy and is understood in a way which is often at odds with the school's role in developing rational preferences and in developing enlightened citizens. Moreover the attempts of schools to promote equality are not sufficient to overcome the inequalities generated by extraschool society.

These failures are quite literally twins. The isomorphism between the commitments of empiricism and the organization of economic activity is sufficient to preclude any suggestion that they are accidentally related. The mechanism of modern empiricism supports bureaucratic rather than democratic forms of authority. Both treat work and rationality as mere instruments. Both seek to atomize their domains into fundamental units. And by rooting learning in unmediated experience and thus missing the educative role of the social environment, empiricism fails to note the miseducative character of current social organization. One can only conclude that empiricism has helped to form and has in turn been formed by our economic institutions. Together they function to make much of our current world seem natural and inevitable and to undermine the realization of the more central commitments of a liberal world view.

If contemporary educators need some basic commitments to guide their activities, let us be committed to developing and applying a pedagogy which has rationality as its central aim and which understands rationality in an adequate way. And, above all, let us make the basic liberal values of liberty and equality the central commitments of our policy. Let us have our schools dominated by our sense of justice.

C. THE NATURE OF LIBERAL EDUCATIONAL REFORM

Let me initiate the discussion of social change in a liberal society by suggesting that change should result from persuasion and that experimentation is a basic part of rational social change.

By suggesting that reform should result from persuasion I mean nothing more profound than that in a liberal democratic society those who wish to promote reform must first convince a functioning majority of their fellow citizens that they are correct. Alternatives to persuasion are essentially the varieties of force and coercion. It should be obvious why liberals should prefer persuasion. Persuasion is the mode of social change consistent with the equal right of everyone to institutions which give a fair chance to protect one's interest, and persuasion is the method of change which takes seriously the notion that the individual is an autonomous and rational agent. Indeed persuasion is the means of change which captures liberals' central commitment to rationality and liberals' belief that social institutions and human life can be improved as a consequence of thought.

The notion that experimentation is an important part of rational social change involves several ideas. One idea is that the best way to get evidence concerning the adequacy of some reform is to try it out. Debate and argument are not sufficient to decide on the merits of an enterprise independent of experience. The focus on experimentation is also meant as a recommendation for small-scale social change rather than attempts at global or utopian reform. It is thus an endorsement of social tinkering.

Why tinkering? Part of the answer is that in principle it is impossible to deduce detailed social arrangements from an abstract view of justice. A view of justice specifies what counts as success in a set of social arrangements. But a variety of different arrangements might succeed in meeting the standards of a view of justice. Which ones succeed and which ones succeed best depend on empirical matters not fully specified by a theory of justice. Institutions must be explored and experimented with.

Current social science does not have the capacity to predict the consequences of global change. If we have learned anything from our own history of attempts at educational reform or from the larger history of social reform, it is that the best intended institutional reforms produce undesirable and unexpected consequences for altogether unanticipated reasons. Little reason therefore exists to suppose that people armed with a blueprint for utopia will be able to produce the consequences they desire.

We should think of social change as a type of problem-solving in which the aim is to discover changes which serve to nudge the current state of affairs in the direction indicated by an adequate theory of justice. This view can be made sharper by sketching a formal model of the process. The model has these components.[2] 1. Basic social commitments: This component would consist of the society's view of justice together with a general description of the kinds of institutions and perhaps of the view of human nature or of social interactions which the view of justice requires or assumes. 2. Policies: Policies are the society's current attempts to realize its view of justice in ways consistent with the view of man, society, and social institutions linked to the view of justice. 3. Results: These are the consequences of current policies.

Rational social change occurs when results are fed back on policies and when policies are thus modified to reflect the particular ways in which their predecessors failed and to indicate the direction of a more adequate realization of the society's view of justice.

We should add that in the typical evaluation of a policy the theory of justice is assumed and is not at issue. Failure refutes particular policies, not the society's view of justice. A theory of justice may, however, be refuted by a history of failure, for a history of failure to succeed in assimilation suggests a need for an accommodation of the basic concept. The model thus suggests the role of tinkering in social change. Tinkering is essentially the process of trying out new policies and modifying them in the light of the results achieved against the background of a more enduring view of a just society. Fundamental change in the view of justice is justified by a history of failure.

The model not only suggests what rational social change is like but suggests also how social change can become irrational. Here I shall mention a single point. To be rational social change must be controlled by the society's theory of justice. When the members of a society lose touch with the substance of their basic social commitments or when they no longer are intensely concerned to succeed in producing a just society, change will become either random (in that it will not be clear what is to count as a successful reform) or change will begin to march to a different drummer.

I have noted this because it seems to me to account for much of the current morass of educational policy. Often educational changes seem to exhibit the lack of a firm grasp of what counts as a free society. In schools, for example, I see little evidence of any serious interest in attempting to produce competent citizens. Indeed, while the objective receives a great deal of lip service, it has come to have an almost archaic ring. Moreover much of educational policy is oriented to economic goals which are not subservient to an adequate view of justice.

I cannot, of course, argue this claim beyond what is already implicit and explicit in the preceding pages. If I am right, however, the most obvious need for developing sound educational policy and rational social change is for Americans to take their social ideology seriously enough to form educational decisions in accordance with it.

Notes

INTRODUCTION

1. John Locke, *An Essay Concerning Human Understanding* (New York: Dover Publications, 1959), p. 302.
2. Ibid., p. 303.
3. John Stuart Mill, "Utilitarianism," in John Stuart Mill and Jeremy Bentham, *The Utilitarians* (New York: Doubleday, 1961), p. 408.
4. Thomas Hobbes, *Leviathan* (New York: Collier, 1968), pp. 98–102.
5. John Stuart Mill, *On Liberty,* (New York: Bobbs-Merrill, 1956), p. 13.
6. John Locke, *Two Treatises of Government* (New York: Mentor Books, 1963), p. 406.

CHAPTER 1

1. See, for example, Richard B. Braithwaite, *Scientific Explanation* (New York: Harper and Row, 1960).
2. On this see Thomas Green, *The Activities of Teaching* (New York: McGraw-Hill, 1971), chapter 3. Green's views on belief systems are reasonably similar to mine. This chapter is indebted to Green's work in ways which would be difficult to specify.
3. For more detailed discussion see Kenneth A. Strike, "Freedom, Autonomy and Teaching," *Educational Theory* (summer 1972): 262–278.
4. See Kenneth A. Strike, "Thinking on Thinking: Some Logical and Ethical Considerations," *Philosophy of Education Society* 27 (1971): 192–203.

CHAPTER 2

1. David Hume, *An Inquiry Concerning Human Understanding* (New York: Liberal Arts Press, 1957) and *A Treatise on Human Nature* (Oxford: Clarendon Press, 1967).
2. R. S. Peters, *Brett's History of Psychology* (Cambridge, Mass.: M.I.T. Press, 1965), p. 693.

3. Some philosophers argue that mental terms do not refer to private events. See Ludwig Wittgenstein, *Philosophical Investigations* (New York: Macmillan, 1965).

4. B. F. Skinner, "The Operational Analysis of Psychological Terms," *Psychological Review* 42 (1945): 270.

5. See Kenneth A. Strike, "On the Expressive Potential of Behaviorist Language," *American Educational Research Journal*, (spring 1974): 103–20.

6. Robert Mager, *Preparing Instructional Objectives* (Belmont, Calif.: Fearon Publishers, 1962), p. 3.

7. Ibid., p. 11.

8. Ibid., p. 15.

9. Robert Gagné, *The Conditions of Learning* (New York: Holt, Rinehart and Winston, 1970), p. 239.

10. Richard T. White, "The Validation of a Learning Hierarchy," *American Educational Research Journal*, (Spring 1974): 122–25.

11. For a discussion see Kenneth A. Strike and George Posner, "Epistemological Perspectives on Conceptions of Curriculum Organization and Learning," in Lee Schulman, ed., *Review of Research in Education* 4 (Itasca, Ill.: Peacock Publishers, 1976): 110–21.

12 B. F. Skinner, *Science and Human Behavior* (New York: Macmillan, 1953), p. 190.

13. See Strike, "On the Expressive Potential of Behaviorist Language."

CHAPTER 3

1. For a variation on this argument see Noam Chomsky, "A Review of B. F. Skinner's Verbal Behavior," in Jerry A. Foder and Jerrold J. Katz, eds, *The Structure of Language* (Englewood Cliffs, N.J.: Prentice-Hall, 1964), p. 553.

2. This line of argument is developed in detail in Charles Taylor, *The Explanation of Behavior* (London: Routledge & Kegan Paul, 1964).

3. Wittgenstein, *Philosophical Investigations,* p. 194.

4. For other examples see Strike and Posner, "Epistemological Perspectives on Conceptions of Curriculum Organization and Learning," pp 129–36.

5. Skinner, *Science and Human Behavior*, p. 250.

6. B. F. Skinner, *Verbal Behavior* (New York: Appleton-Century-Crofts, 1957), p. 420.

7. Ibid., p. 422.

8. Karl Popper, *The Logic of Scientific Discovery* (New York: Science Editions, 1961).

9. See I. Lakatos and A. Musgrove, eds., *Criticism and the Growth of Knowledge* (Cambridge: Cambridge University Press, 1970).

10. See I. Lakatos, "Falsification and the Methodology of Scientific Research Programs," in Lakatos and Musgrove, *Criticism and the Growth of Knowledge.*

11. See Stephen Toulmin, *Human Understanding* (Princeton: Princeton University Press, 1972), pp. 52–84.

12. Ibid., p. 145–54.

13. Thomas Kuhn, *Structure of Scientific Revolutions* (Chicago: University of Chicago Press, 1970).

14. Ibid., p. 144–59.

15. Toulmin, *Human Understanding,* pp. 96–132.

16. I do not, however, use them precisely in Piaget's way.

17. Sigmund Freud, *Psychopathology of Everyday Life* (New York: Mentor Books, 1964).

18. Sigmund Freud, *An Introduction to Psychoanalysis* (New York: Washington Square Press, 1963).

19. Plato, *Meno* (New York: Bobbs-Merrill, 1949). This construction of the problem was suggested to me by Hugh Petrie, to whom I owe much of my interest in conceptual change.

20. Immanual Kant, *Critique of Pure Reason* (New York: St. Martin's Press, 1965).

21. See Noam Chomsky, *Problems of Language and Mind* (New York: Harcourt, Brace and World. 1969).

22. D. W. Hamlyn, "Epistemology and Conceptual Development," in Theodore Mischel, ed., *Cognitive Development and Epistemology* (New York: Academic Press, 1971) pp. 3–24.

23. See Jean Piaget, *The Psychology of Intelligence* (Patterson, N.J.: Littlefield, Adams and Company, 1963).

24. Kenneth A. Strike, "The Logic of Learning by Discovery," *Review of Educational Research* (summer 1975): 461–85.

25. Jerome Bruner, *The Process of Education* (New York: Vintage Books, 1960), p. 14.

26. Ibid., p. 31.

27. Ibid., p. 33.

28. See Lawrence Kohlberg, "From Is to Ought: How to Commit the Naturalistic Fallacy and Get Away with It in the Study of Moral Development," in Mischel, *Cognitive Development and Epistemology,* pp. 151–236.

29. Lawrence Kohlberg, "Education for Justice: A Modern Statement of the Platonic View," in Nancy F. and Theodore R. Sizer, eds., *Five Lectures on Moral Education* (Cambridge, Mass.: Harvard University Press, 1970), pp. 57–84.

CHAPTER 4

1. Mill, *On Liberty,* p. 64.

2. Ibid., p. 71–72.

3. Skinner, *Science and Human Behavior,* pp. 447–48.

4. B. F. Skinner, *Beyond Freedom and Dignity* (New York: Alfred A. Knopf, 1971), p. 181.

5. Ibid., p. 107.

6. Ibid., p. 125.

7. Ibid., p. 136.

8. Skinner, *Science and Human Behavior,* p. 446.

9. Ibid.

10. See, for example, John Dewey, *Democracy and Education* (New York: Macmillan, 1966).

11. Skinner, *Science and Human Behavior,* p. 440.
12. Ibid., p. 441.
13. Skinner, *Beyond Freedom and Dignity,* p. 125.
14. These arguments are developed in more detail in Strike, "Freedom, Autonomy and Teaching," and in Strike, "Review of *Beyond Freedom and Dignity,"* *Studies in Philosophy of Education,* (summer 1975): 112-37.
15. Immanuel Kant, *Groundwork of the Metaphysics of Morals* (New York: Harper and Row, 1964), p. 96.
16. Ibid.
17. Leon Lessinger, *Every Kid a Winner: Accountability in Education* (New York: Simon and Schuster, 1970), pp. 85-86.
18. Ibid., p. 5.
19. Ibid., p. 6.

CHAPTER 5

1. Mill, *On Liberty,* p. 129.
2. See Kenneth A. Strike, "Liberality, Neutrality and the Modern University," in Kenneth A. Strike and Kieran Egan, *Ethics and Educational Policy* (London: Routledge & Kegan Paul, 1978), pp. 22-35.
3. *Pierce* v. *Society of Sisters,* 268 US 510 (1925).
4. *West Virginia State Board of Education* v. *Barnette,* 319 US 624 (1943).
5. John Rawls, *A Theory of Justice* (Cambridge, Mass.: Harvard University Press, 1971), p. 92.
6. See Stephen Arons, "The Separation of School and State: *Pierce* Reconsidered," *Harvard Educational Review* (Feb. 1976): 76-104.
7. *Pierce,* pp. 534, 535.
8. Ibid., p. 534.
9. *Wisconsin* v. *Yoder,* 406 US 205 (1972), pp. 211, 212.
10. Ibid., p. 221.
11. Ibid., p. 215.
12. *Abington School District* v. *Schempp,* 374 US 203 (1963).
13. Ibid., p. 205.
14. Ibid., p. 216.
15. Ibid., p. 218.
16. Ibid., pp. 241, 242.
17. Ibid., pp. 312, 313.
18. Ibid., p. 312.
19. Ibid., p. 313
20. Robert J. McQuilkin, "Public Schools: Equal Times for Evangelicals," *Christianity Today* (Dec. 1977): 8-11.

CHAPTER 6

1. Louis E. Raths, Merrill Harmin, and Sidney Simon, *Values and Teaching: Working with Values in the Classroom* (Columbus, Ohio: Charles E. Merrill, 1966), p. 39.
2. Mill, "Utilitarianism," p. 410.
3. Rawls, *A Theory of Justice,* p. 426.
4. Raths et al., *Values and Teaching,* pp. 35-36.

5. Ibid., p. 36–37.
6. Ibid., p. 38.
7. Ibid., p. 201.
8. Ibid., pp. 56–62 passim.
9. Ibid., p. 74.
10. Ibid.
11. Ibid., pp. 114–15.
12. See, for example, A. J. Ayer, *Language, Truth and Logic* (New York: Dover Publications, 1946).
13. Kohlberg, "From Is to Ought: How to Commit the Naturalist Fallacy and Get Away with It in the Study of Moral Development," p. 165.

CHAPTER 7

1. *Tinker* v. *Des Moines Independent Community School District,* 393 US 503 (1969).
2. See *Goss* v. *Lopez,* 95 S. Ct. 729 (1975).
3. *Tinker,* p. 505.
4. Ibid., p. 506.
5. Ibid., p. 511.
6. Ibid., p. 507.
7. Ibid., p. 512.
8. Ibid., p. 513.
9. Ibid., p. 515.
10. Mill, *On Liberty,* p. 13.
11. Ibid., p. 14.
12. See Francis Schrag, "From Childhood to Adulthood: Assigning Rights and Responsibilities," in Strike and Egan, *Ethics and Educational Policy,* pp. 61–78.
13. Rawls, *A Theory of Justice,* pp. 249–50.
14. *Tinker,* p. 507.
15. Ibid., p. 512.
16. *Pugsley* v. *Sellrmeyer,* 158 Ark. 247, 250 SW 538 (1923).
17. Coleman, *Youth: Transition to Adulthood* (Chicago: University of Chicago ty of Chicago Press, 1974).
18. Ibid., p. 124.
19. Kenneth A. Strike and Robert Serow, "How Tolerant Are High School Students?" *Educational Forum* (Mar. 1978): 327–36.
20. Robert Serow and Kenneth A. Strike, "Student Attitudes toward High School Governance: Implications for Social Education," *Theory and Research in Social Education* (Sept. 1978): 14–26.

CHAPTER 8

1. Rawls, *A Theory of Justice,* p. 426.
2. Max Weber, *The Protestant Ethic and the Spirit of Capitalism* (New York: Scribner, 1958).
3. R. H. Tawney, *Religion and the Rise of Capitalism* (New York: Harcourt, Brace and Co., 1926).

4. The most extensive treatment of the topic is Samuel Bowles and Herbert Gintis, *Schooling in Capitalist America* (New York: Basic Books, 1976). This chapter has been much influenced by this work. The reader should note, however, that I do not subscribe to the more general neo-Marxist orientation of the authors. See chapter 12 for discussion.
5. Ibid., p. 131 (italics mine).
6. Charles W. Eliot, "Equality of Educational Opportunity," in Marvin Lazerson and W. Norton Grubb, eds., *American Education and Vocationalism* (New York: Teachers College Press, 1974), pp. 136–38.
7. Edward C. Elliott, "Equality of Educational Opportunity," in Lazerson and Grubb, *American Education and Vocationalism,* p. 140.
8. John Dewey, "An Undemocratic Proposal," in Lazerson and Grubb, *American Education and Vocationalism,* p. 147.

CHAPTER 9

1. Rawls, *A Theory of Justice,* p. 73.
2. Adam Smith, *The Wealth of Nations* (New York: Appleton-Century-Crofts, 1957), p. 48.
3. Locke, *Two Treatises of Government.*
4. Ibid., p. 309–11.
5. Ibid., p. 409.
6. Christopher Jencks et al., *Inequality* (New York: Basic Books, 1972).

CHAPTER 10

1. *Brown* v. *Board of Education,* 347 US 483 (1954).
2. *Plessy* v. *Ferguson,* 163 US 537 (1886).
3. Ibid., p. 540.
4. Ibid., p. 544.
5. *Sweat* v. *Painter,* 339 US 629 (1950).
6. *Brown,* p. 493.
7. Ibid., p. 494.
8. Ibid., p. 495.
9. Edmond Cahn, "Jurisprudence," *New York University Law Review* 30 (1955): 157–58.
10. *Plessy,* p. 551.
11. William E. Doyle, "Social Science Evidence in Court Cases," in Ray Rist and Ronald Anson, eds., *Education, Social Science and the Judicial Process* (New York: Teachers College Press, 1977), p. 13.
12. See *Stell* v. *Savannah-Chatham County Board of Education,* 220 F. Supp. (1963).
13. *Griffin* v. *County School Board of Prince Edward County,* 377 US 218 (1964).
14. *Green* v. *County School Board,* 391 US 430 (1968).
15. *Swann* v. *Charlotte-Mecklenberg Board of Education,* 402 US 1 (1971).
16. James Coleman et al., *Equality of Educational Opportunity,* 2 vols. (Washington, D.C.: U.S. Government Printing Office, 1966).
17. James Coleman, "The Concept of Equality of Educational Opportunity," *Harvard Educational Review* (winter 1968): 18.

18. See the discussion of the testimony of Harvard's Thomas Pettigrew in *Brunson* v. *Board of Trustees,* 429 F.2d. 820 (1970).
19. *Brunson* v. *Board of Trustees,* p. 826.
20. *Milliken* v. *Bradley,* 418 US 717 (1974).
21. See Robert H. Ennis, "Equality of Educational Opportunity," in Strike and Egan, *Ethics and Educational Policy,* pp. 168–93.
22. Rawls, *A Theory of Justice,* p. 302.

CHAPTER 11

1. See Barry Schwartz, "Comments on 'Justice and Reverse Discrimination,' " *School Review* (Nov. 1976): 189–90.
2. Westinghouse Learning Corps and Ohio University, *The Impact of Head Start* (Office of Economic Opportunity, 1969), 1:18.
3. Ibid., p. 8.
4. Thomas Cook et al., *Sesame Street Revisited* (New York: Russell Sage Foundation, 1975).
5. Ibid., p. 308.
6. *The Impact of Head Start,* p. 9.
7. Ibid., p. 10.
8. See Betsy Levin and Willis D. Hawley, *The Courts, Social Science and School Desegregation,* part II, *Law and Contemporary Problems,* Spring 1975, for a number of reviews on the effects of desegregation.
9. See Thomas F. Green, "Equal Educational Opportunity: The Durable Injustice," in Robert D. Heslep, ed., *Philosophy of Education* (Edwardsville, Ill.: Philosophy of Education Society, 1971), pp. 121–43.
10. *Regents of the University of California* v. *Allan Bakke,* 46 LW 4896 (1978).
11. See Kenneth A. Strike, "Justice and Reverse Discrimination," *School Review* (Aug. 1976): 516–37.

CHAPTER 12

1. See Rawls, *A Theory of Justice,* for extensive discussion of utilitarianism. My account is significantly indebted to Rawls.
2. Rawls, *A Theory of Justice,* p. 302.
3. Ronald Dworkin, *Taking Rights Seriously* (Cambridge, Mass.: Harvard University Press, 1977), chapter 6.
4. Ibid., p. 181.
5. The best traditional exposition of these ideas is Immanual Kant, *Critique of Practical Reason* (New York: Bobbs-Merrill, 1958).
6. Rawls, *A Theory of Justice,* p. 278.
7. Ibid., p. 303.
8. Ibid., pp. 511–12.
9. See James Coleman, "Inequality, Sociology, and Moral Philosophy," *American Journal of Sociology* (Nov. 1974): 739–64.
10. Rawls, *A Theory of Justice,* p. 301.
11. For purposes of this discussion a relevant social group would be one constituted by an illegitimate or irrelevant criterion of classification, such as race or SES.

12. Rawls, *A Theory of Justice,* p. 101.
13. Bowles and Gintis, in *Schooling in Capitalist America,* have a view which roughly corresponds to the one described below.
14. Rawls, *A Theory of Justice,* p. 225.

CHAPTER 13

1. This view may seem to have some potentially tyrannical consequences. I would point out, however, that an expansive application of the idea is precluded by the other principles. So far as I can see, it would not entitle the state to assign occupations or compel people to produce to capacity. Occupational preference or the balance a person elects between work and other endeavors is part of that person's concept of the good. State regulation would be precluded by the first principle. So far as I can see, the view I've suggested requires nothing stronger than the duty to be self-supporting when possible.
2. For more detailed exposition of this view see Kenneth A. Strike, "An Epistemology of Practical Research," *Educational Researcher* (Jan. 1979): 10–16. The model is an adaptation of some ideas suggested by Imre Lakatos.

Index